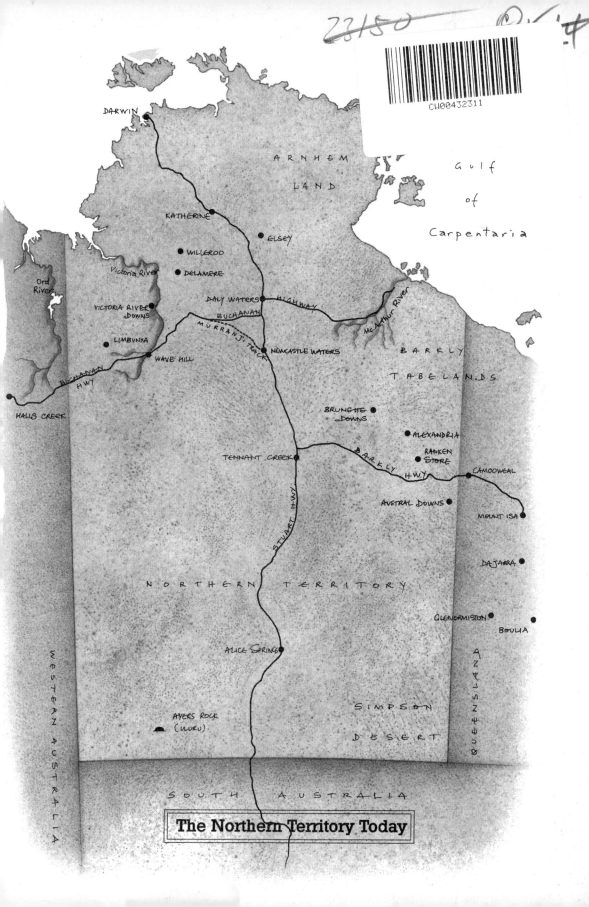

The Northern Territory Today

The author Bruce Forbes Simpson

Author's Note

I WAS FORTUNATE enough to be part of the droving game at a time when it was much the same as in the days of Nat Buchanan. When change did come, it came with a rush. Within a few short years the sound of motors had replaced the music of horsebells, and the day of the packhorse drover had passed into history. In this book I have tried to give the reader an insight into a way of life that is now part of our great cultural heritage.

The men who opened up the Northern Territory to cattle were of heroic mould. It is true that the time and circumstances helped them to achieve greatness, but the spirit to dare and the will to endure were theirs alone. We must never forget them, for their ilk will not pass this way again.

PACKHORSE
DROVER

*This book is dedicated to
the memory of my father Donald Forbes Simpson,
pioneer bushman. And to the memory of my mother,
who faced the wilderness with him.*

PACKHORSE
DROVER

BRUCE SIMPSON

an
ABC
BOOK

Acknowledgments

THE AUTHOR WOULD like to thank the following people for their help and encouragement:
Tim Butler and Ian Tinney of the ABC, Chris Gladwell of the Stockman's Hall of Fame office, Ted Egan of Alice Springs, Alf Chambers of Taroom, Cec Watts of Rockhampton, Bob Gordon of Roma, Jack Charlton of Scone, Dick Scobie of Charters Towers, Peter Treloar of Delaney's Creek, Ced Teece of Rockhampton, Mrs Jeff Hill of 'Glencovie', Munna Creek, Jim Pola of the staff of the *North Queensland Register*, and my daughter Fiona, who did the original typing of this manuscript.

The poems in this book have appeared in various papers and periodicals including Sydney *Bulletin*, the *North Queensland Register*, *Hoofs and Horns*, the *North Queensland Monthly* and the *Longreach Leader*. Many have appeared in the *Bronze Swagman Book of Verse* and other books of collected verse.

Published by ABC Books for the
AUSTRALIAN BROADCASTING CORPORATION
GPO Box 9994 Sydney NSW 2001

First published 1996

National Library of Australia
Cataloguing-in-Publication entry
Simpson, Bruce, (Bruce F.).
　Packhorse drover.

　ISBN 0 7333 0478 8.

　1. Simpson, Bruce (Bruce F.). 2. Drovers – Northern
Territory – Biography. 3. Cattle drives – Northern
Territory – Poetry. I. Australian Broadcasting Corporation.
II. Title.

338.176213092

Designed by Kaye Binns-McDonald
Set by Keyset Sydney
Printed in Australia by APG, Maryborough, Victoria

1995-4.5

5 4 3 2 1

Contents

Foreword

BRUCE SIMPSON IS a unique man. He joins the likes of 'Breaker' Morant and, latterly, Bert Facey and Tom Cole as a true bushman sufficiently articulate and eloquent to relate his personal experiences in literary form. And he covers a unique part of Australia's lifestyle — 'the droving game'. Much has been written about droving: largely the personal experiences of others, related via the pens of professional writers like Mary Durack and Keith Willey. Bruce Simpson tells it in the first person.

Bruce Simpson was a drover — and a 'packhorse drover' at that — right up to the 1960s when road trains were introduced to perform the long hauls of cattle to market. Droving is a bit like the Man from Showy River legend: every second person's grandfather was either the 'stripling on a small and weedy beast' or a famous drover. On closer questioning, you perhaps find that grand-dad walked 100 sheep 50 miles (80 kilometres). But, year after year, Simpson walked a mob of Territory cattle — usually 1000 to 1200 in the mob — over 1000 miles (1600 kilometres) to either the railhead at Dajarra or to the fattening properties 'inside' (as drovers would put it) in Queensland.

They would be months on the road, experiencing incredible privations of heat and cold, living in 'cigarette' swags on a diet of beef, damper and tea, and taking incredible responsibility for a pittance in payment as they battled with this harsh continent. Many of the drovers became callous brutes and the best of them were tough and uncompromising. As Bruce Simpson says, 'You looked after the cattle, the horses, and the men — in that order'.

Yes, Bruce Forbes Simpson is tough and uncompromising. He is a proud, determined man, proud of his Celtic (Scottish in his case) ancestry, and proud of the role played by Celts in the pioneering of the land. He is aggressively determined to retain 'old fashioned' values in this country, and asserts that meticulous effort and the work ethic are the best means of keeping the country sound. He would not use words like 'enthnocentric' himself, but would probably not mind that adjective being used to describe him. He is fiercely nationalistic and deplores any moves by Australians to imitate Americans or English, either in speech, dress, habit or use of equipment. He fairly bristles if he hears Australians sing in half-baked Yankee accents, or use words like cowboy, ranch, corral or stampede. At the same time he was delighted to represent Australia at the Cowboy Poetry Gathering at Elko, Nevada, in 1990, where he had a great time swapping yarns and poetry, and talking horses and cattle with the real cowboys — the ones with huge horny hands, from places like Wyoming, where they still ride horses as they work their ranches.

There have been many wonderful observers of bush life and the 'outback ethos' and many Australians, living in the cities, yearn for and speak nostalgically of 'the vision splendid of the sunlit plains extended'. Thanks to Lawson, Mackellar, Ogilvie, Paterson, Gilmore, Wright and others, Australians can live in suburbia yet turn to the open plains, the dust, the sunsets and the sunrises, and the bellow of cattle and the smell of gum leaves via their literary works. If we want the bush on a more scholarly level, we read McAuley, Hope, Murray, Stewart and Neilson. If you want it straight from the bushman himself, you will enjoy this book.

Bruce Simpson's poems have often been attributed to other people, or to that ubiquitous poet 'Anon'. I published 'The Drover's Life' and attributed it, incorrectly, to Wally Dowling when in fact it was written by Simpson. This is understandable if you know how the 'literary thing' worked in the bush in earlier days. Books like *Such is Life* tell us that itinerants always had a 'borrow book' or a 'swap book' in their swags. You possessed the book until perhaps you knew the content 'by heart'; then you 'swapped' it. It was thus that the bush library operated and people educated themselves. Another habit was to write out in longhand in an 'exercise book' any poems that one sought to learn or liked to recite. Under these circumstances, it often became easier to accept the plaudits on a personal level than explain that somebody else had written the poem. Perhaps a line would be changed or a reference personalised. When Wally Dowling, the Canning Stockroute drover, died, books of poems were found in his saddlebags and it was assumed he had written them. In this way, many of Bruce Simpson's poems have been 'borrowed'; typically, he has 'copped' this as 'one of those things that happen in the bush'.

It has been a thrill and a privilege for me to have assisted in a minor way in having Bruce Simpson's many fine poems recognised and published in this book. Equally, it is wonderful that he has recorded the detail of a droving tradition developed in Australia and unparalleled in the world. Australians, especially schoolchildren, need to be told that the world's biggest movements of stock did not take place in Brazil, or Mexico, or the United States, or Canada or Africa. They took place in Australia.

It is important to note that as a 'packhorse drover', Bruce Simpson carried on the exact traditions, techniques and skills used by the incomparable Nat Buchanan in the 1880s. Sadly, there's no more singing on watch, for 'silent drivers ride the night' as their huge trucks speed over the landscape. Nor are there any more of the monumental drinking sprees in Dajarra, Camooweal, Boulia or 'at the six-mile in Wyndham' as the drovers cut out their cheques. It is no wonder they drank, for it was tough, boring relentless work. Yet they did it, hundreds of them, and never thought of themselves as being clever, or special, or unique.

So why do I think Bruce Simpson is unique? Because not only did he 'go a droving' for so many years, he can speak with absolute authority about the period with the expressive ability of a self-educated man. And because he can write (in respect of his much-loved horse, Actor) poetry like this:

Actor farewell! Till your last long sleep,
May never the creeks run dry,
May the grass be whispering fetlock deep,
Forever, Old Chap, Goodbye.

TED EGAN

Bruce Simpson, left, *with*
Jimmy Charles, right, *with Sam Fuller's*
plant in 1951

The Drover's Statue in the Memorial Park at Newcastle Waters. IAN TINNEY.

The Packhorse Drover

Oh the droving life is a life that's free,
    On the unfenced routes of the back country,
And a packhorse camp is the place to be,
    When they're bringing the store mobs over;
Oh life is happy with not a care,
    With the bush smells strong on the balmy air,
For a whiff of the cook would curl your hair,
    In the camp of the packhorse drover.

Now the drover's bed is a couch to please,
    On the stony ground mid the Bogan fleas,
Or in mud that is up to a horse's knees,
    when the wintry rains drift over;
But life is happy and life is sweet,
    Tho' there's never enough for a man to eat,
And losing weight is a simple feat,
    In the camp of a packhorse drover.

The sky is grey with a hint of rain,
    While the wind blows chill o'er the Rankine plain,
And a ringer swears that he'll drove again,
    When the ceiling of Hell frosts over;
But life is happy and life is good,
    'Round a cow dung fire when there is no wood,
When the damper tastes as it never should,
    In the camp of a packhorse drover.

We watch the mob and we sing the blues,
    And we'd sell our souls for a nip of booze,
As the hours drag by on their leaden shoes,
    And the Southern Cross turns over;
It's a rugged life but we never whine,
    For the mateship found in the bush is fine,
Tho' the boss of course is a hungry swine,
    And a typical packhorse drover.

Packing a mule with water canteens.
A windbreak for the nighthorses can
be seen in the background.

Night Watch on the Dry River Route

THE NIGHTHORSE I was riding picked his way carefully around the sleeping bullocks. As I whistled tunelessly, I looked over the mob of big, aged, store-conditioned bullocks bred in the rough country south-west of Katherine. There was no moon and the Southern Cross was dipping towards the horizon. It was possible to see quite clearly, however, for it is never really dark in the Australian bush, except when there are low, heavy clouds.

Actor walked steadily around the camped cattle with no guidance from me.

He was one of those unique nighthorses that knew as much as any man. The camp was not a good one, but it was the best available. The area was in light timber country with scattered antbeds and some fallen timber. As I rode around the tightly packed bullocks, I could see their big arching horns gleaming softly in the starlight. They were a bad mob; during the week since I had taken delivery of them they had exploded off the night camp in a maddened rush no less than four times. So far we had managed to hold them without loss, but I knew there was no cause for complacency, for when mobs like this rushed, they roared off the camp in a bovine avalanche that crashed over and through everything in its path. It was my first droving trip as a boss drover and with me I had three Aboriginal ringers, a white cook, and my young brother Jeff, who, at the time, was relatively inexperienced. We still had to face the Murranji scrub, but I was confident that we would get the mob through despite the trouble we'd had.

I passed the camp and was riding towards the back of the mob when somewhere behind me a bullock stood on a dry stick. In a split second the mob was on its feet and galloping. I stood up in the stirrups and bellowed, "Whoa bullocks, whoa bullocks'. To my surprise and relief, the mob wheeled sharply and started to ring madly around, just off the cattle camp. The thundering hoofs of the tightly massed beasts stirred up a maelstrom of dust and flying debris. As I called out to the mob to calm them, I could feel the thudding of Actor's heart through the saddle flaps and was aware of my own racing pulse. The surge of adrenalin that triggered a sharpening of the reflexes and an enhancement of the senses was not unfamiliar to me, and I thanked God that the mob had not rushed.

The bullocks were owned by Vestey's, an English company with a string of stations across the Territory and the East Kimberley region. As I rode and sang to the mob, I wondered if the company's directors had any inkling of the problems and perils faced by the men who moved cattle to market. Slowly the mob settled down and my thoughts turned to the train of events that had resulted in me becoming a boss drover.

The Early Years

IT IS PROBABLY true to say that the bush is in my blood. Looking back at my childhood, it is difficult to see how my life could have unfolded differently. I was reared with my brothers on a small selection, one of a number cut off old Pinnacle Station, west of Mackay. The unimproved block was virgin tropical scrub and forest when taken up by my father in 1923, the year I was born.

My parents were no strangers to the bush, although before she was married my mother had led a relatively sheltered life as a station governess in the Mundubbera area. She was a member of a well-known pioneering family, her grandfather John Connolly having been one of the first settlers on the Burnett. He was known as the father of Gayndah and must have been a tough character, for he lived to one hundred and three. My mother told me he smoked a pipe and chopped wood to the very end. My father was born in Australia and was an only child. His father was Scottish, and although his mother was born of Scottish parents, she first saw the light of day in Calcutta, in 1857, the year of the Indian mutiny.

On finishing his education at Maryborough Grammar, my father, against the wishes of his parents, went bush. He worked on cattle stations in the Dawson Valley and on Cape York Peninsula. When World War I broke out, he was managing Bonny Downs, a mixed cattle and sheep property in the Muttaburra district. He enlisted early in 1915, and soon after sailed for France. He won his sergeant's stripes at the front, but late in the war was badly gassed. In 1919 he returned to Australia and married my mother, to whom he had become engaged before sailing.

After my parents' marriage, my father managed Gowan Hills in the Blackall area until he drew the block. My elder brother Keith was born during this period, and in 1923 my mother and he travelled to Brisbane to await my arrival — while my father went to Mackay to take up the selection. The block was far too small to run cattle alone; in North Queensland the talk then was all of sugar growing and the country had been cut up with that in mind.

My father arrived on the selection with one saddle horse and a packhorse. That night as he unrolled his swag under the tall gums, it must have seemed to him like the fulfilment of a dream. For years he had worked on other people's properties; now at last he had his own place. He was not to know that in a few short years the Great Depression would almost destroy that dream.

My father's first task was to fence the selection. He set to cutting and splitting the posts from the giant bloodwood trees that grew in the open forest country. The fencing done, he bought a few head of cattle and a team of horses. The best land for sugar growing was on the creek flats; the deep, rich soil there was covered in rainforest, a tangled thicket of vines, palms and huge trees. Working on his own with a block and tackle, my father cleared enough to plant his first crop.

By the middle of 1923 I had put in an appearance, and my father, keen to re-unite the family, ordered the material for a house and contracted a teamster to bring the load out to the selection. After paying for the building material there was enough money left to purchase a light wagon, a buggy and the necessary farm machinery, but the bank would have to carry the place until the first crop was harvested. It was at that point that unkind fate stepped in. The teamster bringing the load out had an accident as the wagon was negotiating a jump-up. He was taken to Mackay hospital, and the building material was off-loaded on the spot.

It was a few days before my father heard of the mishap. He rode over to find that the whole load had been stolen, not a stick of timber or a nail remained. Cursing his luck, my father, who was now forced to improvise, started on the job with little more than a crosscut saw and an axe. Out of bush timber, he erected a crude two-room house with an open front verandah. It had a dirt floor and a bark roof. My mother, who had been used to living in spacious homesteads, must have received a shock when we arrived. However, she made the best of things and somehow managed to cope. My father, toiling from dawn to dusk to make the selection viable, did what he could to help and knocked up a charcoal cooler to keep perishables from the heat and flies. Under my mother's influence, the rough dwelling soon developed the atmosphere of a home.

To keep the dust down, the dirt floor had to be sprinkled with water and swept each morning. The smell of damp earth still brings back memories of the old home to me. As water had to be carried up from the creek in buckets, my mother did the family wash at a shallow rocky stretch in the stream. Later when water was brought up in a 100 gallon (450 litre) tank on a horse-drawn slide, she used a wood-fired clothes boiler and tin tubs. With no phone or radio, my mother worried constantly about us children. During the Wet, we were sometimes cut off completely for weeks at a time as the normally placid creeks roared on their way to join the Pioneer River.

With the first crop harvested, things looked up a little and my father bought enough galvanised iron to cover the bark roof. This made the place a lot more weatherproof and quite cool.

During the wet season, however, the gap between the bark and the iron provided a snug haven for the green frogs that croaked all night and added to my mother's woes. The selection was lousy with snakes, which at times got into the roof chasing the frogs. I have a vivid recollection, when a child, of seeing a large snake with a frog in its mouth fall out of the roof onto the dinner table.

To beautify the home a little, my mother made hanging baskets for the verandah and filled them with ferns from the creek. She got my father to enclose the area with wire netting, then trained sweet peas to cover the mesh. My mother fussed endlessly over the sweet peas; I don't think any of us realised just how much they meant to her. When she won a box brownie in a competition run by the *Woman's Mirror,* one of the first photos taken was of the sweet peas.

The one thing our home did not lack was reading material. My maternal grandmother owned and ran a large lending library in Brisbane, and mindful of our isolation, she bundled up the books that became too dog-eared for circulation and sent them to us.

We received books of every description, from *Westward Ho* to *On Our Selection,* from *Tom Brown's Schooldays* to *Lasseter's Last Ride.* Long before my elder brother and I could read, our parents often read these books to us a chapter at a time. Later, when I could read myself, a copy of the *Bulletin Reciter* arrived in a parcel. I read it avidly and an enduring love of bush verse was born.

Before the arrival of my two younger brothers, my father added two extra rooms plus a back verandah to the home and put down a wooden floor throughout. The place had been built as a temporary dwelling only; now it was taking on the appearance of a permanent residence. My mother, however, had her own ideas about its future and my father promised her he would build her the home she wanted as soon as he could afford it.

My mother cooked on an old wood stove with a hot water fountain fixed to its side. On cold winter evenings it became the centre of the family's social life. We would all sit around the stoked-up stove while my elder brother and I pressed our father to tell us of his experiences in the outback. We would listen spellbound as he spoke in a quiet voice of cattle duffing, buckjumpers, Aboriginal culture, and epic feats of endurance. He also told stories of Bully Hayes, the notorious blackbirder who shanghaied natives from the Pacific Islands and brought them back in his ship to sell as cheap labour to the early Queensland sugar growers. It was heady stuff to a youngster growing up in the bush and I went to sleep each night dreaming of the time when I would be old enough to seek adventure for myself. The valley in which we lived was surrounded on three sides by mountains. As a young boy I often looked at those hills and promised myself that one day I would find out what lay beyond them.

If those early days were a constant trial to my mother, they were a delight to my brothers and me. The selection teemed with wildlife of every description; there was either a koala or a possum in every tree, sugar gliders feasted on the blossoms of bloodwood and gum trees, while bandicoots, rat kangaroos and wallabies all shared the bush with us. As youngsters we had just about every kind of bush creature imaginable as a pet. Our mother suffered them all, although our echidna sometimes got us into trouble because of its habit of digging holes everywhere.

Beatrice Creek meandered through the property, running clear and cool between the tropical rainforest that lined its banks. The creek teemed with fish, harboured a number of water rats and was home to a family of platypuses. During the summer months we swam in its palm-fringed swimming holes, made crude boats to play at blackbirding, and dived to the sandy bottom to gather imaginary pearl shell. All in all, it was an idyllic lifestyle and I dare say we were as close to nature as it is possible to get.

As we grew older we gave our mother grey hairs by wandering further afield with a mate who knew more about bush tucker than the Bush Tucker Man himself. By the time we were of school age we were virtually capable of living off the land. One of our favourite sports was snake hunting. We would arm ourselves with green sticks about 6 feet (2 metres) long, then whistling to the dogs, we would set out into the bush to do battle with our sworn enemies.

We had two dogs that were expert snake killers. Working as a team, they could deal with any snake, including the king browns and the big red-bellied blacks that in the summer months seemed to be everywhere. The dogs' technique was simple, but very effective — as one teased the snake, the other would dash in and, grasping the reptile in its jaws, would shake it violently, breaking its back. If the snake was a very large one, they would take turns doing this until they had it completely immobilised. We would then move in and administer the coup de grace with our waddies.

We went on these expeditions with bare legs and feet. Looking back, I suppose there was some risk, but we were bushwise kids aware of the dangers. A neighbour's son in our age group was bitten by a snake and died. My mother was appalled by the tragedy, but it did little to dampen our enthusiasm for the hunt. Years later it was discovered that the area was a taipan habitat. By today's enlightened standards there is no doubt that our activities would be classed as environmental vandalism. However, back in those days, when medical help was virtually out of reach, the only good snake was deemed to be a dead one.

The best snake dog we ever had was Pincer. Right from the time my elder brother Keith and I were toddlers she was our constant companion. Pincer was not all that good with stock, but because she was so protective of us, Mother thought the world of her. While out hunting on her own one day, Pincer met the fate of most snake dogs. I don't know what type of snake killed her, but it must have been a bad one, for in her efforts to get home, she crawled only 20 yards from the log under which she had been scratching. We carried her body home and gave her a solemn burial. My mother wept openly, while Keith and I stood silently with constricted throats and dry eyes. Boys did not cry those days.

Each year we travelled to Mackay twice, once just before Christmas, and on Anzac Day. The first part of the trip was made in our buggy, pulled by Dolly, a reliable grey mare. At the railway siding she would be tied up with a nosebag on, until we returned that night.

Christmas was of course always something we looked forward to with relish, for it was the only time we had ham and soft drink. The ham arrived packed in oat husks and stockinet. It was carefully unwrapped and cooked with due ceremony in the cleaned-out clothes boiler. The soft drink was home-brewed ginger beer and a type of hop beer called horehound. The brew was started well before the big day, and usually all went well. There were times, however, when the silence of the bush night was shattered by the sounds of exploding bottles. When this happened, it was panic stations until the remaining bottles had been uncorked. I suppose it was a bit like disarming live bombs, but, then, soft drink in those days was not the everyday thirst quencher it is today.

My mother decorated the house with native plants and gum tips that we gathered for her. The pièce de résistance on the Christmas dinner table was always her great boiled plumduff. We would hoe into it in the hope of finding the threepenny bits she had secreted among the fruit and nuts. Later, in the outback, I had some rather lean Christmases, and looked back with nostalgia at those early Christmas dinners.

Anzac Day was quite different. Although my father never spoke of his time at the front, the Great War — as it was called — exerted a subtle yet powerful influence over the families of all who fought in it. We always arrived in Mackay in time to watch the march. My father, however, never marched himself and wore no medals, just his returned soldiers' badge. After the march he always attended the reunion lunch, then met us in the park, where we would picnic with the families of other returned men.

As a returned soldier my father never received or asked to receive any privileges other than those accorded to an ordinary citizen. Only once did I hear him address in a rather derogatory manner a man who had not enlisted. The incident occurred during a wharf lumpers' strike in the depression years. As the stockpile of unshipped sugar built up, the mills stopped crushing and the industry ground to a halt.

A man who was trying to organise the growers into a strike-breaking gang rode over to enlist the help of my father. When he had finished putting his case, my father looked up at the rider and said, 'Are you asking me to go in and scab on the men I fought with?'

'Well,' replied the visitor. 'We have to keep the home fires burning, you know.'

There was a touch of cold anger in my father's voice as he dismissed the man. 'I'll leave the home fires to you. After all, you got a lot of practice stoking them when we were fighting in France.'

As the would-be strike breaker rode off, I felt very proud of my father.

When my elder brother reached school age, my mother decided to teach him by correspondence until I was old enough to ride to school with him. The nearest school was built beside a road some miles from the nearest township. To shorten the route to the school, my father blazed a track through the bush for us to follow.

In time the bridle track became a well-used road. Riding there was not a problem as we had been taught to ride almost as soon as we could walk. Paddy, our first pony, had died, so it was on Playboy that we rode to school, bareback and double-bank; saddles were out, as my father contended that the only way to learn to ride was bareback. Playboy was a bay horse of about 15 hands. We mounted him by putting our toes in his knee and swinging up from there.

As we were old enough to go to school, it was decided that we should help around the place. Each morning before riding to school we had to muster the work horses and the milkers, then milk the cows, and separate the milk so that my mother could make butter. After a quick swim in the creek, it was off to school for the three Rs, interposed with a bit of mayhem. After school we helped unharness and feed the horses, chopped wood for the stove and generally made ourselves useful. What homework we had was done by the light of a hurricane lamp.

As the 1920s ended, sugar prices fell, banks crashed and credit became unobtainable. As unemployment grew, men carried their swags in search of work. I remember clearly the sad procession of down-at-heel swagmen, many of them returned soldiers, who called at our place in the hope of getting a job or a handout. None went away empty-handed, for although we had little money, we were close to being self-sufficient as far as food went. As the depression deepened, despair and hopelessness seemed to be everywhere and my mother saw her cherished plans for a new home, together with her ambition to send us to boarding school, fade into the realm of impossible dreams.

Despite the depression, I managed to acquire a horse of my own, although I still did not have a saddle. The gelding was a smart-looking chestnut about five years old. He had been kept as a stallion for some time and bore the impressive name of Robert Dean. I shortened his name to Bobby and felt 10 feet (3 metres) tall when I rode him about the district. Before long I found that by touching him on the rump, I could get him to kick up with both hind feet. I regarded this as great fun, and soon had him kicking up so high that the only way I could stay on him was to lean back while jamming my bare feet under his front legs.

My father jumped on him one day to go after some stock; Bobby went into his act and nearly unseated him. Later I was taken to task.

'You've been teaching that horse tricks, haven't you?'

There was little sense in denying it. 'Well, I want to work on stations later and I've got to learn to ride.'

'I see. If I were you, I'd be careful the horse doesn't learn faster than you do.'

I caught the hint of a smile as my father walked away.

One of my more pleasant tasks was to ride into the township of Pinnacle every Saturday to pick up mail and any rations we needed. My father allowed me to use his saddle for the trip, as it made it easier to carry a split bag. A split bag is made by sewing up the open end of a sack bag then cutting one side across the middle; the resulting split bag is thrown over the back of the saddle to provide a roomy pocket on each side. I usually took a short cut to the township, fording Cattle Creek, then crossing the Pinnacle plains past the grave of a young stockman who had been killed in a fall from a horse. I always saluted the headstone as I cantered past on Bobby.

Once upon returning with the mail, I left the saddle on the ground up against a post rather than hanging it up. A cattle pup that I had just acquired got stuck into the lining, tearing it to pieces. My father gave me two options: get rid of the pup or repair the saddle myself. To me, the choice was simple. I cadged some curtain material from my mother and, at a very tender age, was to line my first saddle.

At times stockmen would bring mobs of draughthorses from Charters Towers to sell to the farmers. Whenever I got the chance, I rode around with them. They would yarn about life over the range, and as I listened, I became more determined to see it all for myself.

North to the Territory

I HAD ALWAYS wanted to work in the Northern Territory, and finally I got the chance. But when I threw my gear onto the Northern mail train one night early in 1944, I had little idea of the problems that lay ahead of me. Before leaving Brisbane I had dropped in to the office of the North Australian Pastoral Company and talked to D.M. Fraser, the company's managing director. He greeted me in a friendly manner and listened to my story; he appeared to me to be a man who took a fatherly interest in the staff of all the NAPC's stations. Before I left the office, he told me there was a job as stockman on Alexandria waiting for me and wished me well.

I arrived in Mt Isa three days after leaving Brisbane. I left the train with some relief, and stretched my legs as I looked the place over. Mt Isa, those days, had the raw dusty look of most mining towns in the early years of development. I rolled a smoke and considered a plan of action. The first thing was to find out when, and with whom, I could get a ride out to Alexandria. As the railway station was on the mine side, well away from the town, I decided to leave my gear on one of the seats on the platform. I had less than five pounds to my name; if the worst came to the worst, I could always camp on the platform. I was just walking off when I heard a bellow.

'Is this gear yours?'

I turned to see a railway employee glaring at me.

'Yes. Why?'

'Well, get it out of here before I call the cops.'

'Christ,' I thought to myself. 'Welcome to Mt Isa.'

What I did not realise was that the police had alerted every government employee to be on the lookout for soldiers who were AWL and heading for the Territory.

I picked up my swag and headed for the town. As I crossed the low causeway across the Leichhardt River, I saw ahead of me the friendly facade of the Argent Hotel. Bush pubs are always a good source of information and I needed a drink badly. I pushed open the swinging doors, threw my swag in the corner and headed for the bar. The man behind the bar wandered over in a rather uninterested manner.

'Any chance of a beer?'

'Nope, not until the shift finishes at four o'clock.'

'Any rum?'

He looked at me as if I'd just arrived from Mars. 'There's a war on, you know.'

'So they tell me. What the hell have you got?'

'There's lolly water.'

'Well, that'll do.'

I watched him pour some locally made soft drink into a glass. He pushed it over to me.

'That'll be a bob.'

I gave him a shilling and took a drink of the sickly stuff, then asked him, 'Who runs the mail or loading out to Alexandria?'

'Trying to get to the Territory, are you?' He looked me over. 'We'll, you'd better see Les Peak.'

I finished the drink. 'Where do I find him?'

He told me, and as I was walking out, called me back.

'Don't leave your swag there. These bloody miners will kick it to pieces trying to get to the bar. Leave it by the office.'

I took his advice, and after a couple of minutes walking I found Peak's yard. There were a number of trucks parked, with a couple being serviced. A chap pulled his head out from under a bonnet as I asked, 'Where will I find Les Peak?'

Without answering, he jerked his thumb in the direction of a shed that I could see doubled as an office.

Les Peak greeted me affably and asked what he could do for me.

'I've got a job on Alexandria. When is your next trip out there?'

'Won't be 'till Sunday. It'll cost you two quid.'

'Fair enough. I'll pay you now — the way I'm going, I won't have it later.'

Les scratched me out a receipt, then looked up. 'You'll need a permit.'

'What do you mean?'

He laughed at my apparent innocence. 'The Territory is under martial law. You can't get in without a permit.'

'Well, where do I get a blasted permit?'

'At the manpower office. It's just across from the Argent on the left before you go over the river.'

I thanked him, saying I'd see him on Sunday, and left.

As I walked back to the pub, I realised I had a problem. The permit should not be difficult to obtain, but Sunday was four days away and I had just over two pounds in my pocket. Camping on the river was out, I decided. It was likely that anyone found camping there would be thrown into gaol for life. I came to the conclusion that the sensible thing to do was to see the publican. The permit could wait until the morrow.

When I got back to the Argent I found the area around the bar chock-a-block with thirsty miners struggling to get a drink. It looked like something between a riot and a rugby union ruck. I gave it a wide berth and went to the office, where I found Stewart Summerville, the licensee. I introduced myself and told him everything. He looked at me appraisingly.

'You're not AWL?'

'No, I'm not.'

I unrolled my swag, pulled out a small writing case and set his mind at rest.

'You say you've got a job in the Alexandria camp?'

I nodded. 'You can ring Brisbane and verify it if you wish.'

'That's all right. There's a bed on the verandah, and I'll stand you board. Send in a cheque as soon as you can.'

I thanked him, and with my faith in human nature restored, I took my swag upstairs.

The next morning at ten o'clock I strolled over to the manpower office. I had had a hearty breakfast and was feeling on top of the world. I entered the office and stood at the counter. A middle-aged clerk saw me, but went back to writing something or other at his desk. After a couple of minutes I knocked on the counter. The clerk looked at me as though I'd just broken wind, but grudgingly came over.

'What do you want?'

I was determined to be pleasant.

'I'd like a permit to enter the Territory, please.'

'Do you? For what reason?'

'I've got a job to go to on Alexandria.'

'Have you? Do you have a clearance from manpower?'

I looked at him stupidly. 'A what?'

'A clearance. You just can't go where you please these days. We tell you where you will work.'

'Well, can you organise it? They expect me out there on the first truck.'

'I don't think you heard me. We tell you where you can work. Now, where did you work last, and for whom?'

I thought for a while, then told him, trying not to lose patience.

'Well, you will have to go back there.'

I looked at him incredulously. 'What the hell do you mean?'

'You will have to go back and work where you worked last.'

'Look, I'll say it again. I've got a job. Ring up the North Australian Pastoral Company if you don't believe me.'

'You will have to go back and see the manpower office where you last worked.'

He was beginning to sound like a broken gramophone record. I forced myself to reason with him.

'I've paid my fare out to Alexandria, but I've only got a few shillings left. I can't go anywhere.'

He looked at me sternly. 'That puts you in the same category as a vagrant.'

'No, it puts you in the same category as a bloody cretin. Are you going to pay my fare back and give Summerville the week's board I owe him?'

It was a calculated bluff. For all I knew he may have been able to write out a rail warrant on the spot, but it shook him.

'I'll have to confer with Brisbane on this. You'll have to come back tomorrow.'

I turned and walked out. As I went through the door, he bleated, 'I didn't get your name and particulars.'

I kept walking. Over at the pub, reassured now that I was a house guest, the barman reached under the counter for the rum bottle. A ruddy-faced character in the almost empty bar nodded to me and drifted over.

'Mind if I join you? A man shouldn't drink on his own.'

'No, I'm glad of the company. I've just been trying to talk sense to that dictatorial bastard over at the manpower office.'

'You're wasting your time. Those blokes make Hitler look like Tinker Bell, but they don't worry me — I'm a yard builder and I go where I like, and when I like. I just slip out of town at night and I've got them rooted. That mob couldn't find their arse in two grabs.'

I bought him a rum and thought about what he had said.

That night after dinner I decided to go for a stroll. When I got outside I found that it was drizzling rain so went back upstairs and put on the only coat I had, an army tunic. I wandered up the main street, then returned to stand under the verandah awning in front of the bar. I thought about a drink, but decided against it as the clamour within indicated a full house. I lent up against a post and rolled a smoke. As I lit it, a character in a snap brim hat sauntered up to me.

'A stranger in town?' he said.

I took him to be a bit of a spiv, but nodded agreement.

'I see. Where did you get that tunic?'

'Who the hell wants to know?'

He pulled something from his shirt pocket. 'I do. I'm a demon with the local CIB. Now about that tunic?'

I tried to make myself heard above the growing din. 'It was issued to me.'

'What?'

'It was bloody well issued to me.'

'Have you got your discharge on you?'

'No, not on me.'

'You'd better come up to the station with me.'

'Look, if I was AWL, I wouldn't be stupid enough to wear this in public.'

At that moment the swinging doors of the bar burst open and a struggling mass of humanity almost knocked us both over. I left the local Dick Tracy to sort things out and went up to bed. My sense of humour was being steadily eroded.

The next morning I fronted up at the manpower office again, to be told that no decision had been made — I should return after lunch when my fate would be known. The clerk wanted my name and so on and to keep him happy I obliged, then wandered back to the pub. Over lunch I thought about what the yard builder had said. I was determined to get to the Territory by whatever means, and I would not be sorry to see the last of Mt Isa.

The clerk in the manpower office greeted me enthusiastically when I returned at three o'clock. 'Well, we've solved your problem.'

'Great. I can get a permit?'

'No, you will start work at the Mt Isa mines smelter at eight o'clock on Monday morning. You can work there until you have enough money to pay your fare and clear your debts, then we'll be sending you back.'

He spoke triumphantly, with a gleam in his eye reminiscent of a fox in a fowl yard. If he expected a reaction, he was disappointed. My mind was already made up, I was going to the Territory. Life is full of uncertainties, but as I left that building, I was absolutely sure I would not be reporting for work at the smelters on Monday morning.

I made a beeline for Peak's yard, where I asked the first chap I saw who would be taking the loading out to Alexandria. He told me that Clayton Ewart was doing the trip and pointed to a part-Aboriginal driver standing by an International truck. I walked over and introduced myself. He shook hands and said, 'Les told me I'd have a passenger. We'll be leaving at daylight.'

'Well, I don't have a permit. If you've got a tarp on the back, I'll crawl under it — you don't have to know I'm there.'

Clayton laughed. 'Like that, is it? You'll be right in front. I've never been inspected yet, and anyway, you'll be out before they miss you.'

I thanked him and walked back to the Argent, feeling that the world was not a bad place after all.

On Sunday morning everything went according to plan and we drove across the forbidden border without a hitch. For me, it was the start of a new life. I was to spend the next 17 years on the stations and stockroutes of the North-West. I finally left the outback in 1981, taking my family to Toowoomba.

Alexandria

I ARRIVED AT Alexandria to learn that the stockcamp was out mustering the headwaters of the Rankine River and that the manager, Harry Barns, was back in Mt Isa hospital with a broken arm — the result of a fall from a horse. His son Henry, who was the station bookkeeper, made me welcome. He told me to throw my swag in the quarters as it would be three days before a truck went out to the camp.

After tossing the swag on a greenhide-laced bunk, I had a look around. The station complex was on the bank of the Playford River and consisted of the homestead with its own kitchen, a men's kitchen and the ringers' quarters; other buildings were a thatch-roofed meat house, a blacksmith's shop, a work shed and a vehicle shed. A couple of hundred yards away was the blacks' camp. Its rough shelters housed over a hundred men, women and children. I was told that only about 20 per cent of the Aborigines were employed in the stockcamp and around the station.

Alexandria Station is located on the Barkly Tableland in the eastern part of the Northern Territory. Today the property is still owned by the North Australian Pastoral Company. Over the years the run has been greatly improved by additional bores, paddocks and station buildings. Despite being reduced in area to 16 000 square kilometres through land resumption, Alexandria still has a carrying capacity of over 50 000 head of cattle. When I worked there Alexandria was one of the biggest, if not the biggest, cattle properties in the world. It covered 11 800 square miles (30 560 square kilometres), 25 square miles (65 square kilometres) larger than Belgium. The place was said to carry 80 000 head, but on huge unfenced runs like Alexandria estimates of stock numbers were at best an educated guess. The place was worked by three stockcamps, one at the head station, and one at both Gallipoli and Sudan, the two outstations.

At morning smoko I met Deal Adams. I soon learnt that Deal was a rather

Cammy Cleary was head stockman at Alexandria and one of the best rough riders in the Northern Territory.

extraordinary individual. He was a jack of all trades, and master of them all — a good ringer, capable saddler and a builder of horse-drawn vehicles.

After smoko I strolled over to the blacksmith shop where Deal was busy with an electric welder. I watched him for a while, then when he pushed the mask up to inspect a weld, my curiosity got the better of me.

'What's this going to be, Deal?'

'This,' said Deal, grinning at me. 'This is going to be a rubber-tyred wagonette for the stockcamp.'

I was impressed, and showed it.

'What are they using at present?'

'They're carting the gear around on a big dray I made for 'em.'

'You made it. What about the wheels?'

He looked surprised. 'I made them too, but it's a bit heavy to pull; this will be as light as a feather. Sweeny will handle it, though.'

He looked at me hard and changed the subject. 'You're going into the stockcamp, eh?'

I nodded.

'Can you hang up?'

'I can ride a bit.'

'Well, be careful how you say that to Cammy Cleary. He's the best man on a bad horse I've seen and he'll try you out.'

When I arrived at the stockcamp several days later I was greeted warily by the four whites and with unabashed curiosity by the Aboriginal ringers, Wilson, Johnny, Limerick, Frank, Alec and the others. Cammy Cleary, the head stockman, was a taciturn type of chap, as was Reg Winton, an experienced ringer aged about thirty. Cecil Rose, the other white ringer, was about my age. He was known as 'Yarra', and once he got to know me, he talked quite a lot. He was from Tocumwal, on the Murray River in central southern New South Wales, and one day confided in me that he had not been in touch with his family for years as he could not read or write. I volunteered to write a letter for him and until Cecil left Alexandria I wrote to his mother on his behalf.

The camp cook was Ted Sweeny. He had a very large set of loose dentures that clicked like castanets as he talked. When listening to Sweeny, I half expected him to leap in the air and dance a lively fandango. He always brought smoko up to us when we were branding in the bronco yard; his stock in trade was what Reg Winton called 'Sweeny's jamless jam rolls'.

I was disappointed with the first string of horses allocated to me; the five I had were bits of plonkers with very little spirit. Cleary advised me with a quiet smile that a complete change of horses was due in two weeks. When the 100 odd fresh mounts came out from the station, he gave me five that shut me up. To his chagrin, none of them threw me, although a couple of times it was touch and go. Despite the head stockman's desire to teach me a lesson, I felt I had won his grudging respect, and for the first time felt I was accepted in the camp.

It was about this time that I saw Cammy Cleary ride a station outlaw called Rickety Kate and I marvelled at the ease with which he rode her. He rode long — that is, with long stirrups — his legs swinging with the bucks and only the toe of his boot in the irons. One moment he would reach back and tickle the mare in the flank, the next he would be slapping her on the shoulder. I knew then that his reputation as one of the Territory's best buckjump riders was well earned. He was magnificent on a bad horse, but he was not the best all-round horseman I would work with.

I was intrigued by two fat horses that nobody ever rode. They ran with the plant unworked until the next change was due. I asked Cecil about them, to be told they were supposed to be ridden by the Aboriginals, who had bailed up and refused to ride them. One was a yellow bay horse named Yallaman, a horse that bucked backwards, Cecil informed me. The other was a nuggety black gelding with a white blaze. Coola (wild) Paddy, as he was called, had earlier killed an Aboriginal stockman on Sudan, one of the outstations.

When the two horses arrived in the camp the following year, I worked them both. I found Yallaman to be a top stockhorse; with a bit of encouragement, he gave all his bad habits away and settled down. Coola Paddy, however, was, as they say, a horse of a different colour; he probably should have been shot, for he was hard to catch, difficult to mount, and had to be thrown to be shod. He only threw me once, but he was just as bad at the end of the change as he had been at the beginning.

After I left Alexandria, Coola Paddy put Chuckler, a top horseman, in Alice Springs hospital. He was one of the worst horses I ever struck.

I worked under three head stockmen on Alexandria, Cammy Cleary, Doug Harris and Jack Britt. Early in 1946 I left to work on Nutwood, a Vestey station. Some time before leaving, a bay mare called Cockroach bucked over with me down the bank of the Rankine River, badly injuring my lower spine. I was unconscious for two days, then I went on working. It was an injury that was to play merry hell with me later.

The Number 6 Team at Alexandria Station.

The Cattle Runs

IN THE DAYS before the motorised revolution, cattle work in the North-West was done exclusively with horses. Cattle runs ranged from the vast company stations carrying up to 60 000 head to the 'poddy-dodging' blocks tucked away in the rough hills of the Top End.

The work was hard, with long hours and few days off, but it was never dull. In rough country, the job was fast, challenging, and sometimes dangerous, and young men who had escaped the drudgery of city or farm work took to the life like ducks to water. They relished the opportunity to gain their 'spurs' in an occupation where respect was gained solely on the grounds of personal ability. It was a time when top cattlemen and fine horsemen could be found in every stockcamp.

The mustering of wild cattle in scrub country was the most exciting work on the station. This was done by tracking the cattle until the riders got close enough for the mad gallop through the timber to wheel them, then driving the scrubbers back to the waiting quiet cattle held some distance behind. Often beasts broke away from the galloping mob, and these had to be thrown and tied down until the quiet cattle could be brought up. As these breakaways were often scrub bulls, a great deal of skill and guts was needed to pull them down.

In scrub country, throwing was done on foot: after jumping from his horse, the stockman grabbed the beast's tail, throwing it by pulling the tail to the side as the beast turned to charge. In open country, throwing was usually done from the stockhorse.

Branding in the Territory and the Channel Country was done by 'broncoing', but in most of the Gulf and the coastal hinterland of Queensland the calf-pen method was preferred when branding. Broncoing was introduced into Australia from Mexico around the turn of the century. It entailed catching cleanskins with a greenhide rope that was attached to a harness that fitted over a stock saddle. Straps connected this harness to a collar or breastplate on the bronco horse.

All drafting was done in open camps. The cattle was held on an open flat while the selected beasts were worked out of the mob by the camprider on a camphorse. Once clear of the main mob, the selected beast was controlled by ringers called 'face of the camp men'. These men took the selected beast a short distance to where other cattle were held. Camphorses, like nighthorses, were picked mounts of outstanding intelligence and ability.

As the huge cattle stations of those days were unfenced, neighbouring runs sent stockmen to attend the muster. These men drafted out their cattle, kept them in hand, and drove them back to their respective stations at the end of the muster.

Stockcamp gear was transported by packhorse or wagonette, and some East Kimberley stations used pack camels. Stockmen slept in swags on the ground. The food was plain, mostly beef, or beef dishes such as stews and curries.

Stockcamps were run by head stockmen — older experienced men skilled in every facet of stockwork — and camps ranged in size from six or eight men up to 20 in a big camp. The ratio of Aboriginal stockmen to whites was at times four to one in the Territory.

The changes that revolutionised droving also impacted on station work. Old methods changed, and today stations use aerial mustering and portable yards, and catch scrub bulls with vehicles. Progress finally caught up with one of Australia's last frontiers, and no doubt living conditions have improved in the Territory, but I wonder if the quality of life is as rich and rewarding as it was before the change.

Plant horses at a trough on the Barkly Tableland.

Paddy Lennie's Brumbies

PADDY LENNIE WAS the epitome of the wild Irishman: raw boned, bearded, and anti-social to the point where he could not even fit in with the free and easy ways of the Territory. Paddy was a horse crank who thought far more of his horses than he did of his fellow man. After working on stations on the Barkly Tableland, including Alexandria in the 1930s, he settled on Lorne Creek (a part of Alexandria) with his horses and lived the life of a recluse, shunning human company. Paddy visited the Rankine occasionally for stores, but he avoided setting up a permanent camp and had plants of tucker and rough yards hidden over a large area round Lorne Creek, which he came to regard as his own.

As time passed, Lennie's horses multiplied and began to get out of hand; fewer and fewer carried his 44L brand, and young ungelded colts cut out smaller mobs of mares and began to range over a large area of the station. All Paddy's horses were fine stamps of stockhorses, but interested horse buyers, who offered good prices for his Waler-type mounts, were given short shrift by the Hermit of Lorne Creek. Finally C.A.Y. Johnson, the manager of Alexandria, had had enough. He sought the help of the law and a police muster of the wild mobs of horses was carried out. With the majority of them safely in the Rankine dip yard, the heavy gate was made fast with a chain and padlock, and that, thought the powers that be, was that.

Paddy was a renowned grass fighter and that evening everyone was careful to stay clear of the disgruntled Irishman. But Paddy had other ideas of retribution; when daylight broke, the yard had been broached and Paddy and his horses were back in the fastness of Lorne Creek. Paddy died with most of his beloved horses still free. He passed away at Dunmara, on his way to front the court in Darwin.

When I worked on Alexandria some years later the progeny of Paddy Lennie's horses still roamed the Lorne Creek area. When mustering the bottom end of the Rankine, the stockcamp camped and mustered from the gidgees, on the Rankine River. Cammy Cleary, one of the best roughriders in the Territory, was head stockman, and on this occasion Barney Smyth and an Aboriginal stockman from Avon Downs were attending the muster also, bringing the camp's complement to six whites and 13 Aborigines.

One morning the full camp headed out in the direction of Lorne Creek to muster back to the gidgees, a camp that boasted a rather frail wire bronco yard. When mustering, it was always the custom to ride out behind the cattle then split up and muster back, driving the cattle towards the selected spot.

We had ridden out about 4 miles (about 6 kilometres) when, coming over a rise in the downs, we saw spread out in the hollow before us some 200 brumbies scattered about in small mobs. We were downwind from the horses and they had not spotted us, so we reined in our mounts and sat admiring the spectacle. There were many fine-looking types in the mobs, obviously descendants of Paddy Lennie's stallions and mares. We looked at Cleary. He was rolling a smoke, the reins in the crock of his elbow. Suddenly he looked up at us and grinned: 'To hell with the cattle, let's have a crack at yarding this lot'.

The idea was greeted with quiet enthusiasm by all; who would want to muster cattle when there were brumbies to run? We were all well mounted, as Alexandria, like most cattle stations those days, had magnificent stockhorses. I was riding a big bay gelding by Spaza, a stallion renowned as a station sire. My mount had somehow picked up our restrained excitement and was rearing to go.

Riding back down the ridge, we rode in a great circle to get around behind the horse mob. Our whole group was almost in position when the brumbies got wind of us; then ahead of us and to our left we saw the flying manes and tails of galloping horses making back towards Lorne Creek. As one, we gave our mounts their heads, and the chase was on. I doubt if there is anything as exhilarating for both horse and rider as the wild gallop after brumbies; stones flew from under the shod hooves of our horses and men shouted and urged their mounts on, for there was now no need for stealth.

It was Barney Smyth who finally wheeled them, with Cleary, myself and Reg Winton close behind; but that was only the first round. For the next hour it was one mad gallop after another as stallions broke out of the mob with their mares. It grew ever harder to control them when they hit the timber, but the adrenalin was still flowing and the yard was not far away.

We were in sight of the yard when the mob finally beat us; had we had calico wings out from the gate, we would have got the lot, but as it was, we were lucky to yard some 15 head. Then out of the scrub came Barney Smyth to yard a fine chestnut mare in a remarkable feat of horsemanship; he had raced his horse up beside her as she broke away from the yard, then vaulted from his stockhorse on to her back, steering her back to the yard with his hat.

After unsaddling our horses, we looked over our catch. There was one young black stallion and eight good sorts of mares; the rest, however, were not worth keeping. As Barney was trying to put a horse plant together, it was agreed that he could have what he wanted out of the captive brumbies and we would bush the rest. Next morning, for a dare, I caught and rode the black stallion. Riding an unbroken and unmouthed brumby buck in a wire yard may seem like reckless stupidity, but to walk away from a challenge in the presence of men like Cleary and Smyth would have been unthinkable.

The Rankine Store

THE RANKINE STORE, complete with bottle licence, was on the Rankine (or Ranken) River about 40 miles (65 kilometres) from the Alexandria homestead. It was always spelled Rankine by the drovers and the owners of the store but usually appears as Ranken on modern maps. As it was situated on country mustered by the stockcamp, the store proved, over the years, to be a headache to managers of the sprawling cattle property. Finally, bowing to the inevitable, tacit approval was given to the ringers to have a few days off whenever they mustered past the place.

One hears a lot about endurance riders these days. Once, for a bet, Cammy Cleary rode a horse from Alexandria to the Rankine and back, a round trip of 80 miles (130 kilometres) between sun-up and sundown. He took a bottle of Fowler's rum back as proof. Not bad for a grass-fed stockhorse.

In my time Jim Fowler and his good wife catered to the needs of the drovers and ringers. Jimmy had been head stockman on Alexandria and was a top roughrider who once rode a grey outlaw called The Snake. He was a bit of a showman, handy with his fists, and a real artist with a whip. I once saw a big young ringer challenge Jimmy to hop outside and put his fists up; after a moment's thought, Jimmy agreed, but on his way outside he made a detour through the kitchen, where he emptied one of his wife's pepper pots into his left fist. The bout was a brief one: Jimmy threw a straight left, opening his fist at the end of the punch; the right cross that followed flattened his half-blinded opponent.

Wason Byers, one of the Territory's rougher denizens, dropped into the Rankine one day when we were all there. He was after a couple of chaps, he told us, who he claimed had maligned him. He caught up with them in Mrs Fowler's kitchen, where a leg of goat was roasting for dinner. Wason dropped one of the alleged offenders, then grabbing the other, he sat the struggling ringer on the hot stove top and held him there. For a while it looked as though the night's menu of roast goat would be augmented by roast ringer.

One day at the Rankine, Reg Winton and I got into a debate on rushes. He contended any animals would rush, while I believed highly domesticated ones

The Rankine Store in 1920. NORTH AUSTRALIAN PASTORAL COMPANY.

would not, despite the opinion of a drunken cook who kept relating how he'd seen 30 cats rush and take the side out of a meat house at McArthur River. The debate was an amicable one and I forgot about it until on the way back to the camp, Reg stopped beside Mrs Fowler's goat yard. Mrs Fowler had over a hundred goats that provided meat and milk for the isolated settlement. They were penned every night in a large yard that had an iron-roofed shed in one corner for shelter.

'Now,' said Reg, 'let's settle this rush business.'

He climbed up the fence and then carefully made his way on to the roof of the shed. The goats camped around the yard took no notice of the intruder, until he suddenly leapt in the air, landing with a bellow in the middle of the iron roof. The result was instantaneous and devastating: the goats flattened one side of the compound and disappeared at high speed into the night. Reg made his point, but our reception at the store next day was decidedly frosty.

During those times when we were at the Rankine, we always camped at the one mile waterhole in the river just below the store. It was an easy walk sober, but for those of us who overdid it at Fowlers', it became something between a marathon and an army obstacle course. At one time we had in the camp a cook who earlier had made a fortune at Tennant Creek. He had blown it all in Sydney, with the exception of a top dental plate specially made for him from gold from his mine. One morning we awoke to find our babbler missing. He later staggered into camp, a hungover and heartbroken wreck, crying that he'd lost his fangs. He had apparently got lost and wandered around in circles most of the night. He had had a number of big spits during his drunken wanderings and no doubt his teeth had taken flight on one of these occasions.

After some merriment at the cook's expense, we poured a rum into him and all hands set out to track down the lost dentures. I could not help thinking of Jason and his search for the Golden Fleece, only this time it was the search for the Golden Teeth. Finally one of the group found the cook's last link with his affluent past. The relieved owner picked up his dentures and, after wiping them briefly on his trousers, popped them into his mouth and headed up to the store for another rum.

The Shooting of Palmer Brushe

ONE DAY BEFORE going out to the Alexandria stockcamp I was having a yarn to Arthur Remfrey in his room at the men's quarters. I noticed a hole in the door and remarked, 'That looks like a bullet hole.'

'It's a bullet hole, all right,' he replied. 'In fact it's two bullet holes close together. This is the room where Palmer Brushe was shot.'

I was curious about the incident and pressed him for the details.

Sudden and violent death was not uncommon at one time in the Territory, but the shooting of Palmer Brushe was different; it was a tragic mistake. The man who pulled the trigger had murder on his mind, that is indisputable. The tragedy was that he shot the wrong man, a man who was in fact a good mate of his. The cause of the trouble was the old eternal triangle, at the apex of which was an Aboriginal girl on Alexandria. Cohabitation between whites and Aboriginal women did go on in the Territory; it was supposed to be illegal, but as long as there was no trouble, the authorities were prepared to turn a blind eye. Perhaps the fact that it went on in fairly high places also led to its tacit acceptance.

It must be understood that the men who settled and developed the NT were no saints; they were tough, hard-bitten and lusty characters who worked hard and played hard. There were few white women in the Territory those days, and the few who were there were married and of a very different class. There was a saying in the Top End: 'Necessity is the mother of invention and the father of all half-caste children.' The saying, offensive by today's standards, had more than an element of truth in it. It is true that in the early days of settlement rape and kidnapping of Aboriginal women did, for a while, take place. However, that disappeared when stations learnt to depend on Aboriginal labour and the Territory's mounted police gained control. The liaisons that developed later between white males and Aboriginal women were based on mutual agreement and were at times initiated by the women themselves.

It must also be clearly understood that not all Territorians indulged in promiscuity; many, like Palmer Brushe, did not. In the affair at Alexandria, he was an innocent victim. The main players in the tragedy were Snowy Baker, who in the mid-1930s was employed as a horse breaker on Alexandria; Matey Cotters and

Frank Sweeny, who were also employed at the homestead; and of course, Palmer Brushe himself. A man named Johnson also played a small part.

Baker was a hard man and a typical Territorian; he got on well with Palmer Brushe, who was the windmill expert. Baker became infatuated with an Aboriginal girl on the station and this later developed into a full-blown liaison. Snowy Baker was intensely jealous of anyone who as much as looked at his girl, but there was one man who bided his time.

Baker left Alexandria to take up a block on the Robinson River with a partner. Later he brought cattle from the block back through Alexandria. Baker had a few days with the girl at the station, then drove his cattle on down the stockroute. It was then that Matey Cotters moved in; whether in fact he had been sleeping with the girl before is not known, but he lost no time when Snowy Baker left.

Johnson, who may have been asked by Baker to keep an eye on things, caught a horse after work the next day and rode with the news to Baker's camp on the Buchanan River. Snowy Baker, mad with jealousy, strapped on a revolver, caught a fast horse and headed back to the station. It was well after dark when he arrived and by that time he was in a murderous rage. He tied up his horse and strode to the quarters to settle his account with Cotters.

Snowy Baker always wore long-necked spurs that dragged on the ground and jingled as he walked. On that fateful night those spurs may well have sounded Palmer Brushe's death knell. Cotters, who had the girl in his room, heard and recognised the sound. He fled from his room, ran the length of the barrack-style building and dived into Palmer Brushe's room at the far end. Palmer and Frank Sweeny were sitting on the bed yarning. They looked up in surprise as Cotters slammed the front door shut, gasped out, 'Baker's here', then raced out the back door.

Baker, who had witnessed the flight of his intended victim, approached the closed door roaring, 'Come out, you gutless dingo, or I'll shoot you through the door.'

Palmer jumped up as Frank cried a warning. 'Stay away from the door. He's mad, that bloke, he'll shoot you.'

'It's right. I'll talk to him and calm him down.'

As Palmer reached for the door handle, Baker fired two shots. The bullets crashed through the door, mortally wounding the windmill expert, who slumped backwards to the floor. As Frank Sweeny sat stunned, Baker kicked the door open and sprang into the room. He stopped short and reeled back when he saw the man on the floor.

'Oh God, Palmer, I've shot you,' he cried.

Without another word Snowy Baker wheeled around and walked up to the homestead. He handed the revolver to C.A.Y. Johnson, the manager, saying, 'For Christ's sake, take this. I've just shot my best mate.'

The next morning Baker was arrested and Cotters was found hiding in an old steam engine behind the quarters, where he had been cowering all night.

Snowy Baker stood trial in Darwin and was sentenced to a long term in Fanny Bay gaol. Cotters, who was reviled by many for having caused the tragedy, later left Alexandria and moved to Tennant Creek. When the Japs bombed Darwin in 1942 all prisoners, including Snowy Baker, were released. If Cotters believed that Baker now had two scores to settle with him, he did not wait around to find out. He headed south and dropped out of sight, as did Baker himself.

Palmer Brushe left a wife and family in Winton. Many years later I met them. I also met Palmer's brother Gaynor, who with his sons Ron and Stan had a plumbing business in Winton. All three became very good friends of mine.

The shooting of Palmer Brushe was one of those freakish incidents that should never have happened. It cost Palmer his life, Baker his freedom, and Cotters his reputation as a man.

The Rankine Races

THE FIRST RACE meeting of the Alexandria, Brunette and Creswell Race Club was held at the Rankine in 1922. One of the prime movers in the establishment of the ABC Race Club was Jim Broadbridge, bookkeeper on Alexandria, and the club's first secretary. Other members of that first committee were Dick Holt, manager of Alexandria, Herbert Lloyd, manager of Avon Downs, George Watson, owner of the Rankine store, Bill Reilly, owner of the Landsborough Hotel in Camooweal, and Pat Synott, of Synott Murray and Scholes, who had stores in both Camooweal and Burketown.

A track was laid out near the Rankine store, and a tin shed was erected to act as a bar. Watson built a small dance hall close to his establishment, for George Watson was a good businessman, and race meetings meant money. The high hopes for the meeting were soon realised. Finding gallopers was never a problem, as all of the stations had thoroughbred stallions servicing the station mares, and the bloodlines of some of the stallions were as good as many standing at southern studs. The Territory was full of horsemen ready to ride, bet, drink and dance, so a race meeting was right up their alley. The Rankine races became an instant success and the meeting quickly became the main social event on the Barkly Tableland, with station staff and townspeople alike setting up elaborate camps along the one mile hole in the Rankine River. A piano was set up in the hall and the revellers danced well into the small hours.

There was, of course, a lot of high-spirited fun: I once saw Jimmy Carr throw a large goanna onto the middle of the dance floor during a quick step. The wildly thrashing reptile found it almost impossible to get traction on the highly polished surface, but the dancers had no such difficulty. The quick step turned into a rout, with the ladies leading the charge for the door.

Jimmy Carr was a jocular, rotund individual, with an infectious chuckle and a permanent twinkle in his eye; he was a natural comedian and the perpetrator of many outrageous jokes. Jimmy decided to go into business at one Rankine meeting. His plan was to set up a 'knock 'em down' stall, with himself as the target. He arrived early and purchased a bag of potatoes from Jimmy Fowler, the current owner of the Rankine store. These he boiled in a 44 gallon (200 litre) drum until nearly cooked. On race day he enlisted the aid of a helper whose job it was to hand out the spuds at sixpence a throw. Setting the drum at about 20 paces, Jimmy stood

The ABC Race Club Executive, July 1922. Left to Right: *George Watson, Herbert Lloyd, Pat Synnott, Richard Holt and Bill Reilly.* Front: *James Broadbridge, club secretary.* NORTH AUSTRALIAN PASTORAL COMPANY.

behind it and invited all and sundry to have a go and win five bob with a direct hit.

The sixpences rolled in, the air became thick with flying potatoes, and Jimmy danced and dodged and chuckled behind the drum. Finally, the last potato was thrown and no one had managed to hit Jimmy, but this led to his undoing. He bought another bag of spuds, and confident of his ability to outwit the potato pelters, he saved time by not boiling the new projectiles. The sixpences continued to roll in, Jimmy dodged and chuckled, and the raw potatoes went bounding over the landscape.

All went well until a left-handed Aborigine faced his tormentor with a spud in each hand. Feinting with the right, he drove the left-hand potato at Jimmy like a bullet. It struck him fair between the eyes, knocking him unconscious and out of sight behind his drum. The Aborigine waited expectantly for a few minutes, then turned to Jimmy's assistant and said: 'Well I bin hit 'im all right, but he's a bloody long time paying me.'

After that Jimmy decided that being in business was not all it was cracked up to be and retired, with two black eyes, to Fowlers' to liquidate his accumulated capital. The Aborigines, meanwhile, gathered the scattered missiles for a blow out of potatoes cooked in the ashes.

A rather unusual wrestling match took place at the Rankine one race day. The manager of a Northern Territory cattle station, who was proud of his prowess as a wrestler, claimed he could break any hold that could be put on him and challenged all comers to try their skill. No one seemed all that interested until the heavily built policeman from Anthony's Lagoon was persuaded to take up the challenge. Although the station manager had been on the grog for a few days, he was

*Barney Smythe, a ringer, contemplates his fortunes
at dawn after the race meeting.*

prepared to back himself and money was wagered on the outcome. The policeman was allowed to apply the hold and then the battle commenced.

The two men grappled and struggled for a while, then both fell to the floor, where the station manager heaved and strained in his efforts to break the hold. It looked as if the policeman's grip would hold when the manager, in a last ditch attempt, gave a terrific heave and strained his hardest to break free. He failed to break the policeman's hold — what he did do, however, was to dirty his trousers thoroughly. The policeman sprang to his feet crying foul. He paid up, though, saying that the manager had perfected an unorthodox but very effective method of breaking a wrestling hold.

It was not all beer and skittles at the Rankine, for the race club has seen tragedy. When the horses lined up for the Cup in 1938, no one in the excited and expectant crowd could have had any inkling of the impending disaster. The track at the Rankine was a black soil one that was fire ploughed before each meeting, and the resulting surface was fairly good. There was no running rail in the straight, just a large post firmly set in the ground at the furlong mark.

The Cup had been reduced to a two horse race, with most of the starters having been scratched, leaving the race to the two favourites in what had all the appearances of a match race. George Lewis, one of the Territory's best horsemen, was riding a grey gelding highly fancied by some to win the Cup. However, it was Wynowie, a black mare owned by Tommy Lewis Snr of Avon Downs, that was most fancied by the crowd. Wynowie was a well-bred mare by Brimstone, but she had one bad habit that at times made her difficult to ride. She sometimes threw her head and then reefed at the bit. Young Len Lloyd, her jockey, knew the mare, but in the saddling yard he was reminded to watch her.

The two horses lined up, the judge dropped the flag and the field for the 1938 Rankine Cup was away. For the first half of the race the two were neck and neck, then gradually the black mare inched ahead. With a little over a furlong to go, she looked a winner, then, as she came to the furlong post, Wynowie threw her head, then reefed her young rider half out of the saddle. His head struck the furlong post a sickening blow and the young jockey fell to the track.

I doubt if anyone saw Lewis win the Cup on the grey — all eyes were on the fallen jockey. Help was soon at his side, but little could be done. The young horseman died within a few minutes. The rest of the program was cancelled that afternoon, but at his father's request, racing resumed the following day. That, as his father said, was what young Len would have wanted.

In 1948 the race committee moved the meeting to a new venue on Brunette Downs.

Rankine Reverie

They'll be racing today where the Southerlies play
    And the Rankine goes wandering by,
With the downs sweeping past undulating at last
    To merge with the Territory sky.

From near and from far by packhorse and car
    The bush crowd will gather once more,
There'll be laughter and song from the camps strung along
    The one mile and down by the store.

From the furthest out runs they'll be there with the 'guns'
    And maiden hacks trained for the fray,
Every track good or bad whether main road or pad
    Will lead to the Rankine today.

Though I'm far from the scene with long miles in between
    Old times as I muse reappear,
In my mind I'm again on the course on the plain
    With the horsemen who rode yesteryear.

Oh! I mind well the ways of those old carefree days
    All that came then we took for the best,
For we cared not the cost of a race won or lost
    Though the 'Square A' nags seldom were pressed.

Game Searchlight was one and San-Simeon
    And gallant old Tum Tum the grey,
Ah! no doubt there'll be few of those horses we knew
    That carry the colours today.

Though I couldn't get back to the old Rankine track
    To join in the bush revelry,
This day shall not pass ere I raise a charged glass
    To the Rankine — a grand memory.

Equipment and Dress of the Ringer

ALMOST ALL THE equipment used in the cattle industry had its origins in the British Isles and was adapted to local conditions and the demands of cattle work here in Australia. The one exception was bronco gear. Unlike the pioneering era in America, where the Spanish influence played a major role in the style of both saddlery and dress, there evolved in this country personal gear and equipment that was uniquely Australian.

The Australian stock saddle was based on the English park saddle, and for many years the Australian saddle, although a lot heavier than the park saddle, retained small knee pads placed low on the flaps. It was in Queensland that the stock poley saddle was developed. Saddle makers listened to the men who rode in their products and gradually changes took place. Saddles were produced with knee pads placed up nearer the pommel and at the right angle to allow the rider on a rough horse to 'get under the pads', as it were, if a horse started to buck unexpectedly miles from camp. There were no pick-up men in the bush and no ambulance standing by if someone was injured. The only disadvantage with these saddles was that they were harder to get clear of should a horse fall.

There were, and still are, many fine saddle makers in Queensland. Saddle makers in outback towns, who had the advantage of knowing many good horsemen personally, produced some of the best saddles made. Tim Carr of Charters Towers was probably the best known of these. He made a fairly light saddle with a narrow grip that was famous throughout the back country.

The Australian stockwhip, with its full or half-plaited cane handle, is another piece of equipment unique to this country. A whip was essential on the road with cattle, as it was in most mustering camps. Whips for rough work were often plaited from greenhide or redhide, but it was the 12 or 16 strand 'roo hide beauties that were prized by cattlemen. The most famous of all whip makers was Alec Scobie. All his sons and daughters could plait fine whips, but Alec was the master. His whips were instantly recognisable as he used a hitch, which became known as the Scobie Hitch, rather than plaiting on his whip handles.

As there were four men at most with up to 1500 bullocks on the road, the mob had to be broken in to respond to the crack of a whip. If a mob was spreading out when travelling, the drover had only to ride out and crack his whip and the spreading bullocks would move back into position as one.

A bush sage once said, 'A drover without a whip is like a eunuch in a brothel — both are at a serious disadvantage due to a lack of essential equipment.'

Stockwhips evolved from the buggy or coach whip introduced from England, but later when whip makers established themselves in Australia, they responded to the needs of our pioneers and the stockwhip was born.

Spurs were not used on every horse. However, all ringers owned a pair. The length of the spur neck was usually two and a half or three and a half inches (6–9 centimetres) longer than the English Cavalry spur, because stockmen rode with longer stirrup leathers and with legs forward. Blacksmiths played an important role in outback life. The smithy who made the famous Condamine bells from old saw blades was one; Fred Gutte was another. Fred was employed by Vestey's as a

Glenormiston ringers, left to right, *Ross Ratcliffe*
the late Bruce Hanson, Bruce Simpson and Charlie Trottman.

blacksmith on Wave Hill station in the Northern Territory. In his spare time he made
and sold the famous Wave Hill spurs — acclaimed by horsemen throughout the
North-West as the best spur ever produced.

The humble quartpot played an important part in bush life, particularly on
the road with cattle. As the cook and horsetailer went directly to the night camp,
ringers with the mob boiled their quarts at dinner camp and ate the corned beef
and damper cut that morning. Quarts were small oval billy cans with a deep lid that
fitted inside and served as a mug.

To pass the time it was common practice for ringers to wager on whose quart
would boil first. No one but a new chum, however, would bet against a Jenkins
quart. Made in Charters Towers, the Jenkins quart was handmade in a flattened
oval shape and was approximately 2 inches (5 centimetres) wide. Ringers who
owned them boasted you could almost boil them with a lit match. I'm not sure if
the Towers has an historical museum, but if it has, pride of place in it should go to
the Tim Carr saddle and the Jenkins quart.

All ringers wore belts, not so much to keep their trousers up but to carry
pouches. Every one had a knife pouch carried along the belt so as not to cause the
wearer a mischief. Watch pouches were also common (wristwatches were
regarded as being a bit effeminate those days). In addition, many ringers carried
match box and tobacco tin pouches on their belts.

Scenes from a droving life.
Above: *A drover's wagonette and 'five in-hand' team.*

Above opposite: *A typical drover Andy Zigenbine, a member of a well-known droving family in the 1950s.*

Below opposite: *Road bullocks passing through open timbered country.*

Ringers and other bush workers in Australia seldom, if ever, wore gloves or other protective clothing. Fencers and yard builders did the job with bare hands, as did stockmen when they worked in the branding yard.

Station work and droving in my day entailed long hours in dusty conditions — certainly not the environment for sartorial splendour. Clothing worn in the camps was plain and practical. When in town, ringers prided themselves on looking smart, and although there were a few characters who were regarded as flash, flamboyance in dress among white ringers was seldom seen. Despite this there was a great deal of individuality in dress in the cattle industry, quite unlike the clothing affected by the sheepmen, who dressed in a style that was almost a uniform. Ringers' hats came in all shapes and styles, from the 10 gallon to the 3 inch brim, and the bashes in these hats were just as varied. Shirts worn were of plain colours in flannel or cotton, some with two pockets and all with long sleeves. Trousers in the Territory and North-West Queensland were in stock-cut pattern, while other parts of Queensland favoured jodhpurs (called poop catchers in the Territory). Moleskin, gaberdine and riding twist were the materials used. Those days jeans were called dungarees and were worn only by shearers and navvies.

Leggings were mainly the light pull-on type, although the spring side and concertina styles were still worn. Johnson and Sons riding boots were the favoured brand. Their Kooreelah, Maranoa and Emperor boots were generally worn by cattlemen, until R.M. Williams produced his own well-known Cuban heel boot, which captured the market in a few short years.

The Tasmanian Bluey, an overcoat made from wool, was very popular with drovers and ex-army great coats were also worn a lot. The shorter leather coat or jacket was often seen in later years. There was a lot more wool used in clothing in those days. Wearers of the woollen flannel shirt used to say, 'No matter how wet and cold you are, you're always warm and dry in a flannel shirt'.

Aboriginal stockmen favoured a bit more colour in their clobber; there is an old story about the Aborigine who asked a storekeeper for a shirt and on being asked what colour he wanted, replied, 'Any colour, boss, so long as him red'.

Whether a ringer was droving or working in a stockcamp, his swag was his home. In it were all his worldly possessions apart from his saddlery. Swag covers were made from Birkmere and some were lined and had a pocket at the top for spare clothing that acted as a pillow. Most, however, were merely 8-by-10 tarpaulins in which the ringer rolled up his blankets. Two leather straps went round the rolled-up swag.

Boss drovers looked hard at a man's swag before employing him. If the swag was heavy, it was no job — a bulky swag would not fit well on a packhorse and the man would sleep too soundly and would be hard to wake to go on watch. The lighter the swag, the better chance of a job, and if a man's rolled-up swag could be passed between the spokes of a wagonette wheel, all was well.

Ringers, by and large, were drifters and when a man spoke of greasing the swag straps he really meant he was thinking of moving on.

Forty or so years ago revolvers were still carried by many North-West Queensland and Northern Territory stockmen. Few of these were licensed, but as the hand guns were never taken out of a work situation, no one seemed to worry too much. I had a Smith and Wesson .38-calibre revolver for many years.

Revolvers could be handy at times but were never as effective as a rifle. Looking back, I believe the revolver was as much a symbol as a necessity.

Bulls, Pumpers and Min Min Lights

EARLY IN 1945 Harry Barnes, the manager of Alexandria, asked me and another young chap, Cecil Rose, to take a mob of herd bulls to Gallipoli outstation some 80 miles (130 kilometres) away. The herd bulls were of the Munro breed, low-set shorthorn beauties well known throughout the North-West. We started off with a young Aboriginal stockman called Limerick, and made it to the Buchanan River by the first night. Next day we headed up the Buchanan and continued in easy stages to Gallipoli, taking about 10 days to reach the bore where we were to leave the bulls.

We planned to tail the mob for a few days to settle them down in their new run, so after pulling the packs off at the turkey nest we strolled over to the engine shed to say good day to the pumper. Rather than erect windmills, in those days many of the stations employed men who lived at the bores. They serviced the eight horsepower diesel engines that drove walking beams connected to pump rods and buckets that raised water from the bores. The diesel engines ran night and day and were housed in small galvanised sheds in which the men slept and ate. An eight horsepower diesel makes a hell of a racket and how any of them slept with one a few feet from the bed is beyond me. A ration truck from the station once a week was the limit of any human company. Some of them were avid readers and could discuss, with authority, topics like philosophy, the origins of man, astronomy and alternative religions.

However, our pumper was something else: he had trodden a path at least 6 inches (15 centimetres) deep round the top of the turkey nest, and had a wild look in his eyes. The loneliness had obviously got to him. We boiled the billy and gave him a pint of tea. He took a swig and, looking somewhere over my left shoulder, said, 'A min min took me dorg y'know'.

I looked at him stupidly and said, 'A min min did what?'

'A min min took me dorg,' he repeated without emotion.

Cecil Rose choked on his tea as I thought, 'Christ, we've struck a hard case here'.

The pumper went on: 'It would have took me too, y'know, only I talked it out of it.'

'You talked to it?' said Cecil in a strangled voice.

'Yair,' said the pumper, 'it's friendly like now; comes up and has a yarn to me every night.'

After the pumper had returned to his galvanised hell hole, Cec and I sat and looked at one another. 'The poor bastard has gone troppo,' I said. 'I've heard of min min lights, but never a talking one.'

Cec nodded. 'He's as silly as a cut snake. The sooner we're out of this the better.'

I nodded agreement. I was looking forward to off-siding for the horse breaker when we got back; but we both knew the bulls would have to be settled down first.

That night, after a frugal repast, we were lying on our swags enjoying a smoke when Cec shot upright. 'What the hell is that?' he said.

I looked where he pointed. A light was shining brightly by a point of gidgee and it moved in an undulating way at an angle towards us.

'Well, I'll be buggered,' I said, 'the old bloke was right about the light, anyway.'

I looked over to where Limerick sat crouched over his own fire. 'What name?' I asked him, indicating the light. He rolled his eyes but made no reply.

We watched the min min for half an hour, then it disappeared as suddenly as it had appeared.

After some discussion, Cec and I agreed we would tie up a horse the following night and investigate the mysterious light.

Gypsy was a good style of roan mare that had done some night work, but she seemed to resent the idea of being tied up the following night with no cattle on camp, and stood hip shot and bored as we waited for the light to make its appearance.

Eight o'clock came with no sign of the min min. Eight-thirty passed with still no sign of the mysterious phenomenon. The point of gidgee was south of our position, and as I watched the Cross swing slowly up the night sky, I felt a slight sense of relief that our idea of the previous night may not have to be put into practice. Then, there it was, just off the point of gidgee as before.

'There she is,' said Cec.

'That's it, all right,' I agreed.

Silence for a while. I looked at Cec. He was looking at me. Gypsy stamped a hoof and it sounded unnaturally loud. Limerick slid into the swag and stuck his head under the blankets.

'Well, best of luck,' said Cec. 'I'll keep the fire stoked up.'

I walked slowly over to the mare, untied the reins and swung into the saddle. Once mounted, I felt confidence return. Ringers spend most of their lives in the saddle, and with a good horse under him, a ringer will face almost anything. I urged Gypsy into a trot as we headed for the point of gidgee. The light did not appear to be moving, but was not getting any nearer, and finally we passed the timber with the light looking much the same as it had from the camp. I rode about a mile further, with the light still no closer, then it changed direction, bowling along in a wide arc around me, as though heading back to the point of gidgee. I found it impossible to judge how far away it was — it could have been anything between 50 yards and a mile.

Gypsy took no notice of it, not even glancing at it as I turned her round and rode back towards the camp, with the min min slightly in front and to our right. Halfway back to the point of timber the light stopped, pulsated and went out. I rode on, thinking that was the end of the night's performance when suddenly the mare propped, threw her head up and snorted softly. With ears pricked, she was watching something between her and the camp, and it was obviously something she did not like.

There was still no sign of the light, but I felt the mare tremble slightly and I was aware of the hairs standing up on the back of my neck. At that moment the camp seemed a long way away. Gypsy snorted again and, wheeling away from the timber, took off at a gallop. After a struggle, I eased her back to a canter and we headed back to the camp, wide of the gidgee point.

As I had no intention of pounding into the camp as though the hounds of hell were after me, I reined Gypsy into a walk and glanced back. The min min light was back in position by the point of timber.

I dismounted and, squatting by the fire, told Cec the story, endeavouring to keep my hands steady as I rolled a smoke.

Cec looked at me incredulously: 'But you must have got to it. It never left the point of gidgee. You rode right to it.'

I shook my head. 'I never got close. Did you see it go out?'

Cec looked puzzled. 'The only time it went out was when you rode between it and the camp.'

'Well, mate,' I said, 'if you want to check yourself, the mare is there. If not, let her go. I'm hitting the swag.'

The light did not show again. Two days later we packed up and headed back to the head station.

I have seen three min min lights since then; however, none left the impression that first one did. The word 'min min' is possibly Aboriginal in origin. The light was often seen in the early days east of Boulia close to where the old Min Min pub once stood. The light remains a great mystery of the outback. It still has scientists baffled.

Horse Breaking

IN THE DAYS when cattle stations had hundreds of working horses on the books, the horse breaker played an important part in station life. In a good season a large cattle run could have 40 or 50 unbroken horses waiting for the travelling breaker. These unbroken horses, or colts, as they were generally called, would not have been handled as yearlings, and as some of them would be four and five years old, a breaker needed to be a top horseman.

The horse breaker was usually employed on station wages plus so much per head. As most of the stockmen were themselves fine horsemen those days, a couple of rides out of the yard was usually enough to have the colts accepted by the stockcamp. As most stations required the breaker to shoe the colts as well, a lot of horse breakers employed an offsider. Four to six colts a week was good going for most breakers.

'Simmo', the character in the next verse, was my younger brother, Alan Simpson, who was reared west of Mackay. On leaving school he worked on stations in the Eungella and Clermont districts, but soon turned to horse breaking. Over the next 38 years, he broke in horses in Queensland, the Territory, and in the Kimberley area, drifting further out as station methods changed.

A fine horseman, Alan was breaking in up to the time of his accidental death in 1988 at the age of fifty-eight.

The late Alan Simpson.

Taking the sting out of a fresh horse.

Simmo the Breaker

'Simmo the Breaker is dead, you say!
You must be joking, and anyway,
I've heard of rumours in the past
That Simmo the Breaker had breathed his last.
No, he'll turn up, I have no fear,
In his run-down truck and his breaking gear.'

On a station far in the Kimberleys,
To break in colts with the practised ease
Of a man who has mastered the breaking game,
From Nebo to Derby they know his name.
The best of the breakers without a doubt
To service the stations of further out.

Almost a legend among his peers,
Born out of his time by forty years,
The staunchest mate that a man could find,
They broke the mould when they made his kind.
Reared in the bush when the world was wide,
the horse was king when he learned to ride.

But times are changing and methods too —
Mobs for the breaker of late are few,
Besieged by progress I've heard him swear,
'The Kimberleys are the Last Frontier!
The last retreat of the old bush ways,
There a breaker like me could end his days'.

'But Simmo dead? No, it couldn't be,
The man was as tough as a gidgee tree,
As hard as nails, and it's truth to tell
You couldn't kill Simmo with shot and shell.
Yet you say he's dead, and you swear it's true —
Simmo gone, and I never knew!'

Yes, we scattered his ashes on the breeze
O'er the distant runs of the Kimberleys.
There where the plains and the rough hill meet,
The breaker is home in his last retreat.
When the trade winds sweep o'er the sunlit plains —
When the trees bend low to the monsoon rains —
When the Southern Cross hangs bright and clear
He will be as one with his last frontier.

Protocol and Habits of the Camps

THE RELATIONSHIP BETWEEN bosses and ringers in the cattle country was a lot less formal than on the sheep stations, where a fairly rigid class system was maintained. On a sheep property there was a clearly defined line of demarcation between inside, or homestead staff, and the workers. Fraternisation was not encouraged. Cattle stations certainly had a separate kitchen and dining room apart from the 'big house' for the ringers, but there the similarity ended. Ringers were always on first name terms with boss drovers and head stockmen, and in many cases, on first name terms with the manager. Unlike stockmen on sheep stations, who were home each night, ringers spent most of the year living in stockcamps or on the road droving.

Some managers of cattle stations spent time in the camps and many liked to keep their hands in on a favourite camphorse. Protocol demanded, however, that all instructions to the ringers were given through the head stockmen. Most boss drovers and head stockmen led from the front and the ringers were in no doubt as to who was in charge. Camp cooks, however, were given a fair bit of leeway; keeping the dough roaster happy was in the interest of all. Cooks needed room around the fire to tend to their billies and camp ovens, so even in the coldest weather ringers did not encroach on the cook's domain. If one did, a shovel full of hot coals and a quick flick of the cook's wrist sent the intruder back-pedalling.

There were other unwritten laws in camp life and usually the cook became the self-appointed guardian of these. For instance, no one ever sat on, or close to, the tucker table, and woe betide anyone who sat on a bag of flour or sugar. There were no chairs; ringers sat on their heels or with crossed legs on the ground. Camps were full of tough characters those days, but few challenged the cook. The sight of an irate babbler with right on his side and a fire shovel in his hand tended to discourage any argument.

Setting up camp with horse plant in background.

There is a popular myth that bushmen are careless about personal hygiene; nothing could be further from the truth. It is true ringers often slept in their clothes those days, but they bathed whenever possible and were fanatical about washing before a meal. The reason for this was simple: everyone handled the tucker. A lot of meals consisted of a loaf of bread or damper and a slab of corned meat placed on the table for the ringers to help themselves. Anyone who failed to wash was likely to find himself thrown fully clothed into the nearest waterhole or cattle trough.

In my time in the outback, stockcamps moved regularly and drovers, of course, were on a new camp every night; as a result, toilet facilities were non-existent. When a ringer wished to do what has been euphemistically called a 'No. 2', he merely went a respectable distance from the camp and squatted down. He went down wind, of course. No one who went up wind ever made the same mistake twice.

Toilet paper was also unheard of. In fact paper of any kind was scarce in stockcamps, and limited to the droving contract and waybills when on the road with cattle. But bushmen are masters of innovation: in timber country, straight, even dry, sticks took the place of paper — one reason why experienced bushmen never pick up a stick off the ground to stir their quart pots. In open country, another solution had to be found. Fortunately the downs are strewn with small stones called gidgee stones. They are roughly round in shape and up to a cricket ball in size, and they did the job admirably.

New chums, who had to put up with a fair bit of chiacking, often had ribald comments shouted after them as they trudged away to relieve themselves. Helpful pieces of advice such as: 'Look out you don't wipe your arse with a death adder', or 'Put your belt round the right turd when you're finished' were common. However, new chums survived, and most of them ended up as smart men.

Few ringers felt comfortable with a woman in the camp. Northern Territory ringers had little contact with white women and they tended to regard them with awe and respect — exotic creatures to be worshipped from afar. They were unanimous in their opinion that the camp, with its primitive conditions, was no place for such delicate individuals. There were women, of course, who held their own with men on the stockroutes. The Zigenbine girls, daughters of Harry Zigenbine, were probably the best known of these outstanding women.

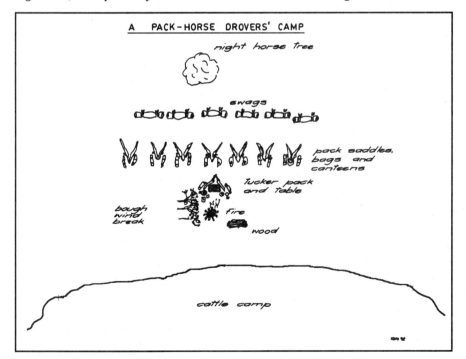

A PACK-HORSE DROVERS' CAMP

The late Bill Yeomans, on horseback, *chats to legendary Rocklands drover Walter Cowan, who is standing by his wagonette.* BILL YEOMANS.

Bush Cooks

BUSH COOKS ARE, to paraphrase Rolf Harris, 'a dangerous breed, mate!' There were, and probably still are, some remarkably good cooks in the outback; and there were also some bloody awful ones. I've known cooks who could bake bread in camp ovens better than any city baker, and I've also known some who couldn't boil water. The one thing they all seemed to have in common was their nature — they all seemed to be crooked on the world. They were, almost without exception, 'death adders' — snaky as hell and just waiting for someone to put a foot wrong. Despite this, if a camp was blessed with a good cook, it was a happy camp.

Camp cooks, whether good or bad, were always, as a rule, clean; however, there is always the exception to any rule. Many years ago I was ringing in a stockcamp where a remittance man who went by the name of Piebald Jack was employed as the dough roaster. One morning when mustering, the head stockman doubled back to the camp to get a pair of spurs he'd forgotten. At the camp he found Piebald Jack with his trousers down, steaming his piles over the tea billy. He claimed the treatment gave him relief; it did not, however, do a lot for the flavour of the tea. The head stockman advised Piebald Jack to move on and steam his piles elsewhere.

The best packhorse cook I ever struck was Jack Brumby, a part-Aboriginal ex-ringer who cooked for Looking Glass Joe Dowling on the road with Nutwood bullocks. Jack was something of a rarity; as well as being top cook, he was a happy, good-natured individual.

Before going droving with Dowling on one occasion, I had been working on Nutwood, a station north-east of Daly Waters and south-east of the Elsey, and it was one of the roughest runs in the Top End, with large areas of thick lancewood scrub and cattle as wild as hawks. The cook in the stockcamp was even rougher than the terrain and a bludger to boot. After a long day of track mustering and scrubber running, we often got back to camp at nine or ten o'clock to find the cook in his swag and a meal of cold corned beef and damper awaiting us. One night when we got to camp we found him awake and complaining bitterly about something or other. The head stockman's reply spoke louder than words; he stood up and knocked the cook clean over the fire. The cook's demeanour improved markedly after that, but unfortunately his cooking did not.

Looking Glass was waiting to take delivery of the store mob we had mustered. I had planned to go in with the mob, so I joined his camp when he took over the bullocks, pleased to leave behind me the cook at the Nutwood stockcamp. With Jack Brumby in charge of the camp ovens, every day seemed like Christmas day to me. The bread he baked was the lightest and finest-textured bread I had ever eaten. He swore he had no secret recipe, yet I never knew him to have a failure.

I watched him when I had a chance and his routine never varied. He would mix up the dough at night in a bread bucket, using flour, salt, yeast and warm water, then he made a thick batter that was left to stand overnight in the bucket. Jack took great care with this part of the operation, covering the bread bucket with a blanket and standing it close enough to the fire to obtain the correct amount of warmth.

First thing next morning Jack tipped the dough out on to a bit of tarpaulin. The mixture had risen during the night and Jack would knock it back by vigorous kneading, at the same time adding more flour. The dough was then put back in the bucket to rise again, and to be carried to the next camp strapped on top of the tucker pack.

As soon as Jack had unpacked, he attacked the dough once more. This time, after knocking it back, he formed the dough into loaves and placed them in the Bedourie ovens to rise for the last time. By the time the bread had risen for the third time, Jack had two shallow holes ready for the camp ovens and had an ample supply of hot coals on hand. After he had shovelled the required measure of coals into the bottom of the holes, in went the ovens, and more coals were placed on the lids. That was all there was to it, but the result was food for the gods.

Most bush cooks could hold their own when it came to repartee. There is an old story about a bush cook who gave up tending camp ovens to start a small pig farm on the outskirts of a western town. A chap who used to employ the ex-cook met him in the main street one day.

'G'day, mate,' he said, 'they tell me you're cooking for pigs now.'

'No,' replied the erstwhile babbler, 'these days I'm cooking for gentlemen.'

The wide range of expertise among bush cooks led to the establishment of a scale to assess their worth. This scale classified cooks much as the Richter scale classifies earthquakes, and considering the gastronomical eruptions caused by some babblers, the comparison is not without merit.

The scale went like this:
Cooks
Cookoos
Baitlayers
Tucker F...ers
Wilful Bloody Murderers

A packhorse drover's dinner table.

Looking Glass Joe

Now the road mobs from Nutwood would gallop all night,
They were big piker bullocks inclined to take fright;
Bred away in the cane-grass and scrub-covered hills,
They were mustered with coachers and plenty of spills.
There was not a boss drover that I can recall
Who had taken them on and delivered them all.

With a rattle and crash through the timber they'd go,
And the first man to tame them was Looking Glass Joe.
Now old Joe with wild cattle was known to be good,
He could lift cleanskins faster than anyone could,
He could front leg a piker with consummate ease
And would wheel a wild scrubber as quick as you please.

He had heard of the Nutwoods and reckoned he'd show
That wild cattle were child's play to Looking Glass Joe.
So he mustered his horses and headed out West,
And the team that he gathered was one of the best;
Jacky Britt and Jack Brumby, and Joe's brother Jack
Were as good as you'd find on the Murranji track.

Billy Thompson went too, so I said, 'What the hell!'
I was ripe for a change so I signed on as well.
Well we picked up the mob, and their rep' was no lie
For a lot of the bastards were older than I.
They were scrub-bred and wary, long-legged and lean,
And the horns that they tossed were the biggest I'd seen.

With a man in the lead so they'd draw nice and slow
We got started for Queensland with Looking Glass Joe.
There were nights when they galloped from darkness to dawn,
There were nights when I wished that I'd never been born,
For they rushed and they rattled through scrubs deep and black
But we wheeled them and rung them, and herded them back.

On the nights when they camped Joe would say to me, 'Son,
You can saddle a nighthorse, there's work to be done'.
Then we mustered the scrubs and the flats for the strays
That had led the wild rushes of earlier days.
There we galloped and drafted bush cattle all night,
To return with our catch in the first of the light.

But I said, 'Joe, you're mad, putting rogue bullocks in
This galloping mob that is hock deep in sin,'
He pushed back his hat, 'Yeah, perhaps that is so —
But I must have me numbers,' said Looking Glass Joe.
What with rushes and musters and long days as well,
I wished Looking Glass Joe and his bullocks in hell.

Well we drove them for four months and one bloody day
We delivered at Morstone, and picked up our pay.
We were proud in the end, I suppose rightly so,
For we'd mastered the Nutwoods with Looking Glass Joe.
Thirteen fifty we took at the start of the drive,
And at Morstone the count, fourteen hundred and five.

Now the store mobs from Nutwood would gallop all night,
They were big piker bullocks inclined to take fright.
Up till then not a drover that I can recall
Had completed a trip and delivered them all.
With a rattle and crash through the timber they'd go,
And the first man to tame them was Looking Glass Joe.

Aboriginal Stockmen

AUSTRALIA, OR MORE correctly the pastoral industry, owes a considerable debt to the Aborigines, both male and female. Big companies employed large numbers of them at very low wages, and the resulting profits must have been substantial. Drovers also employed them at the same low wages; however, at the contract price offered by the same big companies, there seemed little option. Many unsuccessful attempts were made to have the droving price increased, including the 1956 drovers' strike in which I was appointed spokesman.

Despite the exploitation of Aborigines through low wages, the system was not totally without merit. Firstly, they received some reward for effort rather than a government handout. Secondly, they usually worked and lived, albeit as hired hands, in what they still regarded as their tribal area. It is difficult for whites to understand the relationship that exists between Aborigines and the land. If one combines religion and patriotism, I doubt if the combination would come within a bull's bellow of that relationship.

Aborigines made good stockmen, and the older, more experienced ones were highly respected and acted as excellent role models for the young. On every NT station there were Aborigines who were excellent buckjump riders. Despite the fact that many of them could ride anything wrapped in hide, few could be called all-round horsemen, however. Their seat and hands left a lot to be desired and they seldom demonstrated any affinity with the horses they rode.

They all enjoyed fast exciting work, but tended to regard the more humdrum tasks with little interest. A problem for the head stockman was that the majority could not be relied upon when not being supervised, perhaps understandable under the circumstances. Most of the older Aborigines showed an outstanding loyalty to their white bosses, however.

The smartest Aborigines with wild cattle that I worked with were from the Roper River and Hodgson River areas. Their tribal lands teemed with game, wild fowl and fish. As with all coastal people, their physique was far superior to the inland Aborigines, who lived in one of the harshest environments on this planet. That they survived at all says a lot for the resourcefulness and bushcraft of Australia's indigenous people.

FORM 7.   REGULATION 23

THE NORTHERN TERRITORY OF AUSTRALIA

ABORIGINALS ORDINANCE: 1918-1947

RECOGNIZANCE

Be it remembered that on **5th** day of **August** 19**55**

Bruce Simpson of **Camooweal**

personally came before the undersigned Protector of Aborigines in and for the

District of **Elliott** and acknowledged to owe to our

Sovereign Lord the King the sum of **£100** pounds, sterling, to be made

and levied on his goods and chattels, lands, and tenements respectively to the use of

our Lord the King, his heirs and successors, if he the said

shall fail in the conditions as hereunder set out.

_____ *E. T. Shelton* _____

The conditions of the above-written recognizance are that the said

B. Simpson shall return the aborigine **Rusty Walker**

to **Gordon Downs** within **Three months** from the

date of these presents :

AND that the said **Bruce Simpson** shall pay to the

said aborigine **Rusty Walker** wages at the rate of **£7-10-0 with cattle** per week

£5-15-0 with empty plant

whilst employed by the said **Bruce Simpson** in the

Northern Territory of Australia and wages at the rate of **Award** per week

whilst employed out of the Northern Territory of Australia in the State of Queens-

land/Western Australia, then the said recognizance to be void or else to stand in full

force and virtue.

Taken and acknowledged the **8th** day of **August** 19**55**

**Commenced employment with B. Simpson
with cattle on 31st, May, 1955.**

_____ *signature* _____
(Protector of Aborigines)

OFFICE ONLY.

Date returned to District:

Advised by: File No:

*In the 1950s, anyone wishing to employ Aboriginal stockmen had to obtain a licence
and a recognizance like the one above. The system was designed to protect Northern
Territory Aborigines from unscrupulous employers. However well meaning, it
demonstrated the patriarchal attitude of the times.*

The Aboriginal stockmen from the Roper and Hodgson were good trackers and could throw any beast, regardless of age and size. Although the work they did was at times dangerous, it was also exciting and challenging. They were constantly trying to outdo each other and tended to regard the whole business as a game rather than as work.

When throwing a beast after jumping off your horse, as you have to in scrub, timing is vital. The beast has to be caught when it starts to roll in its stride but before it breaks into a trot; by that stage in the chase, the tail is often wet and slippery with hot dung.

Norman was an older man whose experience and presence of mind saved his life one day when he jumped off to throw a full-grown scrub bull. The monster, with horns that could rip a man or horse up in a flash, had broken out of a mob we were running. Just as Norman grabbed its tail, he stumbled and lost his grip on the slippery tail, falling on his back with his shoulders up against a tree. In a split second the bull was at him, shaking its head and blowing snot all over the prostrate ringer. If he had as much as moved a finger, the bull would have disembowelled him, but Norman lay there with the bull only inches away and never blinked an eye until we got the beast away from him.

As Norman calmly remounted his horse Nipper a young Aborigine with me grinned. 'Close up finish that time, ol' man.'

Norman gave him a withering look. 'No more,' he said. 'Mebe bull altogether finish you.'

Splinter, one of the ringers in the Nutwood camp who was with me on that occasion, worked for me years later on the road droving. He was getting on in years then, but just as good a man as ever.

Aborigines are by nature a happy and musical people. In the stockcamps I worked in, I do not remember many nights when the sound of singing and laughter did not re-echo through the bush.

Changes to government policy and higher wages have put an end to all that, and most of the Aborigines once employed on the stations have drifted to our towns and cities.

Tommy Dodd

Tommy Dodd, Tommy Dodd, is your spirit still free
As it was when I met you out on the Barkly?
Riding tall in the saddle, packhorse by your side,
With the confident air of a man who could ride.
I remember the words that the boss had to say
At the Buchanan camp when you reined in that day:
'I've seen some good riders, but honest to God,
The horse isn't foaled that can throw Tommy Dodd.'

I've seen some rough horses, seen many good rides,
I knew Nathan and Cleary, and others besides,
But the horseman I put at the top of the tree
Was long Tommy Dodd of our own Territory,
As good as the best in Australia.

Tommy Dodd, although coloured, a man can go far,
If he only has faith and he follows his star,
With your own culture shattered, when boyhood had flown
The skills of the stockcamp you took as your own.
And they knew, Tommy Dodd, you had mastered those skills
When the wild pikers broke in the scrub-covered hills,
You were there, Tommy Dodd, and your place was the lead
For you rode like a Centaur as one with your steed.

I've seen some rough horses, seen many good rides,
I knew Lewis and Vitnall, and others besides,
But up with the guns at the top of the tree
Was long Tommy Dodd of our own Territory,
As good as the best in Australia.

You have ridden buckjumpers that jarred every bone,
But it seems, Tommy Dodd, that you couldn't be thrown,
From the banks of the Daly right down to the Todd
You were known and respected by all, Tommy Dodd.
Tommy Dodd, Tommy Dodd, is your spirit still free?
As it was when I met you out on the Barkly?
Riding tall in the saddle, packhorse by your knee,
A man in control of his own destiny.

I've seen some rough horses, seen many good rides,
I worked for Sam Fuller and others besides,
But up with the guns at the top of the tree
Was long Tommy Dodd of our own Territory,
As good as the best in Australia.

Whispering Gums

Sentinel gums by the river,
Twisted and gnarled and grey,
Saplings back in the Dreamtime,
Patriarch gums today.
Unmoved by the long years drifting,
Sturdy and gnarled and old,
Unbowed by a thousand tempests,
Unconquered by droughts untold.

Whispering gums by the river,
Close wrapp'd in your own mystique,
You whisper the age-old stories —
If only you could but speak.
The scars on your trunk slow healing,
Scored deep by a Stone Age blade,
Show clearly the desert nomads
Camped long in your spreading shade.
Oft' then when the twilight deepened
On the wind came a rhythmic beat,
The lilting chant of the women,
The shuffle and stamp of feet.

Whispering gums by the river,
Twisted and gnarled and old,
The stories you softly whisper
They never shall be retold.
Ne'er a corroboree fire
Gleams now through the silent land,
From the whispering gums they vanished,
Those who could understand.

Assimilation

A fighting son of a warlike race,
Woodinga strode with a hunter's grace
To the very brink of the cliff's rough face,
    Blue shadowed by afternoon.
He snarled at the white men camped below
Where a precious spring seeped sweet and slow,
Then his challenge rang like a hammer blow,
    For he was a Kalkadoon.

Jimmy Quartpot sweats on the smoko bell
As he cleans the yard at the bush hotel,
Though no one expects him to do it well
    As he's only a flamin' coon.
He'll spend his pay on the cheapest booze,
And the lockup floor is the bed he'll use,
For his wits are all he has left to lose
    And he is a Kalkadoon.

Skull Hole

A grisly name for such a place,
Where big gums shade the water
Deep and cool and clear below,
The cliff face looming over.
A rugged rockhole hidden far
From noise and smog and traffic,
Where pythons slumber coil on coil
Within each secret crevice.
A Bora ground lies scattered there,
Its builders long forgotten,
The big roos pass its ravaged rings
To water at the shallows.
A mystic place it seems at night
When moon-cast shadows shiver,
When Boobook owls along the creek
Call back to one another.
A Goa sub-tribe camped one night,
Not knowing they were followed,
The rock face caught their savage song
And sent the echoes ringing.
At last the dancers sank in sleep,
As night winds fanned the embers
The Black Police threw their cordon round,
Grim-featured, quiet avengers.
The sickly daylight broke at last,
It broke in death and terror,
Behind the Goas loomed the cliffs,
Before them blazed the rifles.
And there upon the crimson sand
Amid their stolen plunder
The Goas learned the White Man's Law,
A brief and bloody lesson.
Now Boobooks call along the creek
When darkness cloaks the ridges,
No campfires glow beside Skull Hole
And there is no more singing.

The Morstone Team

AFTER ACCOMPANYING LOOKING GLASS JOE, who was delivering a mob of
Nutwood bullocks at Morstone, I took a job in the stockcamp there. The station,
situated between Camooweal and Burketown, was a bullock depot owned by
Vestey's. Many of the big store-conditioned mobs from the Territory and Kimberley
region walked in and spelled at Morstone for 12 months before being trucked east
from Mt Isa. Morstone was not in the true sense of the word a fattening depot, but

the spell did wonders for the road-weary bullocks. Morstone is aptly named; the story goes that the original selector, after travelling across the adjoining property called Rocklands, decided that his run had more stones, hence the name.

I found the work on a bullock depot a lot easier than on the breeding places on which I had spent the last three years and I thoroughly enjoyed the change. The stockcamp was a small one by most standards, however all the ringers were experienced men and good blokes to get along with, and as a result the camp was a happy one. The O'Shanassy River ran through the property, heading north-east to join the Gregory. On the open downs country north of the river were large limestone outcrops; these large flagstones were a very real danger when mustering or when draughting cattle on an open camp. Bad accidents did occur and some eight years after I worked on the place, Tommy Burrows was involved in a fall that almost ended his life. It is due solely to Tom's indomitable spirit that he not only survived but came to terms with his resulting disability to become one of the Territory's real characters.

When I was on Morstone, the homestead was situated on the O'Shanassy River. It was a beautiful spot and why the complex was later moved out on to the blazing downs at A bore is beyond me. In one of the vehicle sheds near the yards was an old tabletop wagon, and running in one of the paddocks were a dozen Clydesdale draughthorses. They were fine, big upstanding horses branded FV, the horse brand symbol of Fitzroy Vale, a Vestey station near Rockhampton. No one seemed to know anything about them or how long they had been on Morstone.

They were of particular interest to Ted Keilor and me for as lads we had both gained experience with draughthorses. However, the station work went on and the Clydesdales continued to live the life of Riley in their paddock. The stockcamp was only a small one, and some cattle work had to be done over the summer months, most of the ringers were kept on the books during the slack. There was not a lot to do, and no doubt the manager was thinking of a way to keep us occupied when one morning at smoko he said, 'The area around the cattle troughs needs stoning up badly. We may get stuck into it shortly.'

It was not the type of work that ringers were asked to do those days and the manager's words were greeted with stony silence from everyone except Ted. After we finished smoko, I had a go at him.

'I didn't think you were the type of bloke to have ambitions about becoming a truck-driving navvy?'

'I'm not. Come and have a look at this.'

I followed Ted over to the shed that housed the old wagon. He patted the splinter bar.

'She's as sound as a bell, only needs a bit of axle grease.'

I looked at him in amazement. 'You're thinking about the Clydesdales?'

'Bloody oath. Will you be in it?'

Ted's eyes were shining. I grinned.

'All right, but let's check the wagon over properly.'

We went over the old tabletop thoroughly; the paint was peeling but the woodwork was sound and the two sets of shafts seemed solid enough. The iron fittings were certainly rusty, but, as Ted said, a liberal application of grease would work wonders. The heavy iron tyres were loose on the wooden felloes, but both

Ted and I knew that a good soaking would remedy that. When we had finished the inspection, I stood back.

'Well, Ted, we should be able to get her rolling again, but what about the harness?'

'Come on, then, let's go and have a gander.'

We both knew that there was old team harness stacked at the back of the saddle room.

For the next hour we wrestled with dusty winkers, collars and hames tangled up with backbands and chains. We ended up with seven sets of harness arrayed on the stockyard rails; we also had breechings and saddles for the shafters.

We were admiring our handiwork and grinning at one another like schoolboys when the manager strolled up. He stopped short, looked at the harness, then at us.

'What the blazes are you doing?'

Ted pushed his hat back.

'We're getting ready to stone up those troughs. We'll muster the horses tomorrow.'

The manager's jaw dropped. 'You're both as mad as cut snakes.'

He turned and walked away, shaking his head.

'Right,' said Ted. 'This gear is as dry as a wooden god. You go up and get some fat from the babbler while I look for axle grease.'

I strolled into the kitchen. The word had obviously got around for the cook greeted me with: 'Well, if it's not Ben Hur's offsider. To what do I owe this honour?'

'You can help by donating any old cooking fat you haven't already used to clog up our arteries.'

The cook wasn't a bad bloke; I left his domain with half a bucket of rendered fat, to which I added some stock tar and a dash of kerosene. I returned to the yards, where Ted had armed a few of the more curious ringers with rags, and the big grease-up began. After the harness had been thoroughly treated, we borrowed a lancewood rail from the yards; we then cut a heavy short fork. Using rail and fork as a lever and fulcrum, we removed each wheel in turn in order to grease the axles. After a liberal application of lubricant on the turntable and kingpin, we turned our attention to the ironwork on the two shafts. Finally, we doused the wheels with water and hung wet bags over them.

At the meal table that night we both came in for a fair bit of good-natured ribbing. Ted took it for a while, then addressed the cook.

'You know, I feel sorry for these blokes.'

'Yeah. Why?'

'Well. I know who'll be handling the horses and who will be loading and unloading those bloody big stones.'

The next morning Ted and I mustered the Clydesdales and ran them into the station yards. After smoko we returned to see if the horses had been handled before, and if so, how much they remembered. Draughthorses are cool-blooded types, usually fairly docile — our potential team was no different. We had little difficulty in catching them and found they would lead quite well after a bit of coaching — they had obviously been handled before leaving Fitzroy Vale. Ted and I were delighted, for our plans of becoming teamsters looked like being realised.

'So far, so good,' said Ted. 'Let's get stuck into their manes and tails.'

It took us a while to get rid of the knots and thin out the tangled manes and tails, but when the cook rang the gong for lunch, we had the Clydesdales looking like brewery horses. That afternoon we harnessed each in turn, then using a lead, we got them to snig a heavy log around the big holding yard.

Within two days we had them snigging the log around the station outbuilding and standing quietly when brought to a halt. The manager, who still regarded our activities with amused tolerance, let us have a free rein, and we made the most of the opportunity. It is impossible to spend your life with horses and not feel a great attachment to them. In the fast busy atmosphere of a stockcamp, however, a quick pat and a rub around a mount's ears is about all that is possible; with the Clydesdales it was different. We had time to indulge our great love of horses, and the boyhood memories of horse teams we both shared came flooding back.

A horse team is not guided by reins but answers to the voice of the teamster, who walks beside the horses. There was always some variation in teamsters' commands, but most used 'Gee up' and 'Whoa' to start and stop; 'Gee back' or 'Whoa back' to the team, and in particular the shafters, to back the wagon; and to the leader or leaders, 'Gee off' and 'Gee over' to turn right and left. The leaders are the key element in any team, for they guide the rest of the horses and the wagon. In a small team, one leader is sufficient — Ted and I picked out an active, intelligent bay mare and started training her with light reins. In a couple of days she was answering to our calls without the reins, and Ted and I decided she would do the job nicely.

We were just about to take her back to the yards when Ted had an idea.

'Let's harness them as a team. I reckon they are ready. We'll hook them up to a couple of big logs and see if Princess here can really do the job.'

In half an hour we had them out on the flat working as a team. The bay mare, christened Princess by Ted, needed a little guidance at first, but she soon settled down. She had just swung the team around when the manager appeared. I called whoa to the horses and they stopped obediently.

'Well, I've got to hand it to you two,' said the boss. 'I think the idea of the wagon will work.'

'Of course it will work,' said Ted. 'We're almost ready to give them a trial in the wagon.'

'Yes, well don't worry about that yet. Just keep them going as you are.' He paused. 'I'm getting the agent to send out a teamster on the next mail.'

We looked at him in disbelief — Ted recovered first.

'What the bloody hell do you want a teamster for? We've done all the work. We can handle it.'

'Driving a team is a specialist's job. You can both give him a hand, of course, and keep the horses going until he arrives.'

We both liked and respected the manager, but we knew he was wrong about the team. After he had gone, Ted and I looked at one another in dismay.

'Where in the name of Christ is he going to get a teamster from?' Ted fumed.

'I'm stuffed if I know — it's a bloody stupid idea, but he's the boss.'

We unharnessed the horses and let them go in the house paddock just as the dinner bell went. We both had a wash, and as Ted grabbed a towel he snarled, 'If any bastard has a go at me over this, I'll drive his bloody jaw through the back of his neck.'

I laughed. 'Come on, mate, it's not the end of the world. He's got to find someone who can handle the horses better than we can.'

When we sat down at the table, we found that everyone was on our side over the teamster business. It was some consolation, but did little to dispel our disappointment.

During the three days before the mail truck arrived we drove the team around the homestead paddock and between the station outbuildings. We made the best of the situation, but our hearts were not in it. It was only the rapport that we had established with the horses that prevented us from giving the whole idea away.

In due course the teamster arrived. Ted and I looked him over. When he left us to throw his gear in the quarters, I turned to Ted. 'He's a bit young to be a teamster.'

'Teamster, my arse,' snorted Ted. 'If he's a teamster, I'll carry a boar pig to Bourke.'

The next morning we ran the Clydesdales into the yards, to find all hands and the cook perched on the rails. We shut the gate and joined them as the teamster crawled through the rails. It was at once apparent that he was intimidated by the big draughthorses.

The manager looked at us. 'You'd better give him a hand to catch them.'

'I suppose you'll want me to wipe his backside for him, too.'

Ted had slipped into the yard before the manager could reply. We caught the horses, but the teamster was clearly out of his depth. I calculated that his experience with teams had probably been restricted to a one horse baker's cart. Later that night, the boss sacked him.

Our joy, however, was short lived. Next day the manager informed us that a far more experienced man was coming out on the next mail. It was evident that he was not going to be beaten.

The next teamster certainly showed more promise than the first one. He had obviously handled draughthorses before and seemed comfortable with them. As the days went by, Ted and I wondered when he was going to hook them up to the wagon. He kept putting it off, until finally, at the manager's insistence, we gave him a hand to harness the team to the old tabletop wagon. We had thrown a number of heavy posts on to steady the horses, and to let them know what a load felt like. To my surprise, the new teamster screwed the brake on as well.

'I wouldn't do that,' said Ted. 'Let them get started first. You can always put it on later if it's needed.'

The brake on a wagon is placed just in front and above the front near wheel; it is applied by winding it on with a handle. The teamster reluctantly wound it off, and we called to the horses. They started forward, only to hit the collars and come back. Ted urged them on again and this time they got the wagon moving at a lively pace. The horses would have steadied up themselves, but the teamster panicked; he raced for the brake, and the wagon ran over his foot.

Ted pulled the team up and in a clearly audible stage whisper said, 'The boss isn't having a lot of luck with his bloody teamsters.'

The manager, who had been an interested spectator to the whole show, ignored the jibe. He told us to unharness the team and prepared to take the bitterly complaining teamster into Mt Isa.

We messed about with the horses until he departed, then grinning at one another, we got the team going. To do otherwise could have made jibs of them. The horses started without trouble and took little notice of the wagon rumbling along behind them. We drove them up past the station, along the road to Camooweal, then turned them in a wide circle back to the yards. We both knew that the team had passed its first test with flying colours.

We had them out again the next day when the manager returned. We swung the team off the road and pulled them up as he braked beside the wagon.

'I know when I'm beaten,' he grinned. 'You can take the team out to A bore tomorrow with the ringers and start on the troughs.'

A Mysterious Fire

GLENORMISTON STATION IS one of those cattle properties that is as far west in Queensland as it is possible to go. The run's western boundary is the Territory border; the south-western boundary roughly follows the Toko Range. Although situated in low rainfall, semi-desert country, Glenormiston has an abundance of natural surface water, with the Georgina River running through the eastern part of the station. Quite often the old river would flood out into the channels when there had been no local rain at all.

Further west the run is watered by Pituri Creek. This creek got its name from the pituri plant, a narcotic shrub that grows in the area. Pituri was not only used by the local tribes but was also traded along well-established trade routes to the north. I have picked up many green diorite axe heads on Glenormiston that must have been carried hundreds of miles along these trade routes.

In Pituri Creek there are two fine lakes, Lake Wondita and Lake Idamea, beside which the Glenormiston homestead is built. Both lakes teem with waterfowl, fish and molluscs; before the coming of white men the area must have carried a large Aboriginal population. There is no doubt the tribe would have jealously guarded their fine hunting grounds and the locations where the prized pituri grew.

I found on Glenormiston considerable evidence of tribal activity, including rock paintings, bora grounds and middens. Unfortunately, in 1947, when I worked on the station, there was little else to remind one of the proud Pitta-Pitta tribe that less than 80 years before had hunted and fished along Pituri Creek, as their ancestors had done since before the dawn of history. In a few short years a people and their unique culture had vanished.

When out mustering one morning, three companions and I discovered what I can only describe as the remains of a very old and puzzling fire. With me were Charlie Trottman, a veteran Aboriginal stockman who had been in the district all his life, and two young ringers, Bruce Hanson and Ross Ratcliffe. We were riding along a ridge about half a mile (800 metres) from water. It was a very dry season with little grass about and a dust storm a few days earlier had further denuded the ridge, blowing away loose topsoil.

Charlie suddenly reined in his horse and said, 'Fire here one time ago.'

We dismounted and, sure enough, our horses hooves had turned up burnt ground and scraps of charred material. We could also see bits of old iron lying half buried in the soil over a fairly large area. In 10 minutes we had gathered the iron mounts from packsaddles, as well as steel plates from riding saddles. Other relics included a number of steel clothing buttons.

It was strange that Charlie Trottman could recall no event during his lifetime that would explain the fire, for this was obviously the scene of a major disaster. Someone had lost the equipment of a full camp.

Ross Ratcliffe suddenly spoke: 'I'll tell you what we've found here — it's Leichhardt's last camp. The blacks speared them all and burned their gear.'

Bruce Hanson grinned. 'Perhaps it's the last resting place of Noah's Ark.'

'Laugh if you like,' replied Ross. 'I'll bet I'm right.'

'What about the iron,' said Hanson. 'The blacks would have taken that for spearheads.'

'Perhaps not,' I said. 'The Aborigines soon learnt to use iron, but not before they had been in contact with whites for some time. If the local blacks did wipe out the explorers here, they would have taken the axes and knives, but the shaping of iron would have been beyond them at that stage.

'Anyway,' I added, 'we had better get moving. We're supposed to be mustering.'

'Right,' said Ross. 'But we'll come back as soon as possible with shovels and a sieve. If we can find coins here, that will settle the matter.'

We all agreed to the plan, and as I rode away I saw an odd-looking stirrup iron half out of the ground. Jumping off my horse, I pulled it free, to find its mate lying just below it. The irons were of a design I had never seen before. The bottom bars looked like this:

Bottom of
stirrup irons.

I cleaned them up at the station and later in Brisbane had them chromed. These strange stirrup irons created quite a bit of interest over the years, but when I sold the droving plant, they went with it.

Unfortunately, we never did get back to the site of the fire. The three of us left Glenormiston after I had a disagreement with the manager. I do not know to this day what event caused the mysterious fire on Glenormiston. I do know, however, that iron and steel will survive for very many years in the almost moisture-free air of the semi-desert. It could be that Ross Ratcliffe was right after all.

Where Leichhardt Lies

Is this the land where Leichhardt lies,
Unfound though the years have fled?
Stark red desert 'neath blazing skies,
Where the ghostly pools of mirages rise,
From the claypan's barren bed.
Where is the spot that he lies at rest,
By channel or gibber-plain?
Did he grimly hold to the journey west
Or, disillusioned and sorely pressed,
Did he turn to the north again?
Did he turn to the north as the Israelites
Once turned to the promised land?
Through days of torture and nightmare nights
To a fate unknown went the ill-starred whites
To death in the black men's sand.

This is the land where the whirlwind goes
In the path of the men who fell;
Where the stars are pale and the min min glows,
And the sandhills shift when the storm wind blows
From the south like a blast from Hell.
Sweeping north go the dull red waves,
Storm-crests of a long-stilled sea —
Deep down under in smothered caves
Do they shield forever the long-lost graves,
And the key to the mystery?
Did he die a hero or die accursed
By the comrades he had led?
Did he fall to fever or blinding thirst?
Was he trapped by floor when the channels burst,
And the north-spawned waters spread?

This is the land where the desert blacks
Still wander, a scattered band.
Do they mutter low of the 'debil tracks'
In the long-ago, and of fierce attacks
In the heart of their sacred land? —
Where the fine red dust of the Centre cloaks
In a close embrace and strong,
The spinifex hills by the rock-bound soaks
Where the twisted limbs of the desert oaks,
Are crooning a deathless song.
Is this the land where Leichhardt lies? —
Land of the 'great unknown'.
Grim red desert and blazing skies,
Guard well your secret from questing eyes
For this is his land alone.

Stock Disasters

THE PASTORAL INDUSTRY in Australia has experienced many serious disasters, or smashes, as they are called. These smashes have involved the tragic and often substantial loss of all types of stock from both natural causes and human error.

When one considers the perils faced by drovers from rushes, dry stages, poison plants, sandstorms and scrub, such smashes are understandable. The Murranji Track was probably responsible for the loss of more road cattle than any other comparable stretch of stockroute. The Birdsville Track, with its dry stages and blinding sandstorms, also took heavy toll of travelling stock.

Also understandable are station stock losses from natural causes such as bushfires, floods and drought. There has always been a belief, however, that smashes on stations as a result of human error should never be allowed to happen. In truth, smashes could quite easily occur, and at times they did, for wherever man-made watering facilities were in use, the potential for a smash was present. In my day station waters were inspected no more than once a week, so if a watering facility failed in summer time, two or at most three days were all that were needed for the station to experience a major smash.

A smash involving a large number of stock could be a traumatic experience for those considered responsible. Years ago a mob of station cattle perished on Barkly Downs, and the manager, an efficient and conscientious man, could not live with the consequences and committed suicide.

During the years that I worked on stations I witnessed three smashes on three different cattle properties, and curiously enough, they all involved station horses. Two were the result of problems with man-made watering facilities, while the other was due to a natural disaster no one could have anticipated.

Alexandria had four thoroughbred station sires. The longest standing and the best was a stallion called Spaza, who sired fine stockhorses — true waler types with big tops and clean legs. He ran with his brood mares up the Playford River from the homestead, in a paddock that was watered by a windmill that pumped into an earth tank. A pipe from the tank led to the trough and, like most waters, the mill and tank were securely fenced off; only the trough could be reached by the horses.

Up the top end of Alexandria was some very rough country, and beyond that was a sort of no-man's-land, inhabited by a few reckless characters who were reputed to be a bit careless with their brands. Towards the end of one Wet, the manager asked Cecil Rose and me to take a small pack plant and have a look around up there, a sort of show-the-flag exercise. I've no idea what we were supposed to do if we ran into the hard cases, but neither of us planned to act the hero.

After an uneventful sojourn in the hills, we headed back down the Playford to the station. We called in at the stallion paddock — and rode into the middle of a smash. The stallion was dead, as were most of the mares and foals, and the remainder were on their last legs. The disaster had Cec and I puzzled for a while, for the mill was still pumping, then we saw that a dead foal in the trough had turned the water green and putrid. We saved one foal out of the whole paddock and took turns at carrying the feeble little bundle of skin and bone back to the station. The foal, christened Spondulicks, survived and was reared at the homestead.

Due to the heat, it is impossible to work cattle during the worst of the summer, and stockcamps usually finish mustering well before Christmas, starting up again some time in March. After working in the Glenormiston stockcamp in the latter part of 1947, I stayed on at the station over the slack period, doing leather work and saddle repairs. It was rather monotonous work for someone used to stockcamp life, so when one morning George Bannah invited me to go for a run out to the spell-horse paddock with him, I agreed with alacrity.

Plant horses like this one were often drowned while swimming in hobbles in water holes. If the horse's hind legs got caught over the hobble, the animal had little chance.

The 20 odd mile (30 kilometre) drive over the bush road to the paddock passed pleasantly enough, for George was an affable sort of chap who did not mind a yarn. As the spell-horse paddock was in fairly open country, we could see it long before we reached it. As with the paddock at Alexandria, it was watered by a mill and tank, with the standard fence around them; the only difference was that due to bad ground, the tank was a steel one. As we got a bit closer, I could see what appeared to be horses around the trough, and I had a sudden feeling of deja vu, for horses, unlike cattle, never hang around water after drinking.

I was about to say something to George, when he said in a puzzled voice, 'The place looks different somehow.'

Then: 'It's the tank; the bloody tank's gone!'

And gone it had; one side of it had burst, spilling the entire contents on to the fenced-in area and turning it into a morass. The mill was still pumping into the ruins, but none of the water had run through the fence into the paddock, where stockhorses lay dead about the trough. The few that were still standing stumbled about with hollow flanks and sunken, glazed eyes.

George and I stood and looked at the mess in dismay, then he turned and ran to the truck.

'I've got to go back and get gear and pipe to run the water out to the trough.'

'It'll be too bloody late; they won't last that long.'

There were two 5 gallon (22 litre) buckets on the back of the truck. As though reading my mind, he threw them to me.

'Do what you can till I get back.' Then he was gone in a cloud of dust.

I pulled off my boots and rolled up my trousers, then filled the two buckets at the outlet pipe. The mud was almost up to my knees, but I struggled over the fence and poured the water into the trough. It barely covered the bottom.

Some of the horses were too far gone to respond, but a few others sucked at the small amount of water, and I knew I could save them with a bit of luck. For the next hour I battled back and forth doling out the water to them, for a quick bellyful would have killed the few survivors faster than no water at all.

George duly returned with all hands and I was given a spell with the buckets. As I rolled a smoke, I looked at the pitifully small number we had managed to save, but I felt satisfied that I'd done all that was possible.

The third incident occurred on Lorraine Station in the Gulf, when the splendid station sire Blue Horizon perished in a flood with all his mares and all but one of his foals. Blue Horizon was a New Zealand-bred grey stallion, a stayer of the famous Nazami blood line. He was brought over to run in the Melbourne Cup, but he sustained an injury when being taken off the boat and that put paid to his racing career.

Purchased by Lorraine as a station sire, his first crop of foals were kicking up their heels in the paddock when the Leichhardt River, rising 50 feet (15 metres) in one night, sent down a wall of water that swept them to their death. The paddock was not low lying; in fact, water had never been over it before. A few years later the surviving foal, the last link with the great Blue Horizon, was broken in by my brother Alan.

The Call of the Road

The stockhorses come with the rising sun,
    From the silver-leaf racing hard,
And we watch for the last time as they wheel
    By the gates of the station yard.

For the wind that whispers the white gums through
    Bears a message we must obey.
We will shake the dust of another run
    From our restless heels today,
Then it's off again on the paths of chance,
    In the West that is wide and green,
The channels are draining a record flood,
    Girth high is the grass between.

So we'll say goodbye to the Lorraine run,
    No more on her camps we'll ride.
We will brand no more on the Landsborough end,
    Nor muster Myally side.
Time's tireless fingers have turned a page,
    And a chapter is writ and shut,
As we bid adieu to the 1ZB
    And the mates of the camp and hut.

With his kind eyes searching, a puzzled colt
    May question perhaps the change,
While our favoured pets of the camp must learn,
    The touch of a hand that's strange;
For we leave behind us the good bay mare,
    And the filly by Bengal too,
May they never bend to an unkind will,
    Nor the hands of a jackaroo.

There's a touch of remorse in a horseman's heart,
    Few others could understand,
When it's au revoir to the stockcamp string,
    Farewell to the station brand.
Unfettered and careless, our swags are home,
    For horizons are wide and yet,
There was never a parting since time began
    That did not hold some regret.

But the wind that whispers the white gums through
    Bears a message we must obey.
We will raise the dust on another run,
    Ere the close of another day.
Then it's off again on the open road,
    In a West that is green and wide,
And our destination — it matters not,
    Let chance and the West decide.

R & R in Normanton

NORMANTON HAS ALWAYS played an important role in supplying the needs of those hardy souls who spend their lives working and living on the Gulf Country cattle stations. Situated on the Norman River, the town is roughly 20 miles (30 kilometres) from the coast and has a colourful history dating back to the early days of settlement.

In 1949 a group of six of us from a Gulf station journeyed to Normanton for the annual rodeo and races. We were all ringers, with the exception of Maloney, who was the station's cowboy (an odd job man employed to milk cows and cut wood). Maloney was an ex-jockey who still involved himself at times in the race game and told endless tales of past glories on southern tracks. He was also a victim of the grog, and a typical two-pot screamer at best. We accepted without question that Maloney would need looking after.

The best pub in Normanton for ringers was the Albion, run by members of a well-known Gulf family. We hit town just before closing time and, running the utility in behind the Albion, we trooped into the bar and ordered rums all round. After a couple of drinks we buttonholed the publican, who readily agreed to let us roll our swags out in the backyard and use the hotel facilities. Taking a bottle of OP rum with us in case the mosquitoes were bad, we retired to our swags to gather strength for the days ahead. Work habits are hard to break and next morning I was awake as daylight broke over the Gulf town. I was not, however, the first to surface. Maloney was sitting up in his swag having a boozer's breakfast: a packet of Bex in one hand and a pannikin of rum in the other.

The head stockman reared up out of his swag: 'For Christ's sake, someone take the rum away from that drunken ratbag or we'll have to wet nurse him all day.'

Wardie, who was the closest, reached over and retrieved the half-empty bottle from the protesting culprit. We lay in our swags for a while, yarning and waiting for the town to come to life. Finally Wardie stood up and stretched.

'What about breakfast? Will we try the pub dining room?'

'I don't think so,' said the head stockman, 'not with Maloney. There could be women present.'

'Will we give the Dogger's cafe a whirl?' I said.

Everyone agreed, so the matter of breakfast was settled. The Dogger had been a dingo poisoner in earlier times and the name had stuck. He was, however, a good cook and presided over a clean and well-run cafe; moreover, his servings were reputed to be generous.

After a quick shower and a change of clothes, we rolled up our swags and headed up the street to Dogger's for breakfast. Maloney, lurching along between Don and Arthur, had managed to tuck only part of his shirt-tails into his trousers, and the way his hair was falling over one eye added to his rakish appearance. Suddenly he stopped.

'I think I'll tip the circus,' he announced.

The head stockman propped. 'Listen, you bloody reprobate, you tip anything at Dogger's and I'll have your guts for garters.'

Maloney looked at him owlishly for a second or two then walked on. 'Tipping the circus', as Maloney called it, had become something of an obsession with him. At some time in his chequered past he had seen an entertainer strip a tablecloth from a fully laden table without disturbing anything. Maloney's great ambition was to perform this feat one day.

We forgot about Maloney and his drunken ravings as we strolled to the cafe. The Dogger greeted us warily, but the traditional breakfast of steak and eggs that he placed before us was welcome enough. Steaming in the centre of the table was the grandfather of all china teapots. After washing down the steak and eggs with tea we leaned back in our chairs and had a smoke. It seemed that our stay in Normanton was off to a great start. Finally, we stood up and walked to the counter to pay the bill.

Just as we reached the counter, Maloney lurched to his feet, snatching the tablecloth as he did so. He gave it a mighty heave and fell flat on his back. An avalanche of plates, cups and saucers, cutlery, cruets and the giant teapot followed him to the concrete floor.

For a second or so we stood transfixed, then the kitchen door flew open and out stormed the Dogger, murder in his eyes and a butcher's knife in his hand. The head stockman reacted at the same time. In two strides he had Maloney by the scruff of the neck, lifted him to his feet and propelled him to the door. Before heaving Maloney into the street, he slipped his hand into the cowboy's hip pocket and deftly removed a roll of notes.

The sight of the money did a lot to mollify our host. All in all, Maloney's unsuccessful attempt to 'tip the circus' cost him dearly, but it did little to dampen our high spirits. The rest of the day passed quietly enough, with the only incident being a quickly organised whip-around for funds to bail out a mate who had shown a certain lack of judgment in punching the local sergeant of police on the nose.

The next day was rodeo day. The morning broke clear and bright and full of promise. We had breakfast in the hotel dining room, leaving Maloney drinking with the dawn patrol.

The rodeo grounds were crowded when we arrived at ten o'clock, and the bar area was particularly congested. We finally managed to get a position at the bar, where we ordered drinks and decided that as we were only interested in the buckjump event on later in the afternoon, our best plan was to stay where we were. We had been at the bar for perhaps an hour when the head stockman looked at me.

'Do you know that bloke behind you?' he asked.

'What bloke?'

'Turn around and have a gander,' said Wardie, 'but do it slowly.'

I turned round, stepping to one side as I did so. A character was shadow boxing — punching holes in the air a foot (30 centimetres) or so from where the back of my head had been.

I looked hard at him. 'What's the trouble?' I asked. He said nothing, but continued to dance and belabour empty space.

'It's right,' I said without turning. 'I think he's harmless.'

'You had better make sure,' advised the head stockman, 'before he king-hits you into the middle of next week.'

I stepped forward and clipped the shadow boxer lightly on the chin. He dropped his raised hands and backed away with a hurt expression in his eyes, then was lost in the crowd. I turned back to the bar and picked up my drink, relieved that the situation had been resolved so easily.

'Who the hell was that?' asked the head stockman.

'I don't know. I've never seen him before. He's obviously short of the full quid.'

'Yair,' drawled Wardie, 'but if I were you, I'd keep my eyes peeled for a while.'

The incident was soon forgotten and the time passed pleasantly enough at the bar. I noticed that Wardie was drinking double rums and was well on the way to being drunk.

'Wardie,' I said, 'if you're riding later, you'd better ease up a bit.'

He looked at me and grinned. 'I'm here to enjoy myself. She'll be right.'

Wardie was one of the toughest characters in the Gulf. He hated police and was at times a difficult chap to handle in drink. He had stayed out of trouble this trip, but his past battles with the law were something of a legend. Biting off part of an arresting officer's ear was one of his more celebrated feats in this field of endeavour. Nevertheless, Wardie was a staunch mate liked by all.

By the time the buckjumping event was due to start, our mate was in no condition to ride. However, nothing we could say would change his mind. He had the bad luck to draw a big black horse aptly named Black Angel. It was a horse Wardie may have ridden sober, but drunk he didn't have a bolter's chance.

The black horse threw him face down into the dirt, then bucked over the top of him. Wardie struggled to his feet and somehow climbed the high fence, but he overbalanced at the top, catching one spur to end up hanging head down, dazed and bleeding, like a side of beef in a butcher's shop. We got him down and carried him clear of the fence, when he suddenly came to and shrugged us off.

'Where,' he roared, 'are the bloody coppers who did this to me?'

It was an explosive situation, for the rodeo grounds were crawling with police. Somehow we got Wardie out of the grounds, into the ute, and back to the hotel. There we agreed the best plan was to pour rum into Wardie until he choked down and slept it off. Wardie finally quietened down and our plan was progressing smoothly when a policeman walked down the pub verandah and past the open bar door.

'There goes a walloper now,' said Maloney.

In a flash Wardie was off the barstool and out the door. We tackled him and fell in a tangled heap on the verandah. The policeman spun around.

'What's going on?' he demanded.

We explained to him that our mate had been hurt at the rodeo and was still concussed. He thought for a moment then said, 'I would put him to bed if I were you.'

He was just turning away when Maloney put his bib in again. 'Just as well you didn't try to arrest him. It took six of you coppers to take him in Cloncurry.'

Instantly the demeanour of the policeman changed.

'Who the hell are you?' he snapped.

'He's a mate of ours too,' I told him. 'He's a bit of a comedian, but a bit too drunk to be funny.'

I wheeled Maloney back to the bar without waiting for a reply and was still abusing him when the rest of the group returned to the bar with the still protesting Wardie.

Arthur looked at me. 'Why didn't you tell that copper Maloney was a dangerous escaped lunatic? It might have got him off our backs for a while.'

The head stockman looked at us and shook his head. 'I think the lot of you are lunatics. How the hell I got mixed up with you blokes is beyond me.'

Arthur grinned. 'Fate,' he said. 'Just unkind fate. By the way, hit your kick — it's your shout.'

We finally tucked Wardie up in his swag and left him snoring in concert with Maloney, who had thankfully choked down earlier. I had just walked back into the bar when a chap I had worked with at one time called me out to the verandah.

'Are you going to the ball?' he asked.

'Does it bloody well look like it?'

'Well, you should, mate. This girl, a governess where I work, she wants to meet you. You could do all right for yourself.'

'Pull the other leg,' I said.

'No it's true. She wants to meet the bloke who writes that verse for the *North Queensland Register*. I told her I knew you and she's been on my back ever since for an introduction.'

'Are you fair dinkum?'

'Bloody oath. She's a real good sort, too. I'd do a line for her myself but I couldn't write a poem to save my life. It's up to you. But she hates drink. You'll have to lay off the grog and get cleaned up.'

I looked down at my shirt, torn and bloody from struggling with Wardie.

'Have you got a coat and tie? You'll need them.'

'Where the blazes would I get a coat and tie?'

'Tell you what,' he said. 'There's a hawker in town. I saw his van in that empty allotment up the street. I'm off now. See you tonight.'

I walked thoughtfully back into the bar. There was little money to be made writing verse, but perhaps the fringe benefits would help to make up for that. One thing was for certain — I did not intend to spend a month's wages in finding out. If the governess wanted to meet me, she would have to take me as she found me.

The head stockman eyed me as I walked in. 'More trouble?'

'No,' I said casually. 'I'm going to get cleaned up later and go to the ball.'

Arthur grinned at me. 'I'll bet a bull's pizzle to a Vestey reference that you're on to a sheila.'

The head stockman nodded. 'I think we'd better keep an eye on you tonight.'

'Go and get stuffed,' I told them without rancour. 'But if you do go up to the hall, for God's sake leave Maloney behind.'

I knew the ball would be well attended, for unlike the majority of Territory runs, Gulf stations were home to many of the fairer sex. The floor was crowded when I arrived at the hall, where the dance band were playing toe-tapping music for a gypsy tap. In due course I met the governess, and true enough, she was a bit of a stunner and seemed like a nice girl. She had in tow a jackaroo from the same station who had a long nose and a supercilious look about him, but after a quick appraisal, I dismissed him as serious opposition and asked the governess to dance.

She was light on her feet and danced well. I soon discovered, however, that she was one of those young women who consider it noble and romantic to rescue those misguided individuals who have set out on the pleasant journey down that steep gradient known as the road to ruin.

'Why do you stockmen drink so much?' she asked. 'It's such a waste.'

'Well,' I replied, 'we're a thirsty bunch and after all there is little else to do.'

'Oh, but there is. There are so many worthwhile things to do.'

I grinned at her. 'You could be right. Let's talk about one or two.'

She coloured slightly and said rather stiffly, 'You know what I mean. Why waste your life in the rough environment of a stockcamp?'

I thought it was time to cool my companion's missionary zeal.

'Look,' I explained, 'I'm good at what I do and I enjoy it. Let's talk about you.'

Just then the music stopped. As we went back to her seat, I heard a commotion at the front of the hall and looked up to see that Maloney had arrived. He was waving a bottle of rum and looked as if he had been dragged by the feet through a patch of thick scrub. His entry into the hall was being barred by a large man in a suit. I excused myself and, cursing inwardly, went to his rescue.

The large character glanced at me as I walked up. 'If you know this chap get him out of here,' he said in a stage whisper the whole world could hear.

I got Maloney outside and asked him where the others were.

'I can't find them and I couldn't wake Wardie up.'

'All right, come around to the back of the hall; there's bound to be someone there.'

A group of ringers were drinking by a tank behind the hall. I took Maloney over to them.

'Do you blokes mind if my mate joins you? He's too drunk to get into the hall?'

'No sweat,' one of the drinkers said. 'Here, have a rum yourself.'

It would have been churlish to refuse, so I sat down and took them up on the offer. I yarned for a while, then, promising to see them later, I returned to the dance. The governess and the long-nosed jackaroo were in earnest conversation when I joined them.

'Sorry about that,' I said as I sat down.

'It's quite all right,' she smiled. Then reproachfully added, 'You haven't been drinking, have you?'

Before I could answer, the jackaroo piped up. 'We both detest strong drink,' then he added for good measure, 'I personally despise men who drink.'

I was considering what to do about the jackaroo when a ringer stuck his head in the back door and bellowed, 'Simpson, you'd better get out here. Your mate is starting a blue.'

'Perhaps,' said the governess, 'you should go and look after your friend.'

'Yes,' echoed the jackaroo, 'go back to your boozy mates.'

I stood up. The overwhelming urge I had to rearrange his nose would have to wait. It would be a good idea, I thought, as I left the hall, to strangle Maloney first.

At the back of the hall I met Arthur, who had just arrived. We walked over to where Maloney was sitting with a group around a fire. A chap everyone called 'the professor' was on his feet waving his arms and talking loudly. Maloney looked up as we arrived.

'This clown,' he said, jerking his thumb in the direction of the professor, 'this clown reckons there is gas coming out of that bore. Any silly bastard can see it's water.'

'Is this fellow a mate of yours?' asked the professor.

'Yes, he's under our protection. If anyone kills him, it will be one of us.'

The professor sat down, so I did likewise. I poured myself a nip from Maloney's bottle, then passed it to Arthur. The town's artesian bore was close to the back of the hall and steam from the heated water rose into the cool night air.

'Geologists claim,' said the professor, 'that gas comes out of that bore pipe.'

'Gas, my backside. You're an idiot,' said Maloney.

'Shut up, Maloney,' said Arthur.

'It's true,' went on the expert. 'I've seen the report. It's natural gas, that will light if ignited.'

'You're as silly as a cut snake,' said Maloney. 'If I was 20 years younger, I'd knock the gas out of you.'

I told Maloney to belt up and poured myself another rum. The argument continued until finally Arthur stood up and said, 'Come on, let's go and have a closer look.'

We all trooped over and inspected the bore. The outlet pipe went up for about 8 feet (2.5 metres), then out at a right angle, and the hot artesian water flowed out into a large pond at the base of the bore, then ran out along a bore drain. Someone had placed stepping stones out to the concrete base at the bottom of the pipe.

'We could hoist someone up there and they could try to light it,' suggested Arthur.

'Good idea,' I said. 'Let's hoist Maloney up with a rope around his neck.'

He looked at me and laughed. 'No, I was thinking of you; you're a lightweight and pretty active.'

After a lot of urging, I agreed, as it seemed the only way to resolve the argument. After pulling my boots off, I put a box of matches between my teeth and climbed up on the shoulders of Arthur and another ringer. After a great deal of trouble I got into a position to attempt the great experiment. It was not easy; I had to maintain my balance, take care not to do myself a mischief on the hot pipe and at the same time strike matches.

Whatever was coming out of the pipe was blowing the matches out as soon as I struck them. I was leaning forward to try again when the matchbox slipped out of my hand. I made a futile grab at it, lost my balance, and fell with a loud splash into the water below. It was hot all right. I shot out fast, like a half-drowned, half-scalded rat. As soon as I hit dry land, I made for the fire, dripping water and mud as I went. I was almost there when I looked up and saw the long-nosed jackaroo approaching. He stopped short when he saw me, then, with a horrified expression on his face, he turned and fled back to the hall.

Weeks later I found out that the governess had sent him to tell me she was keeping me the last dance.

On Monday morning we poured Maloney into the back of the utility and climbed aboard ourselves. We were a sick and sorry lot, but we were firmly convinced we had had a great time, although it was doubtful the head stockman shared our opinion.

Where the Girls and the City Lights Are

All's astir in the dawn of this long waited morn,
　　All the ringers are busy and gay;
And we pack up in haste, we have no time to waste,
　　For we go to the station today.
Our hearts they are light, as we girth the packs tight,
　　And our thoughts they are straying afar,
Where the surf meets the sand, where the corner pubs stand,
　　And the girls and the city lights are.

We have mustered the run, all the branding is done,
　　The stockcamp is finishing here.
We have sweated and toiled, but our swag straps are oiled,
　　For a spell at the end of the year.
The wagonette's packed, with the gear neatly stacked,
　　Then we're off with a ringing 'Hurrah',
And a crack of the whip on that oft thought of trip,
　　Where the girls and the city lights are.

The horses we ride take a long swinging stride,
　　For they know that the station's ahead,
They have done the work well, and each one's earned the spell,
　　In the creek paddock where they were bred.
The boys sing a song and the plant jogs along,
　　As we farewell the faint morning star,
And a picture comes clear, of the music and beer,
　　Where the girls and the city lights are.

Though it's thirty miles straight to the home paddock gate,
　　We'll be there tonight, without fail,
For we're chequed up and set, with a good thirst to wet,
　　And tomorrow we catch the down mail.
We'll leave all the packs on the saddle room racks,
　　Well greased with fat and stock tar,
Then we'll swing the door to, like the bellhops will do,
　　Where the girls and the city lights are.

The old station cook may remark with a look,
　　That 'the blasted stockcamp should stay out',
But we'll hand him back cheek, for in less than a week,
　　We'll be dining on oysters and stout.
For we're going straight through, like a bolt from the blue,
　　Though we've visions of Tim Howard's bar,
But we won't touch a drop till we finally stop.
　　Where the girls and the city lights are.

Mulga Corner

There's a spot in busy Brisbane mid the clamour of the town,
Where the bushmen from the outback always gather when they're down;
The buildings loom above it and its traffic signals glow,
And it hardly seems a possie that a Mulga man would know.
Above the roar of motors comes the newsboy's raucous shout,
And it seems a strange location for a man from further out;
The city crowd unheeding hurries by the corner pub,
But they love old 'Mulga Corner' do the pilgrims from the scrub.

When the droving is all over and the branding has been done,
And the mustering camps have finished on each godforsaken run,
When the storms have brought their blessings to the North and to the West,
And the yard builders and fencers and their kind have 'give it best',
When the tired old year is dying and the talk is Xmas Cheer,
Then the townfolk turn to surfing and the bushmen turn to beer,
Then you'll find them flush and happy mid the noises of the street,
Home and hosed at 'Mulga Corner' where the bushmen always meet.

There'll be men from Cunnamulla and Thargomindah too,
With the stockmen off the Cooper and the men from the Barcoo,
There'll be ringers from the Gulf runs where the cleanskin mobs they steal,
There'll be drovers in from Quilpie and the drovers from the 'Weal,
There'll be fencers from Cloncurry who would sink a hole in Hell,
With the Diamantina ringers and Georgina men as well,
From the Isaacs to the Herbert they'll be there to drink their fill,
With the drifters off the Barkly and the lads from Charleville.

There they'll skite and curse and argue and blow down each other's ears,
Till a man would need a shovel to get in to order beers,
And they'll show you how to spur 'em when the outlaws twist and chop,
For the riders at the 'Corner' never fail to say on top.
There the drovers tell of rushes in the gidgee and belar,
Till the mobs get boxed in dozens round the old 'Australian' bar.
There they'll sway upon the bar stools as they draft the wily steer,
And lug a snorting brumby with a beer glass for an ear.

And although the city's murmur and the traffic's clang and roar,
Drift across the bar room from the street outside the door,
You can hear the sound of cattle as they bellow in the yard,
And the storm wind in the mulga if you care to listen hard.
You can hear the stockwhips cracking down the stockroutes brown and bare,
For the spirit of the outback somehow seems to linger there,
It's a little bit of bushland mid the clamour of the street,
And they call it 'Mulga Corner' where the bushmen always meet.

Skills of the Ringer

THE TERM 'RINGER' is derived from the practice of wheeling or ringing a galloping mob of cattle back upon itself. Ringers were employed by stations and drovers as horsemen. They were never employed as general station hands in the Territory or in outback Queensland. Those days no boss out there would ask a ringer to pick up a crowbar or shovel. Most of the work they did was on horseback and all were competent horsemen and cattlemen. In the bronco yard most could take a turn on the bronco horse and all could brand, castrate, earmark and dehorn speedily and efficiently. Some of the more experienced could geld colts and spay cattle, and most were expert in throwing cattle, either from a horse or on the ground. There were some ringers who worked only on stations and some who stuck exclusively to droving, but the majority did both jobs and welcomed the change.

The Australian stockman's seat on a horse leans more towards comfort than style. It is not a seat that a dressage instructor would approve of, but then dressage instructors do not spend up to 15 hours a day in the saddle. The Australian stock saddle enabled stockmen to adopt the forward seat — both body and legs inclined forward. It was important for a ringer to have good hands on a horse; hands held low are essential in pulling a young horse about and teaching the mount stock skills. Freshly broken horses were usually given to ringers after two rides out of the yard, and the young horse's education was then gained in the camp. Bridle reins are an easily read two-way communication channel for a good horseman.

Greenhide or untanned hide played an important part in outback life. Particular ringers won reputations as makers of fine greenhide ropes, and although some were of plaited greenhide, most were made by twisting three strands of hide about 1 inch (2.5 centimetres) wide together. Excellent ropes resulted that were strong and durable and that held a loop well, making them ideal for roping in the bronco yard. Greenhide leg ropes and hobble straps were other items ringers were skilled in making, when time permitted.

Australian tanned kangaroo hide is without doubt the strongest and most versatile leather in the world for its weight. Many ringers became expert at plaiting, and made 'roo hide belts,

Open broncoing on Rockhampton Downs in 1949. PETER TRELOAR.

hatbands and whips in their spare time. The bulk of their work was far superior to that available in shops.

Despite the narrow base of their employment, ringers have proved many times that should the occasion arise, they can turn their hands successfully to just about anything.

The Muse Aroused

THE POETRY OF Paterson, Lawson, Ogilvie and Morant was very popular with ringers in the cattle camps of the North-West. The reason for this was simple; nothing much had changed. The lifestyle they wrote about was almost identical with our own. We had to amuse ourselves those days, and around the fire at night we often recited our favourite bush verses. I preferred the work of Henry Lawson and Harry Morant, who both portrayed the bush in a realistic way; Ogilvie and, to some extent, Paterson tended to be romanticists. However, there were many in the stockcamps who disagreed.

As our lifestyle was so similar to the lifestyle described by the great bush poets, it was a natural and logical thing for many bushmen, including myself, to try their hand at writing verses. The Sydney *Bulletin* was regarded as the bushman's bible those days, and with the optimism of youth, it was to the *'Bully'* that I sent my first literary effort. The paper was renowned for the encouragement it had given over many years to Australian writers. However, the character who put together the answer to the correspondence page pulled no punches; he was frugal with his praise and devastating with his criticism. The page was titled 'The Muse Aroused' and appeared on the inside of the *Bulletin*'s famous red cover. This gave rise to it becoming known as the red page, and owing to its pithy comments, it was regarded by readers as a feature page. In fact, so widely read was the red page that getting a mention there came to be regarded as a kind of literary recognition.

I waited impatiently, then at long last there it was — not my verse in the body of the *Bully*, but my name in the Red Page, with the comment 'pardonable if very young'. I gave up writing verse for a while after that, then I started contributing verses to the *North Queensland Register*, above the nom de plume of Lancewood. A couple of years later the *Bulletin* printed 'Where Leichhardt Lies'; it gave me a lot of pleasure to have the verse accepted, and I hoped that the Red Page critic read it. I received a cheque from the Sydney *Bulletin*, one of their special ones with a parrot in one corner saying, 'Thank God that's paid'. I should have kept it, but in the great tradition established by Henry Lawson, I cashed it immediately.

In 1972 a group of dedicated volunteers under the banner of the Winton Tourist Promotion Association launched the Bronze Swagman Award for Bush Verse, an annual Australia-wide competition. I was lucky enough to win the first swaggy with 'Gold Star'. In 1975 I got the judge's nod with 'Vale Rusty Reagan'.

The Bronze Swagman Award is still going strong, and the Winton Tourist Promotion Association is doing a great job in preserving and encouraging a style of literary expression that is as Australian as gum trees.

Boss Drover

AT THE END of 1951 I went to Brisbane for a holiday. It gave me a chance to get away from the bush while I considered my future. I had spent a number of years working on stations both in Queensland and the Northern Territory, including three years with the same company. I knew in time, had I stayed with them, I would have been offered a management, but the personal restrictions entailed in becoming a company man held little appeal for me.

Droving had always interested me. While working on Alexandria, I had seen the big mobs of aged store-conditioned bullocks walking through from the East Kimberley runs. I had heard yarns around countless campfires of rushes, dry stages and epic trips with cattle to New South Wales and beyond. I knew I needed a new challenge, and becoming a boss drover seemed a logical step. I had worked for some colourful drovers such as Looking Glass Joe, Sam Fuller and Arthur (Spider) Hollins; I had also worked scrub cattle, so I was confident that I could do the job. Becoming a boss drover was not, however, all that easy; it took both money and opportunity, and at that moment, I had neither.

Like most ringers, I never put too high a priority on building a nest egg. I also found that to maintain a reasonable sense of values it was essential to have a holiday in the south occasionally. Now at age 28 I found myself short of a quid, stuck in the city and going nowhere. Dame Fortune, however, is full of surprises, and in the next few days she dealt me a hand that would change my life.

I was having a drink in the Australian Hotel the day after my bout of soul searching when in walked Eric Beaumont. I knew Eric well; at one time he had been the common ranger at Boulia and I had worked his racehorses for him after leaving Glenormiston. We yarned over a round or two of drinks for a while, then pushing back his hat, he addressed me out of the corner of his mouth.

'You goin' out to the races tomorrer?'

'I'm not sure. Do you know something?' Then to the barman, 'Yes, same again.'

Eric waited until the drinks were served, then in a hoarse whisper, he gave me the drum.

'It's the good oil. Great Guru in the fourth — can't be beat.' I thanked Eric and the conversation turned to topics of a less highly classified nature until we parted.

The next day was Saturday and at ten o'clock Bruce Hanson arrived at the boarding house where I was staying. I had known Bruce since our time on Glenormiston, and as the pubs were open, we headed down to 'Mulga Corner' for a noggin. During the session, I told Bruce of Eric's tip and at lunch we grabbed a cab and went out to Doomben. Just before the fourth race, I saw Eric talking to a bookie; he saw me and came over.

'Get on to 'im quick. He's at tens still, but it won't be for long.'

I put a quid each way on Great Guru and joined Hanson at the fence just as the horses left the barrier. Unfortunately for me, the jockey on Great Guru spent most of the race in what can best be described as transcendental meditation and the pair lumbered past the post dead last. I decided that the money I had left would be better spent at the bar, where I proceeded to drown my sorrows.

As Bruce Hanson and I were leaving the course, we ran into Looking Glass

Joe Dowling and his wife. They asked us both back to their hotel for a drink. When we joined them in the hotel lounge, I could see that Joe had something on his mind. After he ordered drinks, he came to the point.

'The road's no place for a gel. I want you to take over me plant.' I sat stunned as Joe continued.

'You can run it on half shares. You shouldn't have any trouble getting cattle. If we're going to make any money, though, you'll have to employ at least three blacks, so you'll need a couple of reliable white ringers.'

'What about me?' said Hanson.

Looking Glass Joe gave Bruce the once over, then looked at me. 'Is he any good?'

I smiled at Hanson's discomfort. 'He'll do me. Where's the plant now?'

'At Thorntonia.'

Joe's brother, 'Armchair' Tom Dowling, was manager on Thorntonia and I knew that Jack Britt was running the camp. I looked at Joe.

'It's a deal. Let's hope the season breaks early.'

'Well, if you're a bit short, I can organise a job for you both on Thorntonia. I'll ring Tom up and let him know you're on the way. You can keep an eye on the plant horses if you're on the place.'

Looking Glass Joe was no fool, and where his horses were concerned, he trusted no one.

Three days later Bruce Hanson and I threw our swags on a mail train and headed for Mt Isa. I was on my way to become a boss drover. Within 12 months of going on the road, I would have a droving plant of my own.

Back to Camooweal

BRUCE HANSON WAS a happy-go-lucky kind of chap who was always good company. He had been working in Brisbane for some years and was delighted at the chance of returning to the outback, to work for me with Looking Glass Joe's plant. As a result of his high spirits, the long trip to Mt Isa was seldom boring. As we approached the mining town I told him of my first experience in the place.

He grinned at me. 'Did the manpower blokes ever catch up with you?'

'No, they never did. Perhaps they believe I am still working at the lead smelters.'

'You'd be nicely leaded up by now if you were. I can think of better ways to put lead in my pencil.'

When the train stopped at the Mt Isa station, we shouldered our swags and retraced my steps on that first visit. The town now was a great deal larger than it had been then, and had an atmosphere of growth and affluence. I noticed with interest that the building once occupied by my friends of the manpower department now housed the AWU. The Argent Hotel, however, seemed unchanged. Its long cool bar still offered relief from the heat, and from dehydration, and there was, of course, plenty of beer on tap. Young Hanson and I had a couple of drinks, then went up to see Peak about a lift to Camooweal.

Since my first visit I had got to know Clayton Ewert, the driver, quite well. He greeted me with a grin.

'If you're going to the Territory, I hope you've got a permit.'

I laughed and introduced Bruce Hanson, adding, 'No, you'll only have the pleasure of our company as far as Camooweal this trip.'

'Well, I'll be leaving early tomorrow morning. Go and say good day to Les — he's always pleased to see someone with a quid.'

We paid our respects and the fare to Les, then returned to the coolness of the Argent bar. We were having a quiet beer when a shift finished at the mine. Hanson looked in disbelief as the crowd rushed the bar. We grabbed our beers and got out, leaving them to it.

We stayed at the pub overnight, and were up at daylight. As we carried our swags out the front of the hotel, Hanson declared he had heard movement in the kitchen. Never one to miss out, he walked in and organised tea and toast for us both. Now well fortified, we tossed our swags on the back as Clayton pulled up. The first rays of the rising sun were striking the top of the tall smoke stack at the mines as we left the town.

The country out along the Camooweal road looked very dry. I had told Clayton of my plan to take Looking Glass Joe's plant on the road and asked him what he thought of the chances of the season breaking. He told me that the signs didn't look good, and they had missed out on early storms.

Clayton passed me his tin of tobacco. As I rolled a smoke for him, I asked, 'What is the old town like?'

'It's bloody lively, just about everyone is in town and will be until the season breaks and the work starts.'

'Oh well, we'll only be there until the Burketown mail goes. You can drop us off at the bottom pub. We should get a camp there, if only on the verandah.'

We arrived in Camooweal to discover that the Burketown mail was undergoing service difficulties. Yamagouchi, who ran the service, had blown up the engine in his truck. Although the mail would of course still get through, passengers, on the other hand, would have to wait for the truck to be fixed.

It's an ill wind that blows nobody any good, and two attractive — and unattached — girls who were working at the hotel at which we stayed did much to occupy our time and ease our woes as we cooled our heels in Camooweal. The days passed pleasantly and when eventually I learnt that the Burketown mail would soon be back in action, it was with real regret that I prepared my departure for the following day. I was just crossing the street from Freckleton's store when Looking Glass Joe and his wife pulled up en route to Darwin. I told him of the hold up.

'Throw your swags in the back and I'll run you out as soon as we've had some lunch.'

When I told Hanson the news, he was less than excited by our turn in fortune.

'What! Go out today! We can't.'

'Why not?'

'I'm on a promise, that's why. I've finally cracked it, and you want me to leave town.'

'I'm sorry, mate, but we've got to go.'

With studied reluctance Hanson rolled his swag and carried it out to the front verandah. I felt sorry for him, for I knew the amount of spade work he had done in wooing the cook at the hotel.

We were soon saying our farewells to the girls, however, and I knew by the look on her face that the waitress with whom I had passed such an enjoyable week was aware of my mate's plight. Then Looking Glass Joe blew the horn and we were away.

Hanson and I put in nearly two months on Thorntonia. I had always got on well with Jack Britt, the head stockman, with whom I had worked on Alexandria and on the road droving. Thorntonia had some rough country on it and it was good to be back in the saddle and handling touchy cattle again. The girls wrote to us both, I think Hanson wrote back, but my mind was more on getting started on the road and I never got around to answering the letters I received from the waitress. There had been some scattered rain about and although the season had not broken properly, I decided to take a chance and start out.

Hanson and I mustered the plant horses, bludged a bit of tucker from Britty and threw on the packs. I planned to go into Camooweal and pick up rations and horseshoes for the trip out west. Hopefully, in the meantime we would get decent rain. Hanson was delighted with the plan, for it would give him a chance to further pursue his courtship of the cook.

On our arrival at Camooweal we found good horse feed on the common close to the Rocklands boundary and set up camp by a large coolibah tree. It did not take long for us to strike up a reacquaintance with the waitress and the cook, although I was taken to task for not answering any of the waitress's letters. They invited us to dine with them that evening, much to Hanson's delight, for when we rode back to the camp together in the small hours, there was a look of satisfied bliss on his face.

As the days passed we were enjoying ourselves too much to hurry with the shoeing of the plant horses. As a result, it took us about two weeks to complete the job. If we were not up at the pub, the girls were down at the camp. I dare say Mrs Toohey, the licensee, was sick of the sight of us. The time finally arrived, however, when we had to get going. We said our farewells to the girls and I promised the waitress that I would let her know where to get in touch with me. I also said I would try and get back for the Camooweal races. In the end, I did neither; although not an easy decision to make, I knew that droving was seldom conducive to romances of a permanent nature. The waitress left Camooweal shortly afterwards.

When Hanson and I left Camooweal we were still hoping that the season would break. However, as the days passed with no sign of rain, we realised we were heading into one of the worst droughts since the turn of the century. The further we travelled, the worse the stockroute became, and obtaining good horse feed was a constant challenge.

Crossing the Rankine Plain early one morning, we witnessed a strange phenomenon. Hanson noticed it first — a bank of low cloud in the south-east that rolled towards us at great speed; it boiled like a giant breaker and swept past not more than 50 feet (15 metres) above our heads. Behind it was a clear blue sky and a brisk, cool sou'easter. I watched it disappear without even laying the dust and looked at Hanson.

'Well, I think, mate, we have just seen the Wet for this year.'

At the Buchanan, we met Boy Beaumont bringing in a mob of Brunette bullocks. He informed me there was no chance of the stockroute remaining open without rain. I had been promised a mob off Eva Downs but began to doubt that the Chambers Brothers would start bullocks on the road under the prevailing conditions.

I arrived at Eva half blind with sandy blight to find my worst fears realised. There would be no droving off Eva Downs. Hanson went back to Brisbane and joined the army, and I took a job on Eva to get feed for the plant. When the rains finally came, I accepted an offer from Vestey's and headed further west.

Drought

Old Camooweal is gripped by drought, the plain is brown and bare,
Relentlessly the dusty streets, reflect the blinding glare;
The burnished sky that's overhead shows little sign of rain,
To us that wait it seems that it may never storm again.
The temperature has passed for days, one hundred in the shade,
While drovers watch with anxious eyes, the clouds that rise and fade;
Their horses still are far from strong, there's nothing on the route,
Impatiently they wait for rain, to head for further out.

The old Georgina's bed is dry, and parched beside the town,
Twelve months have passed since last we saw the grey floods rolling down.
Each evening brings the dry storms up, to split as dry storms do,
While oldsters quote with knowing looks, the drought of 'Ninety two'.
There's little work upon the runs, where cattle losses rise,
And waterholes have given out, beneath the blazing skies,
Now at the bores through night's release, through noon day's blinding heat,
The pump head dips and rises to the engine's steady beat.

Inside, they've had some decent falls and how the herbage grew,
The ringer lads are heading in, in search of pastures new;
We envy them for we must stay, to kick our heels about
The bottom pub with naught to do, but drink and curse the drought.
But all ill winds must bring some good, and eyes of sparkling grey
And loving arms we've found that help to while the nights away.
⁎ time perhaps the rains will come, to flush the dry creeks down,
But Old Man Drought rides high today, above the drovers' town.

Footloose and Free

Old memories gather like moss on the years,
Of triumphs and hardships, of laughter and tears;
But one lingers yet like a snatch of a song
Of an old western river slow drifting along,

A friendly old river that glided and ran
From its hill shrouded source ere the dreaming began.
We were camped on that river, young Hanson and I,
Our swags were our homes, and our roof was the sky.

As footloose and free as the river that flowed
With a plant of fresh horses to take on the road;
On the river the eddies and wind ripples played
And we shod up the plant in the coolibah's shade.
The horse feed was good, life was easy and free
For time mattered little to Hanson and me.
We'd hobble the plant in the last of the light
Then welcome our girls from the township each night.

There we planned and we dreamed, young Hanson and I,
With our girls 'neath the dome of a star studded sky,
Those stars ages old that blazed constantly down
Seemed almost as close as the lights of the town.
The scent of wild clover came fresh on the breeze
That whispered it way through the coolibah trees,
The river and stars cast the oldest of spells
As the bush night re-echoed our Condamine bells.

But the last horse was shod 'neath the coolibah tree
'And dreams are for dreamers,' said Hanson to me,
The road further west held a challenge ahead
'And roads are for riding,' to Hanson I said.
Yet we both were aware of an unspoken doubt
That some day would haunt us on roads further out,
But we threw on the packs as the dawn fires burned,
We kissed both the girls, and we never returned.

North-West Monsoon

We have struggled on with the starving stock,
    When the routes were brown and bare,
When the stench of death was in every breath
    Of the drought-dry dusty air.
We have battled on through the long dry years,
    When the South wind called the tune,
But our hopes revive as the clouds arrive
    With the old north-west monsoon.

We knew some day that the Wet must come
    As the big Wets did of yore,
When the grey floods spread from the riverbed
    To the steps of the homestead door.
A blood-red sunset flamed last night
    And a halo blessed the moon,

Now the dark clouds fly down a windswept sky
    In the van of the big monsoon.

Spawned on a far off Asian coast,
    And nursed o'er the Timor Sea,
The scuds sweep down over bush and town
    And the big drops dance with glee.
The outside channels are running now,
    There's a fresh in the long lagoon,
While the old frogs croak, from their sleep awoke
    By the call of the big monsoon.

The rain on the roof beats a gay tattoo,
    Since we heard it last how long?
The chimneys leak and the old trees creak,
    And our hearts are filled with song.
We can turn our backs on the bad times now,
    And our overdrafts we'll forget,
For the flying scuds and the first small floods
    All heralds an Old Man Wet.

There'll be losses yet to the floods and bog,
    'Ere the rains of the monsoon pass,
'Ere the floods recede and the cattle feed
    Knee deep in the native grass,
But drought's grey spectre has gone at last,
    Though he left us none too soon,
Our hearts are light and we'll sleep tonight
    To the song of the old monsoon.

Packhorse Droving

PACKHORSE DROVERS HAD the reputation of being rather hungry or mean. However, this was more a case of necessity than desire. As everything had to be transported on eight packhorses — rations for up to eight weeks as well as water, beef and horseshoes — it is also not surprising that the tucker in a packhorse camp was a little short of gourmet standard.

Each packsaddle carried on each side a large leather packbag, or in the case of a water pack, a 5 gallon (22 litre) canteen on each side. The total load was distributed thus: two packs carrying water canteens, one shoeing pack, one corned beef pack, one flour pack, one cooked tucker pack, and two dry ration packs. These dry ration packs carried sugar, rice, coarse salt for salting beef, coffee, tea, potatoes, curry powder, tobacco, and cream of tartar and soda.

When packing a horse, the packbags had to be weighed by hand, as an unbalanced load would roll on the horse. As loading like this creates a dead weight, about 50 kilos plus a swag is a fair load for a packhorse.

The cooked tucker pack carried the cook's swag, plus an axe and a small tarpaulin, and a nest of billy cans strapped on top. The rest of the swags went on other packhorses, plus two or three Bedourie camp ovens, a rifle, and a nighthorse peg for open camps to complete the load. When crossing open country, like the Rankine Plain, a small amount of wood was also carried. This was augmented by using dried cow dung.

A packhorse plant gave a drover two advantages. Firstly, the plant gave him total mobility — he could go wherever he wished in order to find grass. Secondly, it made his job a lot easier, if he was shorthanded — the horse plant, usually taken to the next camp by the cook and the horsetailer, could be driven along with the bullocks.

Life on the Stockroutes

WHEN I WAS involved in the droving industry, cattle were still being walked from the West as they had been in the days of Nat Buchanan. Drovers still used packhorses or wagonettes to move their camp gear in the time-honoured manner of the early overlanders.

Mob watering at a stockroute bore.

Killing on Rockhampton Downs. PETER TRELOAR.

The store mobs were still big touchy aged bullocks from the vast unfenced runs of the Territory and the East Kimberleys. It was possible to walk a mob 500 miles (800 kilometres) without seeing a fence, in those days. The size of the mobs varied between 1350 and fifteen hundred. Trips were often of over 1000 miles (1600 kilometres) and four months on the road with a mob was common.

Store bullock drovers usually took 40-odd horses on the road with them, made up of eight pack or wagonette horses, eight nighthorses, and four or five day horses per man. The droving team consisted of three ringers and the boss with the cattle, a cook and a horsetailer. It was unusual for a full team to go right through a long trip. Very often the boss drover ended up being short-handed.

Things were usually lively for a couple of weeks after taking delivery of a mob of store bullocks from the West; this was when most of the trouble with the mob occurred. Things went along a lot more smoothly after the mob were broken in to the road, but it was never boring, as every day brought another stage of the stockroute, and often new problems.

Because of the distance between waters, dry-daying bullocks — that is, watering every second day — was a common practice. If after a dry day there was no water ahead as expected, you had a dry stage on your hands.

Drovers were given a number of beasts as killers at the start of the trip. These bullocks were to be killed for beef as the drover went along. However, in a bad year these beasts soon became too tough to eat, and the drover would succumb to the temptation of filling the beef bags with one of the fat station cattle that grazed by the stockroute.

Getting grass for his mob was the first responsibility of the boss drover. This was never a problem in the Territory, as fenced stockroutes were unheard of out there and no one bothered them but when a drover got well down into Queensland the situation was quite different — fences on both sides of the stockroute lane, and a station hand to 'see the mob through'. Drovers, however, are an enterprising lot, and were usually equal to the challenge. Many a mob 'rushed' at night and ended up knee-deep in Mitchell grass in a grazier's paddock.

Droving was a hard life, but it was a free and easy one that had its rewards.

Song of the Wave Hill Track

Our bullocks are fresh and the season is good,
    For we follow the yearly Wet.
The first mob back on the Wave Hill track,
    And the rain clouds gather yet.
We took our mob from the mustering camp,
    Just on a month ago,
Twelve hundred head and all scrub bred,
    They carry the 050.

Our horses are fat and the creeks are full,
    The feed is the very best;
We'll poke them along with a cheery song,
    And say goodbye to the West.
We camped last night past the timber's edge,
    Where the grasses grow like grain,
Behind our back is the timbered track,
    Before us — the blacksoil plain.

The blacksoil plain where mirages dance,
    And shimmer and then are gone,
Past Brady's grave where the grasses wave,
    The stockroute wanders on,
O'er the rolling downs that rise and fade,
    Past many a river bend,
O'er the tableland where the lone mills stand,
    And on to the journey's end.

But we are young and our hearts are light,
    And the life that we live is free,
With a cheque to spend at the journey's end,
    Not a care in the world have we,
For time and distance are nought to us,
    And the bullocks are feeding slow,
The first mob back on the Wave Hill track,
    Five hundred miles to go.

Downs the River

The season was late when we left with the stores,
Feed scarce as we travelled the Barkly.
Round the permanent holes and the government bores
The tableland stretched away starkly.
We struck early storms as we farewelled the downs,
And the northerlies warned of their coming,
Away in the Gulf from the cumulus crowns
The sound of the thunder came drumming.

How we cursed at the rain when it pelted that night
And added confusion to worry;
How we cursed at the bullocks that bellowed in fright
And flung up the mud in their hurry.
But the morning star shone with a crystal clear light
Through a rift in the clouds ere dawning,
And the butcherbirds welcomed the sun with delight
And carolled their joy to the morning.

We are staging along down the Georgina now
And we water the mob while it's feeding,
By the banks of the holes it is grand to see how
The button grass clusters are seeding.
The scent of the herbage comes sweetly and strong
From the channels all matted with clover,
And water birds circle from each billabong
In the lead of the travelling drover.

The mob rests at noon with the water hard by
The trees where the quartpots are steaming.
Through sunlight and shade 'neath a water-washed sky
The river goes drifting and dreaming.
She winds on her way through the heart of the west
Turning and spreading and slowing,
This river the furthest out bushmen love best
Where the southerly busters are blowing.

Those who drink her pale water as pure as snow,
Be they bushmen or townsmen or rover,
Will some day return where the coolibah's grow
By the tracks of the travelling drover.
For she fashions a spell like a gossamer thread
Yet it holds a man fast and forever
To the creeks that run back through her vast watershed
And the length of the old winding river.

A Tally of Bullocks

SOME OF THE 121 000 head of cattle that walked down the Georgina River route in 1950 are listed below.

DROVER	MOB	FROM	TO
Boy Beaumont	1200 bullocks	Rocklands	Tanbar *
Peter Pedwell	1280 bullocks	Brunette	Dajarra
Barlow Jackson	1242 bullocks	Avon	South Galway *
Fred Barlow	1500 bullocks	Soudan	Monkira *
Ben Benson	1250 bullocks	Alroy	Dajarra
Larry Darcy	1300 bullocks	Helen Springs	Vergmont *
Walter Green	1360 bullocks	Rockhampton Downs	South Galway *
Jack Laffin	1500 bullocks	Soudan	Coorabulka *
Sid Howard	1350 bullocks	Creswell	Dajarra
Arthur Hollins	1500 bullocks	Helen Springs	Winton
Don Booth	1500 bullocks	Alexandria	Coorabulka *
Jack Britt	1400 mixed	Thorntonia	Brighton *
Chas Wolfgang	1200 bullocks	Barclay	Roxborough *
Norm Stacey	1266 bullocks	Victoria River	Walgra *
C. Papworth	1370 bullocks	Wave Hill	Dajarra
Tom Lewis	1626 bullocks	Wave Hill	Winton
Keith O'Keefe	1500 bullocks	Anthony Lagoon	Davenport *
Steve Donovan	1500 bullocks	Wave Hill	Dajarra
Roy McMullen	1250 bullocks	Alroy	Dajarra
Hurtle Lewis	1240 bullocks	Newcastle Waters	Kynuna
Jack Vitnall	1280 mixed	Alice Springs	Davenport *
Doug Scobie	1297 bullocks	Victoria River	Walgra *
Jack Charlton	1600 bullocks	Helen Springs	Dajarra
Reg Tighe	1350 bullocks	Wave Hill	Dajarra
W. Little	1280 bullocks	Elsey	not known
John Darcy	1207 bullocks	Victoria River	Walgra *
Bert Crouch	1250 bullocks	Alroy	Wyandra
Boy Elliot	1200 bullocks	Inverway	not known
Bill Ardill	1365 bullocks	Wave Hill	Dajarra
Splinter Pendergast	1355 bullocks	Victoria River	Walgra *
Edna Zigenbine	1417 bullocks	Bedford Downs	Dajarra

* Fattening properties

Early Overlanders

DROVING IN AUSTRALIA is almost as old as settlement itself. The discovery of a way over the Blue Mountains in 1813 started the movement of stock on the hoof in earnest, and in the next few years thousands of cattle and sheep walked over the mountains to the rich pastures beyond.

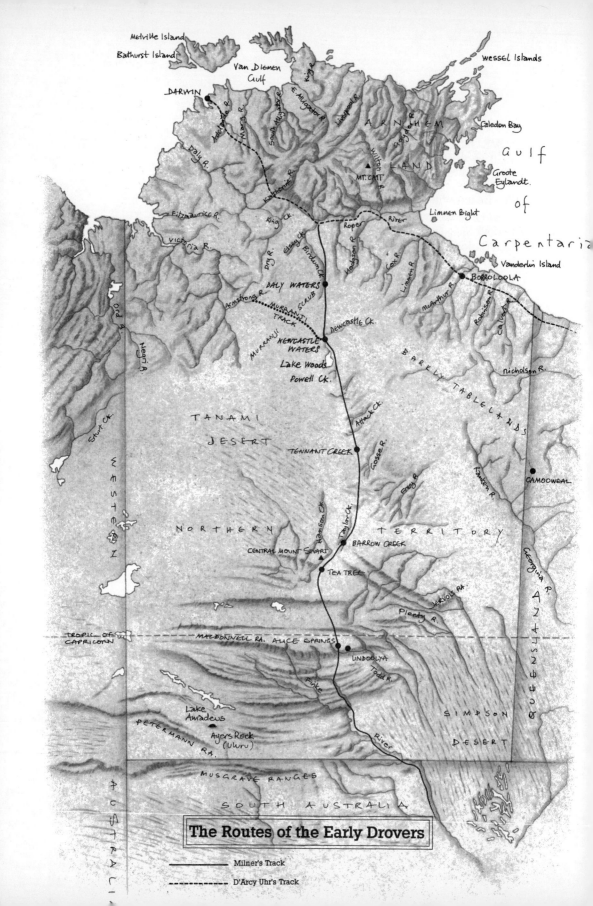

Melville Island
Bathurst Island
Van Diemen Gulf
Wessel Islands
DARWIN
Daly R.
ARNHEM
Caledon Bay
Gulf
MT. CATT
Groote Eylandt
of
Fitzmaurice R.
Limnen Bight
Carpentaria
VICTORIA R.
Roper River
Vanderlin Island
BORROLOOLA
DALY WATERS
Armstrong R.
MURRANJI SCRUB
MURRANJI TRACK
Newcastle Ck.
McArthur R.
Robinson R.
Calvert R.
Negri R.
NEWCASTLE WATERS
BARKLY TABLELANDS
Nicholson R.
Lake Woods
Powell Ck.
Shut Ck.
TANAMI
DESERT
Attack Ck.
Gosse R.
CAMOOWEAL
Ord R.
TENNANT CREEK
Frew R.
Rankem R.
WESTERN
NORTHERN
TERRITORY
Ranken Ck.
Georgina R.
CENTRAL MOUNT STUART
BARROW CREEK
Taylor Ck.
Jervois Ra.
QUEENSLAND
TEA TREE
Plenty R.
TROPIC OF CAPRICORN
MACDONNELL RA. ALICE SPRINGS
UNDOOLYA
Todd R.
Lake Amadeus
Finke
SIMPSON
PETERMANN RA.
Ayers Rock (Uluru)
River
DESERT
AUSTRALIA
MUSGRAVE RANGES
SOUTH AUSTRALIA

The Routes of the Early Drovers

———————— Milner's Track

- - - - - - - - D'Arcy Uhr's Track

Late in 1836 Joseph Hawdon overlanded 300 head of cattle, through Aboriginal tribal country from the Murrumbidgee to the new settlement at Port Phillip. Within 18 months 5000 head of cattle and 150 000 head of sheep were to follow in his tracks.

From that time on, as explorers opened up the interior, overlanders, with their herds and flocks, followed hard on their heels. The Overland Telegraph played an important part in opening up the Northern Territory. It was the OT, or rather the need to supply meat to the workers, that motivated the droving of the first stock to the Top End.

The Milner Brothers left Cooper Creek in 1870 with some 4700 sheep, with Roper River as their goal. The trip took nearly two years and covered almost 3000 miles (4800 kilometres), taking them through the centre of Australia. The journey was not without tragedy as John Milner was clubbed to death by Aborigines at Attack Creek. His brother Ralph battled on, and finally arrived at the Roper in early 1872 with 3000 sheep for the fresh-meat hungry workers.

The government had promised a £10 000 reward for the first party to get meat to the OT workers. However, during the trip there had been an election, and as a result Ralph Milner missed out. It would appear that politicians' promises haven't changed over the years.

The first cattle to reach the Territory was a mob of 400 head owned by Dillon Cox. The mob was headed for the Roper to provide meat for the OT workers. In charge was D'Arcy Uhr, one of the best bushmen in Queensland. He followed the route that Leichhardt took on his first trip, around the Gulf coast. Uhr arrived at the Roper in 1872, only to find the work on the line completed. Cox wanted him to continue to Darwin, but Uhr contended that his job was finished when he reached the Roper. This first ever dispute over a droving contract in the Territory was settled in court with the government resident, Captain Douglas, presiding. D'Arcy Uhr complied with the court ruling and took the mob to Darwin — an epic trip over virtually unknown country. The route he took became the recognised route from Queensland, until the Murranji opened up.

The OT line, completed in 1872, left a number of isolated telegraph stations strung from south to north across the inhospitable centre of Australia. Many of these stations were later to become important towns. The immediate problem they created for the South Australian government in the administration of its Territory was one of supply.

The most practical method, it was decided, was to provide each station with its own flock of sheep for use as a meat supply. Alfred Giles, a noted bushman, won the contract to supply the lonely outposts with mutton on the hoof. He left Beltana in South Australia with 5000 head and started north along Milner's tracks.

At Barrow Creek, Giles met Tim Nelson, who was droving 100 head of cattle to Darwin for killers. Nelson had come from Undoolya Station, a newly established run in the MacDonnell Ranges east of the Alice Springs telegraph station. It had been taken up by Bagot and Smith and was the first pastoral lease in the area.

In 1879 Giles again headed north, supervising the droving of 2000 head of cattle and 12 000 sheep to stock Springvale and Delamere, taken up by Dr W. Brown, in the Katherine area. However, the race to establish properties in the Top End had already been won; Travers and Gibson had already taken up Glencoe on the Adelaide River the year before. The man who stocked it for them was the legendary Nat Buchanan.

In 1878 Buchanan left Aramac with 1200 head bound for Glencoe. Roughly following D'Arcy Uhr's track around the Gulf coast, he travelled up the Roper to Elsey Creek then north to the Adelaide River as Uhr had done. The unfortunate Travers who went with Buchanan did not make it. While alone in the camp near the Limmen River he was killed by Aborigines.

In 1880 Buchanan was again headed for the Territory with 20 000 head, in 10 mobs, to stock newly taken up stations. Buchanan was the first man to take cattle to the East Kimberley region, droving 4000 head to stock Ord River run.

The overlanders who followed in the tracks of Uhr and Buchanan overcame flooded rivers and fever and encountered the wrath of Aborigines whose tribal lands they were crossing. The length of those epic trips, and the problems encountered en route, were enough to crush the spirit of most mortals. The men who travelled the coast road in the 1880s were not supermen, but their indomitable spirit and their vision of the future overcame all adversity.

The building of the Overland Telegraph line, and the men who followed after, played a part in opening up the Territory; it was the coast road, however, that proved to be the vital link.

Many overlanders did a sterling job in those stirring days, but two men stood head and shoulders above the rest.

Nat Buchanan was an Irish Scot, born in Dublin, who came to Australia in 1837. Strong in Buchanan's make-up was the restless spirit of adventure and resourcefulness typical of the Celtic race. He seemed to be as much at home in the trackless back country of Australia as his forebears had been in the wild braes and bens of Caledonia. He had the reputation of dealing fairly with Aborigines, yet like all his peers he saw himself as a flag carrier in the great nineteenth century expansion of the British Empire. Buchanan was in some ways an enigma — a man who overcame the harshest conditions, mixed with and employed hard tough men, yet never lost an innate gentleness — and he always carried a green sunshade.

There was nothing complex about D'Arcy Uhr — a tough, hard-bitten Australian bushman, he would just as soon have a fight as a feed; he was a man who tended to shoot first and ask questions later when dealing with Aborigines. Uhr's trip from Charters Towers to Darwin in 1872 was a feat of bushmanship seldom equalled, and it ushered in a new era. Buchanan's epic droving trip, from Aramac to the Adelaide River six years later, saw that era firmly established.

In the 1880s stations were being established at a rapid rate in those districts west of the tangled scrubs that appeared to be an impenetrable barrier. Running in a northerly direction to the west of Newcastle Waters, the scrub had beaten the explorer McDougall Stuart, and had forced the early overlanders to travel the long and tortuous coastal route. As there was good cattle country on both sides of the scrub, it was only a matter of time before some adventurous character triumphed over the natural barrier.

In 1886 that character arrived in the person of G.R. Hedley. Leaving Newcastle Waters he struck out into the unknown. He came close to losing his life on an 80 mile (130 kilometre) dry stage, but he won through to Top Springs — the first white man to travel the notorious Murranji Track.

Later that same year, after good rain, Nat Buchanan and 'Greenhide' Sam Croker decided to try the short cut. In hand they had 100 horses and a number of cattle that had strayed hundreds of miles from Wave Hill. Sam Croker had tracked these cattle south of the Murranji waterhole, finding surface water after the rain. Enlisting the aid of local Aborigines, who guided Buchanan and Croker to Murranji and Yellow Holes, they made it to Top Springs. The trip from east to west through the scrub proved that stock could travel the Murranji, as long as the waterholes were full.

Although the new track cut hundreds of miles off the coastal route, it proved to be just as hazardous. Neither waterhole lasted long; when full they were fever ridden, and when dry they often proved to be the points of no return for the unwary traveller.

Travellers to the Western Australian goldfields used the tracks extensively, but no cattle were brought back through the Murranji until 1904. It was a good season that year, so Sidney Kidman decided to send two mobs from Victoria River Downs through the Murranji to Austral Downs in Queensland. Both mobs were cows, and Blake Miller went first with 1100 head. Flavelle Smith took the second mob through the Murranji scrubs to Queensland.

Four months later two mobs of bullocks and a mob of cows from Wave Hill started through the Murranji. Jack-Dick Skuthorpe and Steve Lewis were in charge of the bullocks, and Charlie Phillott took the cows. All three mobs were from Wave Hill. Skuthorpe and Phillott drove their mobs to Killarney Station near Narrabri, while Lewis walked his mob to Hergott Springs, going south through Alice Springs. These last three mobs got little water through the scrub.

The following year Walter Rose left Lissadel with bullocks for Queensland. The season was bad and Rose found the Murranji Track closed. Walter Rose was not going to be beaten, however. He turned the mob north to the old coast route and, after many holdups, finally reached his destination two and a half years after leaving Lissadel.

1909 was another bad year, with the Murranji closed to cattle. This did not deter the Farquharson brothers of Inverway Station, out toward the Western Australian border. They drove their bullocks to Top Springs on the west side of the Murranji and spelled them for a few days. Then, after the mob was given a good drink, they headed for the Bucket Hole 120 miles (175 kilometres) away. Thirsty bullocks will march like soldiers as long as you steer them straight. The Farquharsons nursed them by day, and by night they kept the bullocks going with a hurricane light in the lead. It was a great example of guts and cattle work, and they came to the Bucket Hole with only minor loss.

In later life, Walter Rose ran a hotel in Cloncurry. Jack-Dick Skuthorpe died of Gulf Fever on his run on the Nicholson River. Blake Miller, a Kidman man and a fine bushman, later managed Austral Downs. Later still he owned Undilla, a small station between Camooweal and Burketown. There he raised stalwart sons and fine stockhorses. Some of the best horses I've ridden carried the Undilla brand. Charlie Phillott retired to Charleville, and his family became well known in the Winton district.

As a lad I knew Frank Uhr, D'Arcy Uhr's brother. Frank, whose correct name was Herbert George Uhr, was in the Territory in the 1880s and helped stock

Brunette Downs. One year he and D'Arcy left Goulburn in New South Wales with 500 head for Cape York, and after five months on the road they delivered the mob without losing a single beast.

Galloping Bullocks and Dry Stages

Reckless rides through the Murrangi
When little mattered save do or die —
With rushing bullocks the stakes were high
Where the tangled scrub loomed over —
Nursing mobs where the dead men lie —
With grass and water in short supply
For a thousand miles as the crow might fly
To the channels green with clover —
Perishing cattle on stages dry
Where sandstorms rage 'neath a barren sky —
These and more in the days gone by
Were the lot of the old-time driver.

The Elsey Crossroads

THE COASTAL ROUTE travelled by D'Arcy Uhr, and Milner's track up the Overland Telegraph line met near Elsey Creek, a tributary of the Roper, on what would soon become Elsey Station. From that important junction one route went north to the Adelaide River and on to Darwin. Another would later turn south-west, around the Murranji scrub to the Victoria River, then on to Wave Hill and the East Kimberley region. During the 1880s and 1890s the race to acquire Top End land was on with a vengeance. It was a period of explosive development in which the Elsey crossroads became a major focal point.

The first white man to visit the area was the explorer Ludwig Leichhardt, who crossed and named the Roper late in 1845 on his trip to Port Essington. He named the river after John Roper, a member of the expedition who had been speared by Aborigines some months previously. Although grievously wounded, Roper battled on and survived the journey to the sea.

In June 1856 a party led by Augustus Gregory left the Victoria River to explore inland across to the Queensland Gulf Country. The exploration was backed by the British government and the Royal Geographical Society. John Ravenscroft Elsey, a young English surgeon and naturalist selected by the society, had been sent out to join Gregory the year before.

Gregory gave the name Elsey Creek to one of the tributaries of the Roper after the young surgeon and the name was destined to become a household word in Australia long after Elsey himself was forgotten. The young explorer boarded the Alnwick Castle to return to England on 15 March 1857, but on 31 December he died at St Kitts in the West Indies. He was just 24 years of age.

In 1862 the indomitable Scot John McDouall Stuart arrived at the Roper on his epic journey to Chambers Bay east of Darwin. The Murranji had thrice defeated him in his efforts to reach the Victoria River, but on this historic trip he finally cut through the scrub north of the site of Newcastle Waters and crossed Gregory's tracks east of Elsey Creek.

The routes of the three explorers came together at the Roper: Leichhardt from the east, Gregory from the west, and Stuart from the south. The focal point at the crossroads was established. The surveyors of the OT line followed closely the route taken by McDouall Stuart, and within two years of the placement of the first survey peg, stock were moving up the two great stockroutes to the Elsey crossroads.

Workers on the OT line named a number of waters on Elsey country: All Saints Well, sunk in Elsey Creek and completed on All Saints Day 1872; Warloch Ponds (named after a horse); Bitter Springs, at the junction of Elsey Creek and the Roper (later renamed Mataranka Springs); and the Red Lily Lagoons.

The gate to Elsey Cemetery and Nature Reserve. IAN TINNEY.

In 1878 Abraham Wallace was granted the Elsey leases and the following year he was given an extension of time to stock and establish the run. After mustering 2500 head of cattle from Bowen Downs, Mt Cornish and Nive Downs,

Wallace started north with his nephew J.H. Palmer and four others in 1880. Following the coastal route opened up by D'Arcy Uhr, Wallace arrived at his run in April 1881. He camped at Warloch Ponds and built the first homestead close to the stockroute on Elsey Creek. It was the third station to be established in the Top End.

Until the opening of the Murranji Track, the Elsey crossroads saw the greatest movement of stock in the history of pastoral development.

The Stockroutes

A GREAT TRUNK route from east to west facilitated the droving of cattle from stations in the East Kimberleys and the Territory to the Queensland railheads and fattening properties, and to Alice Springs in the south. Three feeder stockroutes crossed the Western Australian–Territory border at Gordon Downs, Ord River, and at Aubergne in the north. The first two met to pass through Wave Hill, where the joined route became the main artery. The northern branch ran through Victoria River Downs to meet the main route at Top Springs. Also joining at the point was the Dry River route, which brought cattle down from the Katherine area.

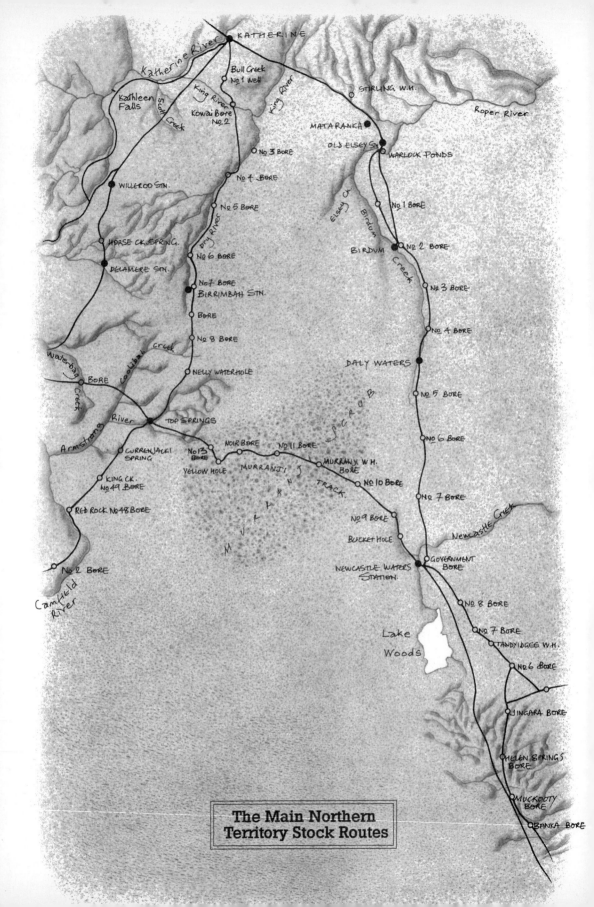

The Main Northern Territory Stock Routes

The combined stockroute then became the Murranji Track. After emerging from the scrub lands, this main route was met on Newcastle Waters by a stockroute that ran from east of Katherine through Daly Waters. The main route then ran south-east over the Barkly Tableland and down the Georgina River to cross the Queensland border at Lake Nash.

Before crossing the border the main route was joined by two other feeder routes; the first, from the Western Gulf, came in at Anthony Lagoon; the second, from Rockhampton Downs and Alroy, joined at the Rankine. Cattle also left the main route at Helen Springs bound for the Alice, and at the Rankine, to cross the Queensland border at, or rather near, Camooweal.

Now if the above makes very dry reading, it also describes what were, for a long time, very dry stockroutes. As drovers were dependent on surface water to water their mobs, droving was restricted to those few months after the Wet. In 1920 the authorities decided to undertake a program to create stockroute watering facilities. Sub-artesian bores were the answer, and over the next few years bores were sunk on most of the recognised routes.

A chap by the name of Peacock, with his son and daughter, put down many of these bores. The plant used was the old percussion type. It was hard work with the drill needing constant attention, and the heavy bits had to be sharpened often, using a forge and anvil. Charcoal for the forge had to be made on the job by burning timber in a covered pit in the ground. The Peacocks were connected with the Jones of Jones' jam fame. Living conditions were rough, but I dare say they were never short of jam for the damper.

Once the bores were down, windmills were erected over the holes. A Japanese national with the unlikely name of Ivan Steel did a lot of this work. Later, during the war, he was interned as a suspected spy.

Earth water tanks were built on the downs, but as the soil in the Murranji was unsuitable, steel tanks were erected there. the contract for putting up the earth tanks or turkey's-nests was given to one of the Territory's genuine characters — Davey Cahill of Shannon Downs. Davey used a monkey-tail scoop and a horse team to do the job. Now Davey never liked to wear trousers when he was working and, although traffic was light in those days, a number of travellers were met by the sight of Davey, swinging on the lever of the monkey-tail scoop, with his bare buttocks flashing beneath the flying tails of his flannel shirt.

With the improvement to the stockroutes the number of mobs walking to Queensland from the West increased steadily. During the early days of the Pacific war, when the Japanese threat was very real, the government introduced a plan to move as many head of cattle as possible out of the threatened areas. This again led to increased activity on the stockroutes.

Many unsuccessful attempts were made over the years to clear a track through the Murranji scrubs. Faced with the Japanese threat, the authorities brought in bulldozers to clear a corridor. This was a short-term benefit only, as the regrowth soon became a problem. Additional bores were also sunk during the war years. Bill Chambers put down Windy Bore and a new bore at Anthony's Lagoon. Bill's father, Sid, had taken up the vacant Eva Downs block in 1936, and Bill and the rest of the family overlanded there in 1938.

The cessation of hostilities did nothing to halt the movement of western cattle to

Queensland; indeed, the demand for beef, due to immigration and a higher standard of living, was responsible for one of the biggest booms in overlanding in our history.

Despite the improvements on the Murranji Track, it remained a headache to drovers right to the end of its use. The scrub in places was impenetrable; night camps were bad; windmills sometimes broke down; and ironwood poisoning added to the other problems. There were good drovers and bad stockroutes in other parts of Australia, but nowhere did the drover feel as alone as in the dark, brooding, and uninhabited scrubs of the Murranji. In the early days men perished from thirst on the Murranji during the dry season and fell victim to fever during the Wet. Murranji waterhole is more of a swamp than a hole, and there are reputed to be at least 20 men buried there. It is not a pretty spot.

The Murranji

It lies a silent, stagnant swamp o'erhung with brooding trees,
Beside the lonely road that winds out to the Kimberleys.
The wild dogs chorus there each night from scrub on every side,
And there in torment and alone some twenty men have died.
The wild blacks called it Murranji before the white men came
To blaze the road and stockroute west that bears its sinister name.
A pest plagued swampland in the Wet — a mud hole in the Dry,
Both thirst and fever, deadly foes, then stalked the Murranji.

They stocked their stations further out, and brought their bullocks back,
With water fifty miles apart across the dreaded track.
Through endless scrub with packhorse plants they travelled day and night;
When fever struck no mortal man could help them in their plight,
With brains awhirl they lent upon their mates who rode beside,
Who nursed them and who buried them in rough graves where they died.

The Halls Creek diggings boomed out west and further every week,
The rumour of the riches spread — good gold up at 'the creek'.
A few made fortunes overnight, with gold the stakes are high,
Both others staked a final claim beside the Murranji.
And often troopers on patrol or drovers passing through,
Would curse the spot and start upon the task they had to do;
The scattered bones were gathered then, the sun-bleached skull was found,
Another coolibah was marked beside another mound.

They came from many climes and lands, they steered by many stars,
Their paths converged to meet and end beneath these coolibahs.
One was a Swede who'd travelled far, he was of Viking blood,
He'd won his spurs in other lands in blizzard and in flood.
The craze for gold was in his veins, he swore he'd beat the track;
He reached the Murranji at last with aching legs and back.
He stayed a while to drink and rest and wash away the sweat,
And by that twisted coolibah the Swede is resting yet.

Two were but lads from New South Wales who rode to meet a mob,
The 'Never' held no fears for them, 'twas just another job.
Ah! reckless youth than reckons not what carelessness can cost,
They heard the Murranji was low — they gambled and they lost.
One found his final resting place by way of English pride,
For England shipped her wayward sons then when the world was wide.
A lone, aloof remittance man, none dared to ask him why,
Ere fever stilled those guarded lips beside Murranji.

They all left family ties somewhere, knew hopes and dreams and fears;
How many mothers' heads have bowed through waiting down the years?
No crosses stand, no railings guard each long neglected plot,
The names unknown, they slumber in one acre God forgot.

This message written on one of the tanks at Government Bore Number 11 on the Murranji stockroute reads: 'C. Prendergast past here with 1082 head of galloping Newrys.' IAN TINNEY.

Taking Delivery

BEFORE A DROVER took delivery of a mob in those days, each bullock had to be inoculated against contagious bovine pleuropneumonia, commonly known as 'pleuro'. This was done by inserting a 'seaton', or short length of woollen yarn soaked in serum, in the soft tissue at the end of the beast's tail. The instrument used in this very minor operation was a large bladed needle with an open eye at the point of the blade.

As a result of this compulsory requirement, every station, no matter how under-improved, had at least one set of yards with a crush or race. As well as being inoculated, each beast was bang-tailed (the tassel on the end of the tail was cut short) to denote that it was a road bullock.

After the mob was put through the yards, it was ready to be handed over to the drover. The bullocks were counted by stringing them out between the manager and the drover, and when the number was agreed on, the droving contract was signed. The contract set out the price per head per hundred mile (160 kilometres) the drover was to receive, as well as the distance per week (water permitting) the drover was to travel. Most contracts also specified payment for holding time when drovers could not travel due to a direction from a stock inspector or other authority. This was usually commensurate with the contract rate for mileage lost. Waybills showing brands and earmarks of the mob together with a permit to travel were also handed to the drover.

Once the contract was signed and the drover had taken delivery, he was on his own — completely responsible for the well-being of the bullocks and the delivery of the full mob at the destination. As a drover was not paid for droving those bullocks lost during the trip, delivering anything less than the full mob would result in financial loss to the drover as well as possible damage to his reputation. A drover who made a very bad delivery by finishing the trip hundreds short, or by arriving with the bullocks in very poor condition, would be unlikely to be employed by that pastoral firm again. He may, in fact, find it hard to continue as a contract drover.

Contract drovers, knowing that future work depended on their reputation, set their priorities accordingly — the bullocks came first every time. Experienced ringers used to droving knew and appreciated this, and if anyone did grumble, the boss drover was quick to remind the culprit of the facts of life on the stockroutes.

Song of the Droving Season

On the runs of wide horizons, where mirages haunt the sky,
They are mustering the road mobs and the busy days slip by,
Reckless musters through the ranges o'er the plains that stretch before,
And the dust clouds slowly spiral from the drafting camps once more.

In the dawn light from the stockyard comes the sound of action too,
And the bang-tail knives are flashing as the bullocks rattle through,
Then the drovers take delivery where they count them on the plain,
And the restless mobs go stringing down the stockroutes once again.

Down the Wave Hill track they're coming twelve and fifteen hundred strong,
And the lonely nights are gladdened by the watch's lilting song.
Dusty pads are wearing deeper — wearing deeper as they wind,
For the Vestey mobs are walking with the 'Bull Heads' close behind.

Baldys, Shorthorns, wild-eyed pikers — mobs of every breed and brand,
From the wilds of West Australia to the Barkly Tableland.
While the bullocks of the Gulf runs are awalking with the rest,
Oh! the blackened quarts are boiling on the stockroutes north and west.

Down the rivers too they're stringing to the flats of channel grass,
And the brumbies wheel and whistle as the bullocks slowly pass.
Stringing down the lonely stages as the dust wrack swings aloft,
From the rolling downs of Avon, and the hills of Yelvertoft.

Dusty mobs from Alexandria, from Brunette and Creswell, too,
Placid top fats for the rail heads, rangy store mobs walking through.
Mobs for sale and mobs to fatten on the river flats inside,
Oh! the good old days still linger where the outback drovers ride.

Slowly mobs are feeding camp-wards as the evening shadows fall,
And the horse bells' mellow music drifts with twilight overall.
By the plains and scrubs and rivers where the western stars burn bright,
The friendly fires are glowing in the drovers' camps tonight.

Nighthorses and Night Watching

THE PICK OF a store-cattle drover's plant was his nighthorses. These were fast, sure-footed horses with good eyesight, and the temperament for the important and often dangerous job of controlling touchy mobs at night. Good nighthorses were invaluable to a drover, as he depended on his reputation for future work. In a bad rush the quality of the nighthorse was often the deciding factor between holding the mob and disaster. Experienced nighthorses knew exactly what was expected of them. On a pitch-black night a drover had to depend to a large extent on the nighthorse to get to the lead of a rushing mob. Good nighthorses seldom put a foot wrong.

As there were no yards or fences on the outback stockroutes, watching the mob at night was an essential part of droving store bullocks. The mob was fed to the camp towards dusk and gradually pushed together until they formed a compact mass in front of the fire. Some drovers camped the mob up to 100 yards from the fire; others liked to have the bullocks close, leaving just enough room to ride between them and the fire.

The hours of darkness were split into watches, with the length of each watch depending on the number of men available. Two and a half hours was normal with a full team. Drover's time was always set on six o'clock sundown, as this did away with having to adjust the watches due to the shortening or lengthening of the days. The boss drover always did the last or daylight watch — the horsetailer, the first.

The man on watch rode round the mob singing, reciting or whistling. This had a calming effect on the bullocks and prevented them from taking fright as the rider loomed up out of the darkness. A well-known drover once took delivery of bullocks from Brunette Downs, and in his employ he had a young chap who had never been on the road. Before the lad went on watch, the boss explained to him that he had to sing to the mob. On being informed that the lad knew no songs or poems, and could not whistle because he had lost his two front teeth, the boss scratched his head and said: 'Well, lad, these are Brunette bullocks and the Brunette brand is 505, so go out and tell 'em that'.

Throughout the trip the young chap chanted: '505 is the Brunette brand, the Brunette brand is 505'.

I don't suppose the bullocks minded: after all, he was singing their song.

Goodbye Old Chap

You may rub your head on my coat, old chap,
        As you stand by the gate in pain,
While I loose the knot in the greenhide strap
        That you never shall wear again.
You may nudge my hand as you've done so oft,
        In the days that have gone for aye,
For you'll carry me never again on watch,
        Round the mob at the break of day.

You will draft no more as the grey dust swings,
        From the camp on the blacksoil plains;
You will prop no more by the stockyard wings,
        When we yard for the cattle trains.
No more you'll wait for the mob to splash,
        By the light of a storm lit sky,
Mid the thunder's roar and the timber's crash,
        Round the camp in the Murranji.

Ne'er again by the nighthorse break you'll doze,
        In the chill of a winter night,
When the south wind moans and the back log glows,
        And the stars wink cold and white.
We may find another with swinging gait,
        To hack through the trucking town,
And there'll be others to quietly wait
        By the break as the sun goes down.

We may find another to match your pace,
        Through the scrub when the fireworks start,
But never another to take the place
        That you hold in a horseman's heart.
Your mates have stood on the camp since dawn,
        You are watching alert and keen;
The packs are on and the girths are drawn,
        But the fence stands there between.

The plant is off on the road again,
        And here by the paddock gate,
In the days to follow, and all in vain,
        You'll whinny and watch and wait.
And often out on the Wave Hill track,
        When the evening shadows fall,

Our thoughts will turn to the gamest hack,
And the best nighthorse of all.

Actor, farewell! Till your last long sleep,
May never the creek run dry,
May the grass be whispering fetlock deep,
Forever, Old Chap, Goodbye.

Selecting and Setting Up the Camp

IT WAS VERY important, when droving touchy bullocks, to select the best possible camp site, but quite often drovers had to make the best of a bad situation. Camping a mob on drummy or hollow ground was something drovers avoided like the plague. If bullocks took fright on that sort of camp they would gallop all night. In scrub or timber country, drovers picked the most open spot clear of standing or fallen dead timber. The noise of a dry branch snapping would be enough to start a rush.

Wherever possible, drovers looked for a camp with reasonable feed close by so that the mob could be fed up to the selected spot. If bullocks had not had water during the day, it was important to camp them upwind of any half-dry, inadequate waterhole.

Drovers always put the fire between the camp and the bullocks. Behind the fire was the tucker pack and 'table'. In a packhorse plant the 'table' was a bag or small tarpaulin laid on the ground and the packs were set out in a line, side on to the bullocks and beyond the fire. If the drover had a wagonette, it was used in place of the packs. The men unrolled their swags behind the wagonette or packs, and close behind the camp the nighthorses would be tied up. Drovers relied on the fire to split the mob should the bullocks rush towards the camp.

Road bullocks being moved off camp as the sun comes up.

*Cattle camp at sundown with the 'kitchen' in the foreground. Pic Willets' camp at
Glenormiston on the Georgina River, July 1992.* IAN TINNEY.

Bullocks have been known to go over a camp. A mob of Territory bullocks
once flattened a wagonette camp at a spot called The Dead Dog on Austral Downs.
I've never seen a mob go over a camp, but I have seen both end packsaddles
flattened as the bullocks split around the fire.

When a mob was playing up, the safest place to be was on a nighthorse, but
usually there were only two or three nighthorses tied up. If you missed out on
getting a nighthorse, the next safest place was either by the fire or up a handy tree.
If the bullocks were giving trouble, everyone slept with one eye open.

A character called 'Snuffler' was once on the road with a galloping mob.
Snuffler, who was a smart, conscientious ringer, was always first out to help the
man on watch wheel the mob. After 10 days or so of this, Snuffler had had enough.
On this particular night away went the mob again, passing quite close to the camp.
The boss and one ringer flew up a nearby tree, and when they had reached a safe
height, they paused to listen.

'Christ, boss,' said the ringer. 'Listen to 'em go. That's a bad rush.'

'She'll be right,' replied the boss. 'Old Snuffler will wheel them.'

'That's what you think,' said a voice from above. 'Old Snuffler is just one
branch ahead of you bastards.'

Rushes

RUSHES WERE A fairly common occurrence when droving the aged, touchy bullocks from north and west of the Murranji Track. A rush is the Australian term for what the Americans call a stampede. To the uninitiated a rush can be a terrifying experience. Most were at night and often in difficult or scrubby country. The causes were many and varied, and sometimes there seemed no apparent reason for the bullocks to take fright.

The sight of 1500 big bullocks exploding from a massed camp, with a noise like thunder, was not one that drovers relished. When a mob rushed there was only one thing to do, regardless of scrub or broken ground — that was to ride like blazes until the lead was reached. This could at times take 1 or 2 miles (2–3 kilometres), and once there, the idea was to ride in on the leading bullocks shouting or, if the country allowed, cracking a whip. This had the effect of turning the lead around, and back on the bullocks galloping behind.

Once the lead was wheeled like this, the mob began to ring and the rest of the bullocks caught up. If there were two men on watch, as there sometimes were with fresh mobs, it was important that both men rode up the same side of the rushing bullocks. A man on each side or wing could lead to disaster and was called 'Chinaman Laning' a mob.

There was always the chance of a 'Chinaman Lane' developing with inexperienced men, particularly if the mob was being double watched at the time of the rush. I never liked the idea of double watching, where two men rode towards one another, met, then turned around to ride back and meet on the opposite side of the mob. If the mob rushed, they either went in front of both men or behind them both. Either way, in the heat of the moment, both men were likely to try for the lead and a lane would result.

A far better way to double watch was to have both men riding in the same direction, but on opposite sides of the mob. This way, when bullocks rushed, they went in front of one man only, and that man took the lead. His mate did not change direction but rode round and backed the lead man up.

A lane could take rushing bullocks miles from the camp and could result in a slower rider having the leading bullocks wheel over the top of him. If a drover got caught with a lane, he really only had two courses of action open to him: firstly, he could pull out immediately, and leave the job to the other rider; secondly, he could cut through the galloping mob where it had thinned out, putting both men on the one side of the bullocks. The latter was a last resort and was fraught with danger, but at times it had to be done.

When bullocks were rushing, it was important to have someone keep the fire blazing brightly. This was to protect the camp and to let the men with the mob know exactly where they were in relation to the camp.

A mob would sometimes take fright without actually rushing. The bullocks would jump or splash then pull up of their own volition. Although it was important to get to the lead quickly, if a rush developed experienced drovers always waited until they were sure of just what was happening.

After a rush the boss drover always counted his bullocks the next day to make sure none had been lost. If the mob was still too stirred up to get a count, he track rode in a circle beyond the area the mob had covered the night before. Quite often after a bad rush, injured bullocks would have to be destroyed.

Rushes ending in human death were rare, and when one considers the risks, it is a wonder there were not more.

My First Rush

I HAVE BEEN involved in dozens of rushes — some very bad ones — during my years on the road. The first one, though, I can recall very clearly. I suppose it has similar memory triggers to most first time happenings, like the first girl one kissed or the first time one got full — but also I was without doubt indirectly responsible for the rush.

I was on the road with a boss drover with 750 spayed cows. It was not a long trip — about a month. The camp was a packhorse one, with a cook and a horsetailer, and the boss and I were with the cattle. Travel was slow due to the very stony nature of the route, and to make matters worse, the boss would leave me early in the afternoon and ride on to get a drink of tea from the cook, meeting me again when I got the mob within feeding distance of the night camp.

I was flat out keeping the mob moving, up one wing and down the other and across the tail. One afternoon I lost the fall off my whip, and in frustration, I put a few small stones in my quart pot; I found that by rattling this, I could keep the cattle moving over the stones faster than was possible with a whip.

As the days went on, I found I had to put larger stones in the quart to get the same result. I also noticed that the spayed cows were becoming very nervous and jumpy because of the constant rattling, and I was careful never to use the goad in the presence of the boss.

When the crunch came, I was on watch riding a bay mare who, like me, had never been in a rush. I was looking at them at the time, but they went so fast, I do not remember seeing them get up. The mob passed quite close to the camp, and the bay mare and I were going after them at somewhat less than full pace when the horsetailer flew past us and shouted over his shoulder: 'Back me up.'

The mare, taking a lead from the horse ahead, stretched out at a gallop. It was timbered country, but not thick scrub; nevertheless, it took us over half a mile to wheel the mob. As soon as we turned the leaders around, a mob split off behind me, and it was on again. This time the mare and I took the lead, with the horsetailer backing me up. Spayed cows are noted for splitting like this and it took some time, with first one of us in the lead and then the other, before they steadied up.

For the rest of the night the horsetailer and I watched the mob where we stopped them. Near daylight the boss jogged up saying he had been checking to see if any cows had split off the tail — and I was young enough to believe him. The mob rushed every night until we trucked them a week later, and after that first night, I must admit I enjoyed the excitement immensely. I dare say, however, that the spayed cows were pleased to see the back of me.

After trucking the cows we retired to the pub, where I heard the boss skiting about the smart lad he had with him. He would not have been so generous with his praise if he'd known it was me who caused the problem in the first place.

Gold Star

The sun went down and the storm clouds rose,
    Dark browed with the threat of rain,
As they put the mob through the netting fence,
    To the camp on the blacksoil plain.
'Twas a short half mile 'cross the plain just there
    From the hills on the western side,
To the gloomy depths of the myall scrub,
    Where scarcely a man could ride;
Near a mile across and as bad a scrub
    As ever a stockman saw,
Then a bluegrass flat and a twelve foot drop,
    To the river that ran before.

As quiet as milkers the bullocks seemed,
    As they moved on, feeding slow,
With heads all turned to the cattle camp
    In the sunset's ruddy glow.
But a spark remains in the quietest mob,
    That can leap to a roaring flame,
In the maddened rush as the ringers know,
    Who have followed the droving game.
They had splashed a bit when we took them first,
    As the Gulf mobs often do,
But they settled down to the dull routine,
    Of the road in a week or two.

For they learnt the lesson the drovers teach,
    To the tune of the whip's barrage;
And seldom it was that a mob played up,
    When Mac was the man in charge.
For he'd served his time when the game was tough,
    In the days when the West was young;
When a man was judged by his bridle hand,
    And his skill when the scrubbers rung.

A sunburnt son of the far North-West,
    Where the fenceless stockroutes are,
And the pride and joy of the drover's life,
    Was his chestnut mare Gold Star.
I had heard tales told in a hundred camps,
    Of Mac and his chestnut mare.

From the Gulf coast down to the New South side,
    Ere I ever met the pair.
A thing of beauty she was to see,
    And a tower of strength to ride,
With a lean game head and a lion's heart,
    And a free and swinging stride.

There was never a nighthorse foaled, Mac swore,
    That could stay with the chestnut mare,
Through scrub or holes in the mad pell-mell
    Of a rush 'neath the lightning's flare,
For a dozen years she had served him well,
    And always the mobs were held;
But he rode her only at odd times then,
    When the fresh store mobs rebelled.
A favoured pet with the plant she ran,
    From the bridle and hobbles freed,
But she watched the mob with her soft ears pricked,
    As it spread on the plain to feed.

Mac came to me as I hobbled up,
    By the camp in the failing light;
And I heard him say as I caught the bay,
    'Better tie up the mare tonight'.
'Better tie up the mare' was all he said,
    But he spoke with a troubled frown,
And I saw him glance at the thunderheads,
    That had grown since the sun went down.
I went on first round the sleeping mob,
    While the quarter moon on high
Was blotted out by the leaden clouds,
    As the watch dragged slowly by.

It was Jim's watch next, and stepping down,
    By the fire I called his name,
Then the heavens split in a blinding flash,
    And the whole camp seemed aflame;
I stood transfixed by the startled bay,
    Then cursing I swung around,
For merging low with the thunder crash,
    Was another grimmer sound.
I offered a silent prayer of thanks,
    For a nighthorse that knew the job,
As the bay horse reefed at the bit and raced
    Round the wing of the rushing mob.

But the lead was off to a flying start —
    A start that was far too great,
And even then as I urged the bay,
    I knew we would be too late.
They hit the scrub with a splintering crash,

And strong on the storm wind borne,
    Came the pungent breath of the fear crazed mob —
        The tang of the hoof and horn.
I had eased the bay to a saner pace,
        And pulled out a little wide,
When I heard Mac's shout, then his chestnut mare
        Was galloping by my side.

'Ride as you never have ridden, lad,
        No matter what risk or cost,
We must beat them out on the further side,
        Or half the mob is lost.'
Mac was never a man to flinch at night
        In scrub, or to ease the pace,
And I'd never relive for a thousand mobs,
        The span of that nightmare race.
A gully loomed in a lightning flash,
        It was strewn with stumps and wide,
But the old mare rose in the lead of me
        With never a change of stride.

As game as ever she took the jump,
        We were but a length between,
But the power and strength of her quarters then
        Was not what it once had been.
She landed badly and blundered on,
        Striving to rise in vain —
She turned clean over while time stood still,
        Then the darkness closed again.
The bay horse lit and his shod fore feet
        Struck fire from the jutting stone,
With a backward glance and a bitter oath,
        I rode on through the scrub alone.

Rode on alone through the windswept scrub,
        Though that dark clad rider 'Death'
Rode stirrup to stirrup with every stride,
        And I cursed him with every breath.
The roar of the storm and the timber's crash,
        Was a Hell's own mad refrain;
And I threw the reins at the bay horse then,
        And rode like a man insane.
The bay was bred where they know a horse,
        And value the old game breed,
But we burst at last from the myall scrub,
        Too far from the flying lead.

Then high and shrill rose a horse's wail,
        That died in a kind of sob,
And Gold Star passed like a bird in flight,
        Down the lead of the rushing mob.

The Poley saddle was empty then,
    And the loose irons swung beside,
No brown hands gathered the flying reins,
    To steady and urge and guide;
Her mane and tail were as burnished brass,
    In the lightning's vivid flood,
And the foam that she flung from the bit-rings back
    I saw then was red with blood.

With a wicked light in her kindly eyes,
    Ears back and her teeth laid bare,
She wheeled them back from the river's edge
    With nothing but yards to spare.
She wheeled them back from the yawning brink
    Till they rung on the narrow plain,
And I rode and sang till they settled down,
    With their backs to the slanting rain.
I was looking round for the chestnut mare,
    But never a shadow stirred;
When I heard Jim's voice and the song he sang
    Was the finest I'd ever heard.

We watched them there through the lonely hours,
    Till the dawn broke chill and grey,
And showed the spot by the timber's edge,
    Where the chestnut night-mare lay.
Jim called to me and I rode across
    As he knelt by the dead mare's side,
She had wheeled the lead as her life blood flowed,
    The faster with every stride.

We buried Mac as he would have wished,
    For he does not sleep alone,
By the posts and railings that guard his bed,
    Stands a rough built mound of stone.
They rest together the man and mare
    Where the shy scrub cattle feed,
On the narrow flat by the river's bank
    Where Gold Star wheeled the lead.

Boomerang Brady

BOOMERANG BRADY, SO called because of a bowed leg as a result of a horse falling on him in his youth, was renowned as a horseman in both Queensland and the Northern Territory. When Boomerang set out on his last ride in December 1923 he had not long recovered from an accident that had almost cost him his life. Lying in the bush for over two days, as a result of a fall from a horse, Boomerang was almost finished when found by stockmen from Newcastle Waters. One of his rescuers, Wally Langdon, was to later win fame as a member of the proud Northern Territory Mounted Police when he and an Aboriginal tracker captured Tiger, an Aborigine who had gained notoriety as a troublemaker.

When Boomerang Brady left Newcastle Waters later in December 1923, he was heading for Queensland with a racehorse in his plant that he swore would beat the best gallopers at Mackay, his destination. Unfortunately Boomerang never made it. Crossing Eva Downs he became sick and finally fell from his horse and died on the road on Christmas Day 1923.

Boomerang's only companion was an old Aborigine who must have been shattered by the tragedy. However, he took his boss's watch and 26 gold sovereigns from the body and covered it with a small tarpaulin, then rode on to report the death. It meant a ride of over 60 miles (100 kilometres) to Anthony's Lagoon, as Eva Downs had been abandoned two years earlier. At Anthony's Lagoon the Aborigine reported Boomerang's death to Constable Bill McCann, the policeman stationed there, and handed him the valuables taken from his boss's body.

The Wet had just begun in the Top End and it was a week before McCann could get back to bury the body. There, without ceremony, he dug a grave in the middle of the road and Boomerang went to his last rest with a few short words. The grave remained unmarked for some time, with the road making a detour around it. The Territory was a hard, rough place in those days, and I've heard jokes told of the grader driver who, in attempting to straighten the road, brought about the resurrection of Boomerang Brady. However, the detour remained, and later a sister of Brady, Mrs Whittaker, had a headstone and fence erected to mark the final resting place of one of Australia's best horsemen.

Boomerang's grave is on the stockroute and, at the end of a day's stage, drovers always camped there and tied their nighthorses up to the grave's fence. I'm sure Boomerang would have welcomed them.

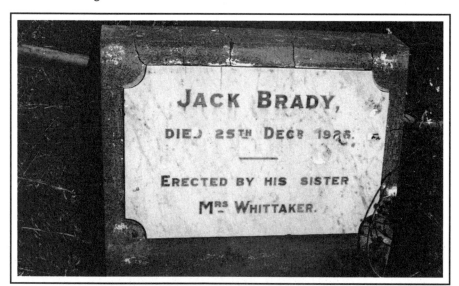

The headstone of Jack 'Boomerang' Brady's grave. IAN TINNEY

Brady's grave, now protected by a picket and wire fence, is beside the road on Eva Downs. IAN TINNEY

The Drover's Yarn *(or Brady's Ghost)*

A drover it was that told this tale,
    In the bar of the top hotel;
He hooked a boot in the brass footrail
    And his gaze through the doorway fell.
'Back in the thirties it was,' said he,
    'In the days when me beard was black.
I was coming in from the VRD
    With a mob on the Wave Hill track.

'Fifteen hundred all built for speed,
    Lean gutted and wild as Hell,
They sulked by day and refused to feed,
    They were demons when darkness fell,
For they galloped as only a scrub mob can,
    And most of you fellers know
A man needs horses like Peter Pan
    When the Bull's head bullocks go.

'I've seen some stags that could carve it out,
    But that mob just seemed to fly.
We lost two hundred, or there about,
    As we came through the Murranji.
And the camp I had, if you'd call it that,
    Would have driven a saint to booze,
A one-eyed cook and a myall black
    And a couple of jackaroos.

'But we battled out on the downs at last
    And I knew that the rest we'd save,
For they settled down and the worst was past,
    When we camped by Brady's grave.
My two gun horses were on that night,
    They could gallop both fast and true,
My favourite bay, whose name was Flight,
    And a big black horse called Blue.

'The mob fed up like a milking herd,
    Contented as stags could be,
They camped at once and they hadn't stirred,
    When I went on watch at three,
But a deadly stillness a man could feel
    Was over the camp that night —
Not a bullock moved, they seemed scarcely real
    In the pale moon's eerie light.

'I often had seen those signs before
    And I knew that the harm was done.
Then the bay horse leapt to the muffled roar
    As the whole mob went as one.
I swung Flight into a racing stride,
    To wheel 'em before they spread,
When the old horse swerved in his tracks and shied,
    And I gasped as I turned my head.

'For passing close in the dim half-light
    And riding a coal black steed,
A phantom rider, all glowing white,
    Was racing to swing the lead.
It was Brady's spirit, I knew full well,
    As the ghostly pair sped on,
And the black horse flew like a bat from Hell,
    The way that the lead had gone.

'Well, I followed up in a kind of daze
    As the spectre wheeled the lead,
And we flogged them back through the dusty haze,
    To the camp with surprising speed.
They steadied down when we got them back,
    But I knew by the eerie glow,

That Brady's ghost, on his nighthorse black,
    Was still riding to and fro.

'I'll admit I never was scared so bad,
    And I've seen some queer things too,
But that mob of bullocks was all I had,
    So what was a bloke to do?
The sky in the east was growing pale,
    And the phantom had gone from sight,
When there came from behind me an anguished wail
    "It's perishing cold, all right".

'I jumped as shot, then I wheeled about,
    For the voice was one I knew,
And the sight I saw was without a doubt
    All the stranger for being true,
For strike me dead as a gidgee post
    The "steed" was poor old Blue
And the spectre I thought was Brady's ghost,
    Was a naked jackaroo.'

Tracking Lost Road Bullocks

COMING IN ONE year with bullocks from the West, I camped 3 miles (5 kilometres) back from a bore on Anthony's Lagoon. I was short-handed; my younger brother Jeff was doing both the cooking and horsetailing, while John Schondrock and David, an Aboriginal ringer, gave me a hand with the cattle. The mob was a bit stirred up, having been put through the government cattle dip on Anthony's the day before, and walked off camp a lot that night, keeping us busy until about midnight. I stayed out with David for a little while, then, as the mob seemed to have settled down, left him to it and rode into the camp to catch what sleep I could before doing the last watch.

I'm not sure what woke me, but when I looked out, I could see bullocks all over the place. Jumping on a nighthorse, I started putting the mob together. There was no sign of David, but I had no time then to worry about him. I caught up with the lead half a mile on towards the bore, on the edge of the timber. As I pushed the bullocks back on camp, I almost rode over David asleep under a tree. His horse had pulled away as the mob moved off camp and was found back with the horse plant.

Next morning I looked over the bullocks; the lead was there all right, but the mob did not look right; then I saw that bullocks from the front of the right wing were missing. Groups of bullocks tend to take up the same position in the mob during the trip. On counting the mob, I found I was 87 head short. I sent John Schondrock off to see if he could pick up the missing bullocks quickly, while I settled the mob down again on what feed there was.

John rode back about ten o'clock and said that the bore was lousy with bush cattle, and that he had seen nothing of the missing 87 head. Realising that tracking the missing mob would probably be an all-day job, I caught a big brown horse with an easy gait and the guts to go until he dropped. I instructed Jeff and John to wait until mid-afternoon to water the mob, when the bush cattle would be easy to shift, then to feed the bullocks back to the same night camp if I had not returned. Stowing a bit of damper and beef in my saddlebag, I mounted the brown gelding and trotted off.

When tracking missing road bullocks there are three factors that, if known, can be of great help. Firstly, the tracks of cattle that have been on the road for a while are easily identified, as their toes are worn down from constant walking. Secondly, road bullocks will stay together for some time; it may be weeks before a group of road bullocks will split up among bush cattle. Thirdly, road cattle, if they escape from a drover, once they are out of country they know will almost always travel into the prevailing wind.

I gave my horse a drink at the bore, where at least a thousand head of station cattle waited for the day to cool off before going back out to feed. I knew they would have obliterated any tracks left by my bullocks, so I rode out in a wide arc about 3 miles (5 kilometres) from the bore. Tracks of the station cattle heading into the water still covered the pads and I failed to pick up any tracks of road bullocks. Sure that the missing 87 head would have to be further out, I doubled back in a wider arc about 5 miles (8 kilometres) from the bore, and picked up the telltale tracks of my missing bullocks about two o'clock. It was easy tracking for a while, enabling me to follow them at a trot. Later, in more difficult country, tracking became slower, but late in the afternoon I rode up on the missing bullocks camped in a patch of scrub. They were lying down, contentedly chewing their cuds, and rose to their feet with marked reluctance when I started them up for the drive back to camp.

After watering the 'absent without leave' mob at the bore, I got back to the camp with them about ten o'clock. Everything was under control; the main mob was on camp and there was a rough meal cooked.

One of the first things I did on my return was to pay off David. I gave him his cheque and some tucker and told him to carry his swag out to the road and wait for a lift. It meant from then on there would only be three of us with 1350 bullocks and 40 head of horses. However, both Jeff and John were top men, and, like most drovers, I preferred to work short-handed rather than depend on men who could not be relied upon.

Horsetailing

THE HORSETAILER WAS an important member of the droving team, as he was responsible for the well-being of the 40 or 50 horses in the drover's plant. Without fit horses, a drover would soon be out of business, and as a result, good horsetailers were always in demand.

In a bad season, a horsetailer would have to take the horses out a few miles from the camp to get good horse feed, and often he would take a blanket with him and camp with the horses. Before daylight the horsetailer would unhobble the horses and drive them to the camp, where he would catch the horses needed for the day's work. After breakfast, when the cattle had left the camp, he and the cook would pack up and start off, providing, of course, no horses had cleared out during the night.

A boss drover would often leave it to an experienced horsetailer to pick the camp for the coming night. On reaching the selected spot, the cook and the horsetailer would unpack, and he would then gather wood for the cook and cut boughs for a windbreak for the fire. After selecting a nighthorse tree close behind the camp, if the weather was cold he would build a bough windbreak to protect the nighthorses from the cold wind.

After taking the horses to water, the horsetailer turned them out to feed, and if no shoeing had to be done, he could relax for an hour or two. As the bullocks neared the camp, the horsetailer hobbled the horses out for the night and caught the nighthorses. After watering and hobbling the horses that had been ridden that day, the horsetailer did the first watch, providing, of course, he did not have to camp out with the horses. Hobbles were carried by each horse on a thin strap placed around the mount's neck.

To locate the horses before daylight, each plant of horses carried five or six bells. An experienced horsetailer could go straight to his own horses even when other horse plants carrying bells were hobbled close by. Although bells may be identical to the eye, each bell had a minute difference in tone that an experienced man could identify.

Caught in the Wet

WHEN I WENT out to the West in 1955, the mob I was to take was not yet ready, so I was enlisted to run a scratch camp with my own men and station Aboriginal stockmen. By the time the mob was ready for delivery, I was almost out of tucker — you cannot carry a hell of a lot on eight packs. Unfortunately it had been a late Wet and the station loading had not arrived; rations on most of the western runs were in short supply. I scrounged what I could, including a bag of last season's flour, and started the long trip to Queensland on 31 May. It would be 13 October before we delivered the mob.

I was lucky in having a good team of ringers that year: Kevin Ryan and Ron Condon were cooking and horsetailing; Luke McCall and two Gordon Downs Aborigines, Rusty and Tommy, and I were with the mob. The first damper made with the scrounged flour was a disaster. When cut, the middle was a glutinous mess that stuck to the knife. The cook explained that the flour was full of weevils, and on inspection this proved to be no exaggeration. The weevils had obviously devoured all the nutriment in the flour. My suggestion to the cook to throw the flour out and cook the weevils did not, I'm afraid, meet with any enthusiasm, but there was little anyone could do.

As we were short of everything, including tobacco, I decided to take a short cut between Inverway and the police station at Old Wave Hill; it would knock at least two days off the normal trip down the stockroute. Mick Cousens, a top bushman, had told me of the short cut earlier in the year. It meant heading straight bush in a rough easterly direction for about a week, then turning north and following the Victoria River to Old Wave Hill.

The weather had looked threatening for almost a week, and a few days into the short cut, down came the rain in torrents. The whole of the Top End was inundated, with over 10 inches (250 millimetres) falling in a couple of days. We had to hold up for three days, as travel was impossible due to bog and flooded creeks. To make matters worse, the last of the tucker was gone and we were without tea and coffee. The only tobacco we had was the chewing tobacco favoured by the Aborigines. We did, however, have meat, but only fresh meat, as we had run out of coarse salt to make corned beef. As a result, we had to kill a young beast every couple of days, then work the two Bedourie ovens overtime to cook as much as possible before it became flyblown. Fresh meat can be very welcome in a drover's camp, but a diet of nothing but fresh meat *sans* table salt soon palls.

Finally, we were able to move the mob on — albeit slowly. It was a very frustrating time for the men, who were sick of the sight of fresh meat and were itching to get to Wave Hill and once more resume a normal diet. We had been travelling two days when, on the second night, I lay back on my swag and was promptly bitten between the shoulder blades by a redback spider that came from God knows where. After dispatching the spider, I called for a volunteer to perform the old cut-and-suck routine. At first no one seemed all that interested, then Rusty Walter stepped forward with a gleam in his eyes that made me wonder if the fresh meat diet had, in some way, affected his mind. His intentions, however, were good and he attacked my back with gusto, and a half-sharp razor blade. He soon had the blood flowing like Irish whiskey at a wake, and as a finale to the operation, he whipped a wad of chewing tobacco from behind his lower lip and applied it with a flourish to the wound. Next morning, apart from a sore back, I was as fit as a fiddle.

For the next few days we were in conkerberry country and the bushes were laden with the small blackberry-like fruit. To say that the men made the most of the opportunity to vary their diet would be an understatement; every time I looked over at a rider, he would be off his horse with his head stuck in a conkerberry bush. I can't say I blamed them.

The day before we crossed the Victoria River, we were feeding the mob over a well-grassed flat that had steep breakaway gullies running through it. I had blocked up the lead, and glancing back, noticed one of the Gordon Downs ringers was missing. When I saw the back of his horse visible in one of the breakaways, I assumed he was answering a call of nature and went on steadying the lead. Next time I looked over, there were two horses in the breakaway and I saw Luke McCall riding over to investigate. As I watched, I saw Luke ride into the gully, dismount, and disappear as well. Intrigued now, I waited to see what would happen next. After five minutes nothing had happened at all — the backs of three horses were in sight, but no men. The mob was feeding quietly so, unable to restrain myself any longer, I rode over to the breakaway. There I found my team sitting in a patch of watermelons. Three or four ripe melons were broken open beside them, their hands and mouths were full, juice ran down their chins, and there was a look of absolute bliss in their eyes. I lost no time in joining them.

Before turning north we had to cross the Victoria River, now running in full flood due to the recent rain. I sent the horses and packs further up the river with Ron Condon to find a shallow crossing, and prepared to swim the mob across. When swimming cattle, it is vital to put them into the flood in a straight formation and to keep them swimming in a direct line for the further shore. The force of the water will bend them downstream, but on no account must they be allowed to ring, for if this happens, losses from drowning cannot be avoided. It is also important to be mounted on strong swimmers that will allow the rider to remain in the saddle, enabling him to see if the mob is swimming as desired. As a precaution, the stirrup irons are crossed over the pommel and bridle reins are checked to make sure the ends are untied. When swimming, a horse is steered by splashing water either side of his head.

We were all riding good swimmers, and after discussing tactics with the lads, we started the mob for the river. With myself out front to give the mob a lead, two men on the downstream wing, one upstream and a man on the tail to force the mob along, we put the cattle into the water. It is important to select a suitable spot on the opposite bank for easy access from the water for the cattle. This cannot be done before it is evident how far the current will sweep the mob downstream, but fortunately, at the spot we selected to cross, this did not pose a problem. Everything went to plan and the crossing was made without loss.

We finally reached Old Wave Hill — so called because of the wavelike formations on the hillsides. The cook and horsetailer had got some rations from the police station and met the cattle at dinner camp. There was a billy of tea by the fire, an opened tin of jam and freshly cooked johnny cakes. Hardly the stuff a gourmet's dreams are made of, but to us it was a banquet.

After numerous pints of tea and a couple of smokes, I rode over to the police station to give notice and to present my waybills for inspection. The young constable there seemed quite concerned for our welfare, saying we were a week overdue and had been posted as missing. As there had been no sign of us on the stockroute, he had been about to organise a search for us. I thanked him for his concern, but made no mention of the short cut. Then I rode back to the mob thankful in the knowledge that there was again tucker in the camp, and that I had a team of men who would stick to me through thick and thin.

An Unexpected Dry Stage

DRY STAGES OF up to 60 miles (100 kilometres) are always a matter of concern to a drover. Nevertheless, they can be negotiated without too much trouble if the drover is aware of what is ahead and has prepared for it. An unexpected dry stage that occurs due to circumstances beyond the drover's control and leaves him short of preparation can at times be a serious problem.

I struck one of these unexpected stages coming in with western bullocks one

Number 11 Stockroute Bore on the Murranji.

year. A lot of cattle from the western runs are used to watering at springs and creeks and take some time to adapt to watering from troughs at stockroute bores. The mob I had was particularly stubborn; they would not drink at all at Red Rock Bore and at King Creek Bore drank very little. The next three waters were springs, then there was just one more bore, called Pussy Cat, before I entered the Murranji scrubs. The mob drank well at the first two springs; however, the night before Top Springs — the last of the natural waters — the bullocks rushed and were stirred up all night. As a result they were very toey at Top Springs and kept taking fright and galloping back out of the water. When I finally gave up, very few had had any sort of a drink and most had had no water at all. This situation did not concern me greatly, as I considered that the drier they were when I reached Pussy Cat Bore, the better chance I had of breaking them into trough watering before we reached the Murranji, a route watered solely by stockroute bores.

It was late in the afternoon when I took the mob off the water and went out a few miles and camped. I had checked at Top Springs on the water ahead at Pussy Cat and had been told it was low but that there was ample to give my bullocks a good drink. Next morning the mob fed a little, but, being thirsty, soon started walking, and this suited me. I steadied the lead to let the tail keep up and we made good progress. It had been threatening rain all morning and rain is the one thing that can cause a smash on a dry stage. Bullocks will try to turn into any wind coming off rain, making progress almost impossible; if rain falls, they will scatter after puddles — all in all, a hell of a mess.

We had covered about 5 miles (8 kilometres) when I was surprised to see my brother Jeff, who was horsetailing, lapping back to the mob. He reined in beside me and said 'There's no water for the mob at Pussy Cat. I was flat out getting horse water. You'll have to go on to No. 13 or turn back.'

After a few well-chosen words, I thought things over. The way the weather was, I could not afford another dry night, so it was either go back to Top Springs or try to make No. 13 bore in the Murranji scrub before dark. The bore was still about 20 miles (30 kilometres) away and I had to make a detour around Pussy Cat Bore, and then get the mob up the stony jump-up to the Murranji tableland as well. No drover likes to turn back. I looked at the sky. The rain was still holding off.

'Is the plant still at Pussy Cat?' I asked Jeff, and he nodded. 'Right,' I said, 'go on to 13 and set up camp at the bore; see if you can get a spot within two or three hundred yards; water the horses and hobble up early, then come back; we'll need a hand.'

He looked at me doubtfully. 'Do you think you can make it before dark?'

'I don't know,' I said, 'but we'll have a moon for an hour or two, and we'll probably need it.'

After Jeff had ridden off, I looked over the mob. Most of them had been without water for two days and had walked 25 miles (40 kilometres) since their last drink, but the die was cast. Thirsty bullocks will give you their best and it is important not to get impatient with the slower ones on the tail of the mob, even though it means holding the lead up at times to allow the tail to catch up — very frustrating at a time like this when you can see the time ticking away.

We finally got back on the stockroute pads after passing wide of Pussy Cat Bore and headed for the jump-up, still some miles away, but standing out plainly with its dark, tangled crown of scrub. It was late afternoon when we got the last of the bullocks up the steep ascent and faced the last 7 miles (11 kilometres) through the Murranji scrub. The bullocks were distressed now and at times a low moaning sound ran through the mob, but despite this, they still walked well. Their instinct told them there would be water somewhere ahead.

Jeff met me about 4 miles (7 kilometres) out from the bore and, as I had arranged with the rest of the team, he and I cut off 200 of the leaders and took them on ahead to the water. The sun had gone when we got there, but I allowed myself the luxury of a smoke as I watched the bullocks as they were drinking greedily at the long trough.

Jeff grinned at me. 'At least the bastards have learnt to drink at a bore.'

I nodded. 'I'll go back and get another couple of hundred. When these have finished, feed them out towards the camp. I'll turn the next lot out to you.'

I trotted back and met the mob about a mile out and cut another 200 off the lead, instructing the three men with the rest to block them up about a quarter of a mile (400 metres) from the bore. It was almost dark when I returned to the trough, but a weak quarter moon cast some light through the overcast sky. A fire was blazing in the camp and as soon as the small mob had watered, I pushed them out to where I could just see Jeff tailing the lead bullocks.

The watering went on without mishap, but as we turned the last of the tail bullocks towards the camp, a few spots of rain fell, and the watery moon was slipping down behind the dark scrub line. We slowly pushed the bullocks together in front of the camp. The lead had had a bit of a pick on the rough feed, but the tail would have to wait for the morrow. Jeff had already tied up four nighthorses, and as I changed to one, I thanked God for having such a reliable mate with me.

I decided to double watch the mob, for although the bullocks were full of water, they were still hungry and jumpy from the long drive. The rain steadily got heavier and by ten o'clock it was coming down in sheets. We had our hands full with the mob and when the rain eased off a little around midnight, the fun really started. The bullocks crashed into the scrub, first in one direction, then in another. There were three of us out with them at that time and when we finally got them settled down, I asked Jeff to go into the camp and stoke up the fire, as it was almost out.

He tied up his nighthorse and was almost at the fire when the mob rushed straight at the camp, and I did not have a hope of wheeling them in time. It was a horrible moment for me, as I knew the four men in the camp, including my brother, did not stand a chance.

It was my brother who saved the situation: with no time to stir up the fire, he snatched up a torch the cook used, and by flashing it at the bullocks, split the mob round the camp. It is one night I would rather forget but when daylight finally came we still had the mob. A drover two days ahead of me was not so lucky: he lost over 200 head that same night.

Drovers' Towns

BEFORE ROAD TRAINS took over, droving made a significant contribution to the economy of a number of outback towns. Trucking centres, in particular, received a large injection of funds during the droving season. Mobs of sheep, fat cattle and store bullocks from the Gulf Country and the Territory converged on these railhead towns to fill the seemingly endless rakes of rail trucks.

Towns that had dozed peacefully through the slack months re-echoed to the sound of shunting engines, shouting men, bellowing cattle and the crack of stockwhips. Businessmen in the town smiled in anticipation, for the jingle of their tills would soon mingle with the sounds from the trucking yards. The streets filled with train crews and bearded, travel-stained drovers and their men, who, unlike the drivers of road trains, would stay a while in town and spend their money with the reckless abandon of sailors in port. Many of the drovers used the trucking towns as a base for their operations, but there were other towns not on a railhead that became well known drover's towns; of these Camooweal was the most celebrated.

The explorer William Landsborough passed by the present site of Camooweal in his search for Burke and Wills. He named the Barkly Tableland and, in his report, commented on the suitability of the country for grazing. Landsborough also named the Herbert River (later renamed the Georgina) and two fine waterholes in this river, Lake Mary and Lake Frances, he named after two of his nieces.

The first settler in the Camooweal district was John Sutherland, who arrived at Lake Mary in 1865 after an epic trip, with 8000 sheep, from near Rockhampton. The local Aborigines received a rude introduction to jumbucks when Sutherland's perishing sheep rushed through their camp in the middle of the night to drink at Lake Mary. Sutherland called his new run Rocklands, and for a few years he prospered. However, isolation, low prices, sickness, and resentful Aborigines proved too much. By 1868 early pioneers like Sutherland, Nash, Ranken (or Rankine) and Lorne had all abandoned their runs and retreated east with what stock they had left. Some of them were to leave their names for all time on the map of the Northern Territory.

Despite the problems of isolation, the Tableland country was too good to remain neglected for long; within 10 years Nat Buchanan had restocked Rocklands for Tetley and Crosswaite with cattle from Mt Cornish. Other settlers soon followed.

The town of Camooweal had its beginning in 1882 when J. (Mick) Cronin arrived at Lake Frances, 4 miles (7 kilometres) south of Lake Mary, with a horse team and a wagonload of supplies. Cronin was aware that the area was in need of a store, so unloading his wagon, he set up a business on the present site of the town. A hotel followed in 1883, opened by a man named Kennedy. Mick Cronin and his family were to play an important part in the future of the frontier town.

Drovers selected Camooweal as a base for two very good reasons: firstly, it was within a few miles of the Territory border, so it was an excellent jumping-off point for the Territory drovers; secondly, the town was surrounded by a common that could carry up to 1200 drovers' horses over the slack months.

The annual horse muster was a spectacular event, full of colour and hard riding. On the first day the downs country west of the town was mustered, then the timbered half on the east was cleaned up on the second day. Each day, the horses were drafted through the yards, with the common ranger presiding. Arguments over horses were usually settled in the time-honoured manner, without resorting to legal debate. Drovers used the yards to break in colts and to take the sting out of fresh horses, and nods of approval or shouts of derision registered the results of each contest.

When the drovers had sorted out their plants and shod all the horses, they headed out to pick up the mobs they had been offered. The trip out to take delivery could take over six weeks, and very often the Camooweal storekeepers — Tom Cronin, son of Camooweal's founder, and Joe Freckelton — would stand the drovers the cost of tucker and horseshoes until they returned.

Camooweal, as with most frontier towns, was in its heyday a fairly wild place. The police, most of whom understood the hardships of bush life, tolerated the high-spirited antics of ringers, which would probably not have been accepted elsewhere.

A large number of drovers lived in Camooweal and many owned homes with nicknames as colourful as the owners. 'Rum Jungle' was one, for obvious reasons; another, for equally obvious reasons, was christened 'The Sanatorium'; another situated in Beaumont Street was known as 'The Ringer's Roost'. I was the owner, or more correctly the co-owner, of the Roost. When I first bought the place for a modest sum, I thought I was getting vacant possession, as stated in the contract of sale. I soon found, however, that a few million white ants were already firmly entrenched in the residence. It took them some years, but with a single-mindedness that had to be admired, they finally ate the bloody place to the ground. Before that happened, however, the Roost saw many good times; it was an open house to anyone who cared to throw their swag over the threshold.

The long defunct Barkly Tableland Shire Council had its headquarters in Camooweal those days and its night cart serviced the town. One slack day, when the Ringer's Roost had its usual quota of non-paying guests, the driver of the night cart put in a complaint regarding the termite-ravaged condition of my outside dunny. Archie McInnes was the Shire Clerk. Archie was a bit of a character who I often had a drink with at the top pub. He sent me a show cause letter, stating that a threat of this nature to the life and limb of the night cart man was of vital concern to the council. I replied promptly, advising him that all correspondence should be addressed to the real owners of the Roost: the termites. Honour was satisfied all round and the termites proceeded to devour the show cause letter.

Many old drovers and ringers retired in Camooweal to live out the remainder of their lives in familiar surroundings. There, as elder statesmen of the droving fraternity, they held court in the pubs (Camooweal boasted two, those days), drinking rum and recounting epic battles with buckjumping horses, rushing bullocks and dry stages.

Wirrawarra Mick was one old boss drover who spent his last years in the 'Weal. Mick had been a top horseman and a fine cattleman, but what set him apart from his peers was his ever-ready wit. Advancing years and copious draughts of rum often left Wirrawarra Mick legless and, for his own protection as much as anything else, he often spent the night as a guest of Her Majesty. Next morning the sergeant's wife would stoke a meal into Wirrawarra and he would be released from *durance vile* just before the pubs opened.

I had not seen Mick for some time when I met him one morning making a beeline from the cop shop to the bottom pub for his first phlegm cutter of the day.

I greeted him with: 'Good day, Mick. What are you doing with yourself these days?'

Wirrawarra propped and fixed me with bright, but somewhat bloodshot, eyes.

'Doing with myself?' he quipped. 'I'll tell you what I'm doing. I'm serving a life sentence in nightly bloody instalments!'

A Tale of Termites

Stranger, please pause by this old bungalow,
For it hides a grim battle that ebbs to and fro,
A primitive struggle devoid of romance,
'Twixt the Camooweal drunks and the giant white ants.
No quarter is given, no mercy displayed
In this fight to the death with the termite brigade,
But if their rampaging is not soon reduced,
You can all say goodbye to the old Ringer's Roost.

There are termites to left and termites to right,
And their molars are grinding by day and by night;
They raid and they ravage and plunder unchecked,
And they're larger, much larger, than one would expect.
By wall plate and rafter they stealthily creep,
And God help our hides if they catch us asleep,
And if we can't turn their attack mighty soon,
We'll be under the stars by the change of the moon.

There are white ants below and white ants above,
In the floorboards and battens and rafters they love;
They deploy to the left and attack from the right,
And their molars are grinding by day and by night.
They break up our parties and ruin our rest,
And they are, in a nutshell, a damnable pest,
And if we can't deal them a kick in the slats,
I fear it's the end of these bachelor flats.

We've tried every method to stop their advance;
We've fought them with poison and baton and lance,
But it does little good, for in thousands they breed,
And they sharpen their fangs as they look for a feed.
An expert once called in to give us a quote,
But as soon as he entered they sprang at his throat;
He fought himself free with the leg from a bed,
And one flick and 'I'm going,' he screamed as he fled.

They're ravaged our larder, our furniture too,
And one night they punctured a carton of brew,
Then the word got around to the whole of their tribe,
And they bunged on an orgy I couldn't describe.
They've cleaned up our woodheap, our outhouse as well,
The 'Man who comes round' said he'd see us in Hell;
They've eaten our moleskins and eaten our Bex —
Two novels by Thwaites and a pamphlet on sex,
And if very soon we don't stop their advance,
Then I'll transfer the deeds to the flamin' white ants.

The Drovers' Strike

BOSS DROVERS WERE independent contractors, in competition, to some extent, for the mobs that stations planned to put on the road during the droving season. Despite this, there was never, to my knowledge, any undercutting of the contract price. The competition was limited to the reputations of the drovers and to the suitability of their plants. Many stations seemed happy to stick to the same drovers for years, providing they did the job.

The company that moved the most cattle out of the Territory and East Kimberley region was of course Vestey's, and because of the scale of their operation, many drovers got a start in the industry with cattle from their stations. Vestey's were not, however, the best of payers; their contract price of four shillings and sixpence (45 cents) a head per 100 miles (160 kilometres) had, in 1956, remained the same for some years, while other stations were paying five shillings (50 cents). Because of the length of the trips a few of us did, we were happy enough, but not all Vestey drovers were in the same position.

Early in '56 I was shoeing the plant at the Ringer's Roost in preparation for the trip out West when I looked up to see a group of Vestey drovers entering the yard. I straightened up and greeted them.

'Good day. I thought you blokes would be flat out like me.'

'We're not going out.'

'What do you mean?'

'We're digging in our toes. Vestey's can get stuffed. We won't work for four-and-six.'

'This isn't a joke?'

'No bloody fear. We're going on strike. Are you with us?'

I sat on my heels and rolled a smoke. 'I don't know. What are your plans?'

'Well, we're on strike, and we want you to act as spokesman. You've had a good education.'

I let that pass through to the keeper. Because I wrote a bit of verse, they obviously regarded me as something of a Rhodes Scholar.

'I'm with you on one condition: you've got to stick it out. You've left it a bit late; we're all short of a quid and it's not going to be easy.'

They assured me they were all solid in their determination to toss the biggest pastoral company in Australia. I told them to organise a meeting of Vestey drovers in the billiard room at the bottom pub for eight o'clock that night, then continued shoeing the horse I had been working on.

Every Vestey drover in town was at the meeting that night. It was agreed that minutes of the meeting be kept, and that I should be elected in the approved manner. After the preliminaries were out of the road, we got down to business. A motion was passed requesting me to send a letter to Vestey's head office setting out our claims, together with another to Gilbert MacIntosh, Vestey's road boss in Mt Isa, requesting a meeting in Camooweal. Both these letters were to be signed by all present, with the signatures in a round robin.

I was further empowered to organise the Vestey drovers at Elliott and Newcastle Waters. After some discussion, the meeting agreed that as the strike was not of a general nature, drovers were free to accept cattle other than Vestey's if the price was similar to what we were fighting for. It was a decision that was to have serious ramifications.

Next morning I put into effect the decisions from the meeting and sat back to await results. I received confirmation from Newcastle Waters that everyone there was behind us; but if we expected panic at head office, we were bitterly disappointed. The powers that be at Vestey's Sydney office simply ignored us, well aware that time was on their side.

A deputation met with Gilbert MacIntosh as planned. However, he could not see us gaining a price rise and warned us that the company would, as a last resort, bring in drovers from Queensland to lift the cattle. Mac was a top bloke who had come up the hard way, and he was sympathetic, but he had a job to do. Later that day I received a wire from Vestey's head office confirming that the price was to remain at four-and-six.

I called a meeting for that night and advised the drovers of our lack of progress. They were just as adamant as ever that they would not work for four-and-six, and swore if the company engaged scab drovers, they would belt piss and pick handles out of them and bush their horses. I advised them against violence, while at the same time, I felt greatly heartened by the spirit they showed.

The weeks dragged by with the stand-off continuing. The company showed no sign of weakening, so the Camooweal storekeepers were approached for help and, to their credit, both Tom Cronin and Joe Freckelton agreed to stand by the striking drovers.

I decided to try my luck with other stations. Before becoming a boss drover, I had worked for years in stockcamps, including two years on Alexandria and one year on Glenormiston, both owned by the North Australian Pastoral Company. I wired their Brisbane office and received a reply next day offering me 1500 Alexandria bullocks at five shillings per head; delivery in six weeks time. In accepting the mob, I felt that I had perhaps let the others down, despite the decision of the first meeting.

One of the drovers, who had been on the grog, was told by a town wag that we had won and the strike was over. He hurried back to his camp, packed up and headed for the Territory. When we learnt of his departure, a few of us commandeered a vehicle and set out to bring him back. We did not expect any trouble as we realised he had acted in all innocence, and the bottle of rum we took with us would help dispel any awkwardness created by our action. We caught up with the bolter just through the border fence; he was confused, shame-faced and badly in need of a drink. After a couple of rums, he told his men to take the plant back to his camp, then climbed into the vehicle for the trip back to Camooweal.

The deadlock over the price continued, with no sign of Vestey's agreeing to our demands. Mac advised us that although the company was considering bringing in other drovers, there were still mobs available if we wished to accept four-and-six a head. They had us over a barrel and they knew it. The point of no return for the season's droving was rapidly approaching, with the chances of a successful end to the strike becoming less likely every day.

Despite assertions of solidarity, I was aware of a weakening of resolve among some of the drovers. Many of them had not been successful in obtaining other cattle, and I realised they felt that they were bearing the burden for everyone. Their attitude was not without some justification, and the decision of the first meeting was coming back to haunt us. Gradually, interest in the strike waned. One by one, the drovers accepted the inevitable and headed out West at the old price. The strike was virtually over, but Noel Willets better known as 'The Pic', still held out. We had a yarn the day before I was due to leave for the Alexandria mob.

'What do you reckon I should do?' he asked.

'There's only one thing to do mate; throw the packs on and tell Mac you're going out.'

'I dunno. I don't want to scab.'

'You're not scabbing; the bloody strike is over. Everyone else has gone.'

'Yair, I suppose you're right. I'll see if the Limbunyas are still available.'

The Pic wandered off and I got on with preparations for my own trip.

That afternoon I received a wire advising me that due to an outbreak of three day sickness on Alexandria, all droving had been cancelled. I read the telegram again, and with dismay, I realised its full implication; the plant was shod and ready, I had engaged men and had ordered rations, but what I didn't have was cattle to pay for it all. Mac had advised me early in the strike not to stick my neck out too far as spokesman; in hindsight it seemed like damned good advice, for I felt that the sword of Damocles was about to fall.

I thought things over for a while, then decided the time had come for me to bend the knee and tug the forelock. At the post office, I rang Vestey's Sydney office and asked for the head of the company.

He finally came on the line with a curt 'Yes?'

'Simpson here,' I said, 'the spokesman in the drovers' strike.'

'Yes, I know that. What do you want?'

I gritted my teeth. 'I was wondering if you had any cattle from the West still available?'

'I thought you had Alexandria cattle?' There wasn't a lot he didn't know.

'I did have. The mob has been cancelled.'

'Hold the line.'

I held the line and waited. He was going to make me sweat a little. Fair enough, I thought.

He picked up the phone. 'Can you start out immediately?'

'Yes.'

'There will be a mob of bullocks ready at the Ord by the time you get there. You know the price?'

'Yes. Four-and-flaming-sixpence.'

'Correct.' The line went dead.

I walked over to the top pub. The Pic was at the bar having a quiet drink by himself, so I joined him and told him the news.

'Fair enough. I've got the Limbunyas, so we can travel out together.'

I raised my glass. 'Here's to overseas interests and absentee owners.'

Frank Martin, the publican, strolled over and gave us a quizzical look. 'I didn't think you chaps would be celebrating.'

'This isn't a celebration,' said the Pic. 'This is a wake.'

Bullen Creek

WHEN I TOOK delivery of one mob of Ord River bullocks, Billy Hart was the only experienced man I had with me; the cook and the other two young chaps I'd employed had never been droving before. The Ords, like most Western bullocks, would rush; however, they seldom split and once you wheeled the lead you usually found you had the whole mob. But wheeling the lead was not all that easy at night, for the Ords galloped hard and fast, crashing through or over everything in their path.

The head stockman and two ringers came with us for two days to give me a hand, but we were on our own, with the bullocks still playing up, when we arrived at Bullen Creek, and Bullen Creek was not a good camp. There were some bad cattle camps that I felt relatively comfortable with, but this was not one of them. Boss drovers are a down-to-earth breed not usually subject to fanciful premonitions, so I found it difficult to explain my feelings about Bullen Creek. In the end I put it down to fatigue and forgot about it.

The cattle camp was on a rather narrow flat with stony ridges on the right, a creek and breakaway gullies to the left and in front, and a jump-up behind. I strung the mob down the jump-up well before sundown, feeding the bullocks along the flat to give them plenty of time to become familiar with their surroundings before dark. At dusk the bullocks came together on camp without trouble, about 10 yards in front of the fire, where the cook was busy with his camp ovens.

I had placed the camp as close as possible to the jump-up so we could take full advantage of the good galloping the flat provided. After talking things over with Billy, I decided the best way to control a rush would be to turn the mob up on to the stony ridge; it would result in the laming of a few beasts but the alternatives left us little option. I told the two lads of the strategy, and advised them that if the mob rushed they should pull out of the road and leave things to Billy and me. I felt sure one of us would have to be on hand all night.

Billy had tied up four nighthorses. Two of them had seen many bad rushes and could be relied on to wheel any lead. The other two were younger but both showed the qualities needed to make top nighthorses. Charm, a clean-legged bay mare, had received her baptism of fire during the last trip. The last horse to be tied up was a big brown gelding I called Brown Harlequin. Originally an O'Hara Gap brumby, he was one of those unique horses that could be used anywhere; he was an excellent camphorse and had taken to nightwork like a duck to water. Sure footed, like all brumbies, his speed and intelligence at night had made him invaluable. He did, however, have one fault; if you let your hands drop onto his wither he would buck a town down. When I was drafting cattle on Gordon Downs he had caught me by surprise and had thrown me very convincingly. Because I knew the brown horse so well, I usually rode him myself.

I did the dogwatch on Harlequin while Billy took the day horses out and hobbled them where he'd left the plant, well clear of any possible trouble. When he returned he had a quick meal with the others then rode out to join me, both of us riding in a clockwise direction on opposite sides of the mob. It was a clear, moonless night with the Southern Cross hanging brightly above the ridges to the south, and despite my earlier misgivings the mob was quiet enough to suggest we may have a trouble-free night.

A little after eleven I decided to go in to the camp to grab a quick meal before Billy was relieved by one of the new chums. I stopped to wait for Billy to ride around to meet me.

'I'll slip in and grab a quick feed while I've got the chance, Billy.'

He nodded. 'I'll be right. I'd like to see a few more bullocks on their feet, but I don't think we'll have any trouble.'

I agreed with his observation; the more bullocks that were awake, the less likelihood there was of a bad rush. Billy had been with cattle all his life and I appreciated that having him in the team offset, in many ways, the lack of experience of the others.

'If they do go,' I said, 'we'll just have to hit them quickly. We've not a lot of flat to play with.'

I watched Billy ride on around the mob, then I turned the brown horse and rode slowly into the camp. I had almost reached the nighthorse tree when Charm woke from a doze and shook herself. Despite having the surcingle over the top flaps and the irons knotted over the saddle, the noise was enough. With a crash like thunder, the mob was away.

I gave the brown horse his head and rode for the lead, knowing that Billy would come around the mob and back me up. Harlequin streaked down the flat in pursuit of the flying lead, with the timber and broken ground close to our left. Although the mob had not had a big start, the lead had almost reached the end of the open flat before we caught it. I rode in hard, shouting to wheel them quickly, taking the risk that the mob would not split behind me. The bullocks hit the ridge at full gallop, sparks flying from the flint stones underfoot while the air was filled with the acrid smell of seared hooves and clashed horns.

At the top of the ridge I swung them to the right again, along and down the slope to join the rest of the mob galloping below. Glancing back, I saw that Billy had kept the rushing bullocks in line behind me. The tail caught up as we held the ringing mob near the bottom of the ridge and gradually, to shouts of 'Whoa bullocks!', they steadied down and finally stood with heads up and sides heaving. The first round had gone to us, but the fight was far from over. It was not yet midnight.

When we had eased the mob down on to the soft ground we found ourselves halfway along the flat and in a far worse position than before. Most mobs can be put back on camp after a rush, but the Ords were not like that; I knew from past experience that they would constantly break back around us if we tried. We were committed to watch them where they were, with only half the flat to wheel the mob in.

Twenty minutes later the mob rushed again. This time we hit them quickly, bending the lead on to the ridge before the wild-eyed leaders had gone too far. The mob continued to take fright and splash and it seemed that the stony hill, although doing nothing to calm the mob's panic, was causing the bullocks to baulk at facing it at a gallop. I hated to think what it was doing to their feet, but needs must when the devil drives.

I noticed that the bullocks were taking fright from within the mob itself and this convinced me that some beasts had broken, dangling horns that were causing them to panic whenever they moved their heads. We could do nothing to remedy the situation until daylight when the injured bullocks would have to be thrown and the horns removed.

Billy and I watched the mob until one o'clock when I decided it was high time we changed to fresh horses as we had a long trip ahead of us. As I rode around the camp side of the mob, something freakish happened: Harlequin trod on what must have been a loose, angled stone and it flew like a bullet, striking a bullock on the edge of the mob. It was on again.

This time there was no stopping them quickly, for the mob took on the flat and the hill with the same frenzied determination. When we finally steadied them up at the end of the flat, Harlequin was lathered with sweat but as game as ever. The mob continued to ring, dust flying from the churning hooves. Then, for no apparent reason, the mob rushed again, and this time the lead stormed down the flat straight for the camp.

Billy, who was riding the fresher of the two horses, set out after the bullocks at a flat gallop. To me, backing him up, it seemed like an eternity before he drew level with the big wild-eyed pikers in the lead, and swung them past the camp and on to the ridge. As Harlequin galloped past the fire, I saw the cook standing there ashen-faced, a fire stick in his hand, 20 yards from the thundering mob. Once the bullocks were wheeled on the stony hill, the fight went out of them. They stood wary-eyed and exhausted, but the muted bellowing that ran through the mob showed they were about as stirred up as it was possible for bullocks to be. It would take very little to start another rush.

After half an hour I got a chance to talk to Billy and sent him in to the camp to get one of the young chaps to relieve him on Charm. While he was waiting for the lad to take over, I rode into the camp and changed horses. I rode back out on Kite, an Undilla-bred bay gelding and a nighthorse I was sure would be equal to the task ahead.

The bullocks were now a little to the right of the camp at the bottom of the ridge, and for once I abandoned my firmly held beliefs regarding the double watching of cattle: I felt I could not afford to be on the wrong side of the mob if there was further trouble, so I sent the young chap to watch the far side of the mob while I stayed on the camp side.

The next two hours passed without any major trouble but the mob was still restless, making it plain we were not yet home and hosed. At half past three I sent the young chap in to get his mate to take over from him, reminding him that Harlequin was not to be ridden again. I did not see the new rider come out to the cattle as I was riding away from the camp at the time, but a little later I saw Billy standing at the fire waving to me. I rode over to him and asked him what was up.

'I've just checked the nighthorses. That bloody young fool has Harlequin. He's probably half asleep.'

'Thanks, Bill. I'll whistle him over.'

I turned back to the mob and had ridden only a few yards when I heard the rattle of stones from the side of the hill. The noise was instantly lost in an explosion of sound as the mob roared past the camp. The bay gelding went with them, ears pricked and reefing at the reins. I looked over at the mob. I had little chance of wheeling them before they crossed the flat and as yet there was no lead. The bullocks were galloping in a solid phalanx heading straight for the rough going.

As the mob stormed through the timber and over the gullies, I saw bullocks going down under the weight of the maddened mob, for 1350 fear-crazed bullocks create an almost irresistible force. The mob was still rushing on a wide front, a sea of tossing horns and flying hooves. I had gained a few lengths on the mob and decided to take a calculated risk; shaking the thong of my whip loose, I swung it with all the power I could muster.

The whip-cracks rang out like rifle shots above the tumult and the result was better than I had hoped, for the mob veered sharply to the right, then crashed back in the direction of the flat. I cracked the whip again to keep the rest of the mob turning, then set out after the leaders. The bay horse took the broken ground in his stride but almost went down over a fallen tree. He kept his feet somehow, but in doing so, rammed my knee into a leaning limb, tearing my moleskins and gashing my knee. I felt the blow at the time, but the pain did not come until later.

I saw the lead racing along the bottom of the ridge away from the camp as the bay horse gained the flat. He stretched out after them and caught the vanguard, turning them up the ridge. I thought the mob would steady quickly on the stony ground, but it was as though they knew this was the last throw of the dice: when I wheeled them at the top of the ridge, they fought me all the way back along the slope, dust and stones flying in their wake.

They finally threw it in and stood 50 yards from the camp. They were obviously distressed and many of them were tonguing, but for the first time that night I felt I had the upper hand. There was another rider out with the mob and from his voice I knew it was Billy, but the young chap was nowhere to be seen. Billy waited by the camp for me to ride around the mob to him.

He greeted me with: 'Harlequin came in to the camp riderless as I rode out to give you a hand.'

'Bloody hell,' I said; then added, 'Billy, did you hear a sound on the side of the hill just before the mob went?'

'Yes, I did. If the brown horse threw him — ' He stopped.

We looked at one another in dismay. The bullocks had swept over the whole hillside in the last frenzied rush and if the lad had been thrown and injured he would not have stood a chance. I turned Kite without another word and rode up the hill, hoping against hope that we were wrong. I went slowly, zigzagging across the slope, and three-quarters of the way along the ridge I saw something ahead of me. I dismounted to find the lad's hat almost cut to ribbons by the trampling hooves of the galloping mob. It looked as though he had been thrown there; if the mob had gone over him, his body, or what was left of it, would not be too far away.

Leading Kite, I began to search the torn-up slope carefully, and the further I went from the hat, the more hopeful I became. Then I heard it: a feeble cry from the bottom of the jump-up. I mounted and rode over. I found him standing beside a tree about 50 yards from the camp. He looked up at me, ashen-faced with blood seeping from a cut in his head, but by this time my relief had given way to exasperation.

'What the hell happened?'

'I don't know,' he said in a shaking voice.

'Then I'll tell you. You rode the wrong bloody horse. You went to sleep and he threw you. You're lucky to be alive.'

He hung his head and said nothing.

'Why didn't you go to the camp?'

'I was afraid and my head hurts.'

'All right. Go to the camp now. Wake the cook and get him to patch you up. It's almost time for him to boil the billy.'

I rode back to the mob and told Billy the news.

He grinned. 'I'll bet you ripped it into him.'

I nodded. 'We can't afford stupid mistakes like that on the road. Not only did he risk his own life, he put the whole show in jeopardy.'

Billy rolled a smoke. 'I reckon he won't make that mistake again.' He turned away from the mob to light the cigarette, shielding the blaze of the match from the bullocks with cupped hands. When Billy had the smoke going to his satisfaction, he leant down and patted Charm's neck. 'You've got a good'un here. She went through the rough-going like a breeze.' He glanced at the eastern sky. 'Must be time to get the horses.'

The morning star was blazing brightly above the horizon, a welcome herald of the coming day. 'Right you are, Billy. I'll be okay here.'

As he reached the camp, a dingo howled on the top of the jump-up. The long, drawn-out lament cut through the crisp morning air like a knife. The big horns tossed and the bullocks stirred uneasily, but they stayed on camp. Like me, they'd had enough galloping for one night.

The stars gradually paled and at long last the darkness lifted. As I rode in to the camp in the light of a new day, I saw that the surrounding landscape bore clear evidence of the night's feverish activities. I unsaddled Kite and walked stiffly to the fire. I felt no great relief at having held the mob; at that moment I was just too knackered to care.

Outback Humour

THERE HAS ALWAYS been a lot of humour in the outback, and droving certainly had its fair share of wags.

The large steel tanks erected at the mills on the Murranji Track became a medium for charcoal-wielding scribes. Many pearls of wisdom, witticisms and quips appeared that brought answers, denials and additions from other drovers. Unfortunately, most of these were never meant for publication.

I remember one verse on a Murranji tank that was a parody of an old army song. It went like this:

> Goodbye Mr So-and-so
> Farewell Vestey's too
> Since we've been a-droving
> We've been stuffed about by you
> This droving is a failure
> A failure and a farce
> As far as we're concerned you can
> Stick it in your arse.

Drovers had the habit of picking up the bleached skull of a bullock and on it writing a biting obituary to the long-dead beast. Here are a couple of examples:

> Here I lie for my race is run
> Driven to death by 'Twenty-One'.

> My cruel fate was a thing of sorrer
> A bovine victim of 'Wirrawarra'.

The skull would then be placed in a tree beside the stockroute for all to see. Twenty-One and Wirrawarra were the nicknames of Territory drovers; in fact, Twenty-One was my nickname.

Boss drovers, by and large, were a colourful lot; one chap who sported a huge black beard would stalk into a bar and announce himself by roaring:

> Steel to the heels and leather to the knees,
> Wild and woolly and full of fleas,
> Bad women and buckjumping horses
> Are all the same to me.

Another chap would introduce himself by singing a sad little ditty to the tune of 'The girl I left behind me':

> I'm up to my knees in Mitchell grass
> I'm up to my knees in clover
> I'm up to my balls in bloody debt
> And I'm a Vestey drover.

Bushmen have always been past masters at creating their own entertainment, without the aid of television, portable radios or regular newspapers. When drovers hit town after months on the road, they tended to let their hair down. Pranks like shutting goats in outside toilets, riding horses into the bar, and posing as wealthy graziers for the benefit of the barmaids were, to the perpetrators, nothing but good clean fun.

Townspeople, who saw only the larrikin side of the revellers, resisted any temptation they may have had to ask them home for dinner. Hotels and cafes, however, welcomed the nomads with open arms. As a result, the girls employed at these establishments became the focus of attention. The ardent and often inebriated young Lochinvars from the scrub seldom got to first base, but life was good, the beer was cold, and the West was wide.

The End of the Trip

THE BIG MOBS of store-conditioned bullocks that walked in from the East Kimberley and Northern Territory stations were of no use to the market until they were topped up on properties known as fattening depots. The Queensland Channel Country was ideal for this purpose, and many store mobs went down the Georgina River route to these stations.

Many other store mobs were trucked away by cattle train from Dajarra to the coastal fattening depots. Dajarra, in its heyday, was one of the biggest trucking centres in the world. Other store mobs were for sale while on the road, and the drovers travelled the stockroutes until the owners managed to sell the mobs.

As the drover was employed on a contract of so much per head per 100 miles (160 kilometres), the final count was very important, since it was on the number of bullocks delivered that he was paid. The final count was either done through the trucking yard, or carried out by the boss drover and the original owner.

Drovers with store mobs were often on the road for four, five or six months, so after delivering a mob, it was not surprising that most of them lived it up a bit.

The Dajarra pub, once Mecca for thirsty drovers at the end of a trip, has been quiet since the railway closed but it still serves the locals and the occasional travellers.
IAN TINNEY

At the Trucks

The cook's fire glowed in the drover's camp as the Southern Cross swung down,
Ere the first light spread and the shadows fled from the camp and the trucking town.
They had trucked the tail of the store mob down and bade it a glad Godspeed,
And could hardly wait for the stockyard gate to close on the restless lead.

A thousand miles from the West they'd come, from the land where the runs are wide,
Where the wild donks bray at the close of day from the hills where the pikers hide.
They'd travelled far from the scrubs and hills through the land of the grey galah,
On camp each night in the failing light and awake with the morning star.

A thousand miles from the Kimberleys, where the stockroute miles are long,
They'd wrapped the days in a dusty haze and the nights they'd wrapped in song.
Not the kind of song that a rocker sings who clutches a microphone,
But a song that slips from the watcher's lips in a soothing monotone.

Now the journey's end is a short half mile and wide is the open gate,
While spreading slow comes the dawn's first glow as the drovers smoke and wait.
An engine shrills, it's a sad, strange sound to these drifters born to roam,
And the echo brings, as it sharply rings, a sudden thought of home.

But it's time to go and they quietly start the bullocks up from camp,
As they move ahead, from the engine shed comes the glow of a shunter's lamp.
The end of the long hard road's in sight and the open gate is wide,
With the plant before so the mob will draw, they move like a flowing tide.

A dawn wind stirs and the grey galahs rise up from the carbeen trees,
Then the big heads rise and with wary eyes the bullocks sniff at the breeze.
They baulk and ring, then the mob draws on and the drovers steer them straight,
Till the leaders go with an even flow through the jaws of the stockyard gate.

With the last beast through, the gates swing to, and the heavy chain's made fast,
Then the lads slip in with a cheery grin for the trip is done at last.
The mob runs well and the trucks soon fill, for the coastal depots bound,
But the sun is high and the men are dry when they climb from the empty pound.

Now a dusty throat is a thing to note in a land that is parched and dry,
And to die of thirst is by far the worst of a thousand ways to die.
But Milligan's bar is down the street and the beer that he pulls is cool,
There a man might drink till he couldn't wink nor sit on a bar-room stool.

So they troop away for a round of drinks, just a couple to slake their thirst,
Things look less grim in the shadows dim and the publican shouts them first.
The sun goes down on the trucking town with the men still drinking hard,
But the cook has sunk in the corner drunk with his features slightly marred.

A dashing ringer, well primed with rum, gives the kitchen maid a hand,
And it's plain he's not now a man forgot in a lonely, forgotten land.
They will whoop it up in the trucking town, and each bush pub along,
The lonely track to the far outback will share in the drink and song.

For this is the life that the drovers live, with none but themselves to please,
Who bring the stores to our crowded shores from the far off Kimberleys.
It's God's own country, the drovers say, out there where the pied-geese call,
Where the reckless thrive, and the fit survive and the others go to the wall.

To the Barmaids

Six months we've been with Fuller's plant and we have just returned,
Two thirsty Barcoo immigrants, to bust the cheque we've earned,
So barmaids have the beer on the tap, and flex your dainty arms,
Bring solace to our perished souls with beer and girlish charms,
For things are dry on Thunder Lakes and drought is in the air,
But you can pour the glass that makes the old world seem so fair.

The days were hot when first we left en route for Jundah town,
The weather Gods, as if bereft, sent showers drizzling down.
We swam the raging Thomson, mate, with flooded packs and bags,
And dined that might on damper straight, and slept without our swags,
But soon we started on the job with Braidwood's Jundah Jack;
We mustered up a breeder mob, and took them on the track.

We've travelled many miles since then and seen a sight or two,
Been held, and spelled and quarantined, and often shown through.
We've mustered fats on Thunder Lakes, and branded on Retreat,
Watched bullocks in the freezing cold, and drafted in the heat.
Three weeks ago our work was done, we trucked a mob away,
Then headed homewards with the plant from down Yaraka way.

We turned the horses' heads for home, and every stockhorse knew,
And as they moved with eager stride we turned our thoughts to you.
Now past and gone our troubles are for we are back in town,
To skite around the Central bar and drink our quota down;
Our mates they took a ringing job, bull tossing in the scrub,
But that can't hold a candle to bull tossing at the pub.

Though oft we've drunk the waters of the Thomson and Barcoo,
To slake the thirst that we have now we need a stronger brew,
So barmaids have the beer on tap, and flex your dainty arms,
Have cold the amber nectar that deceives but never harms,
For things are dry on Thunder Lakes and drought is in the air,
But you can pull the draft that makes the old world seem so fair.

Drovers' Mail

WHEN BANJO PATERSON wrote the famous line, 'Clancy's gone to Queensland droving and we don't know where he are', it was no exaggeration. Getting mail to a drover on the road with stock was at best a hit-and-miss operation. Not that drovers had a lot of letters addressed to them. Most were bills and, despite the time lag in payment, the creditors knew the risks were slight. Storekeepers were few and far between on the outback stockroutes, and no drover could afford to gain the reputation of being a bad payer.

1954 was a census year. When the census form was to be filled in, I was droving down the Georgina, then across and down the Wills River route, with a mob of Territory bullocks, en route to Brighton Downs on the Diamantina. It would be honest to say that my concerns regarding the population of Australia were not, at that time, keeping me awake at night. However, on reaching camp one night, the cook waved a large, important-looking document under my nose and said with a grin, 'You, as the bloody householder, are supposed to fill this bastard in tonight'.

After a quick meal, I dug in the swag and finally found a battered biro; armed with this, I attacked the census form and, amid a great deal of ribald advice, finally

Camooweal to Borroloola Mail in 1916. NORTH AUSTRALIAN PASTORAL COMPANY.

completed it. The description of the building caused some concern for a time, but bushman are an enterprising lot. As the cook had told me the form would be collected at Dajarra, I stuck it in the saddlebag and forgot about it.

However, at Dajarra no one wanted to know about it. I made unsuccessful attempts to unload it on the publican, the storekeeper, the postmaster, the policeman, and anyone else I thought may be interested in the population growth of Australia. Finally, I rode back to the cattle in disgust, with the cursed form still in the saddlebag. In Boulia, I had no better luck; by that time the census was old hat, and the form and I rode on.

I finally arrived back in Camooweal after finishing the year with a mob off Chatsworth and flung the census form into a cupboard. The termites immediately laid into it and, pricked by a guilty conscience, I wrote to someone (I forget who) and asked for advice. I never received an answer — perhaps the letter is still being shunted between outback post offices.

The census form is still with me. A dozen times I have been about to burn it and then held back. Some day someone may call and collect it, and then the population figure for 1954 will receive a rightful and long overdue adjustment.

Horse Dealing

FOR CENTURIES HORSE dealers have suffered from what can best be described as a bad press. It is not unreasonable to assume that this dubious reputation has been thoroughly earned, for most horse traders would cheerfully sell their grandmothers for fish bait. Of necessity, at times horse dealers have had to deal with their peers, and on those occasions, it was inevitable that one of them would find himself in the invidious position of being hoisted with his own petard. Drovers, who were inveterate horse dealers, sometimes found themselves the victims of this cruel fate. There was little that could be done, however, other than to accept the blow philosophically, for it was no use crying over spilt milk, or spavined horses.

When heading well down into Queensland with Territory bullocks one year, I was on the lookout for fresh horses, as few of the plant were becoming leg weary. I knew that Byron Nathan had retired on a small block on the Georgina, and Byron had always owned good horses, so I let it be known on the bush telegraph that I was in the market to trade.

In the plant, there was a nice-looking bay filly that I was keen to get rid of. She was out of a pack mare of mine and had been broken in while we camped, waiting to take delivery of the mob. Right from the outset, she developed the habit of bucking with her head in the air, and she dealt out a damn good hand. A horse that bucks like this is difficult to ride, because it is impossible to put any weight on the reins, or to get a feel of what the horse is going to do. The filly had finally settled down due to tiredness, but I knew she was going to be a real problem after she had had a spell.

The day we passed Byron's selection, I saddled the filly and rode over to see him. We yarned for a while, then got down to business. I told Byron the filly was a bit leg weary and I would like to swap her for an older, seasoned horse. He asked me what she was like and I told him she had settled in well to droving but might have a root after she'd been given a spell. Byron nodded, then walked around the filly. He picked up all four feet and checked her mouth, then, turning to me, he said he had a black mare in the yard he was willing to trade.

We walked over to the yard where a fine-looking black mare was standing. She had a good girth, straight clean legs and fine quarters. I looked at her teeth and saw she was rising seven years old; good for at least another five or six droving seasons. With studied reluctance, I agreed to the deal. We swapped receipts, then, leaving the filly in the yard, I saddled the black mare, saluted Byron and rode off.

Before I had ridden 200 yards I realised we had caught one another. The mare had been foundered in front and almost fell twice before I reached the mob. No doubt Byron was smiling to himself, but he was yet to deal with the bay filly after she'd had a spell.

The worst deal I ever made was with the legendary Sam Fuller. I had worked for Sam in the past and we were good mates, but friendship, unfortunately, was never a factor in horse dealing. I had five older horses in the plant that were nearing the end of their working lives, so between Winton and Longreach I swapped them with Sam for three big fat horses. Sam swore they were as quiet as ladies' hacks. God knows where they came from and, knowing Sam, I didn't bother to ask.

Within 24 hours, I wished I'd never seen them. They were hard to catch, harder to ride and cleared out every night, giving a clear indication that wherever they had come from was preferable to their present situation. I got rid of them at the first opportunity.

Some time later I ran into Sam in a hotel in Longreach where he was entertaining a crowd in the bar with songs, yarns, lies and his own ingenious method of making music. He greeted me like a long lost brother and bought me a beer. We yarned for a while, then he asked the question I knew he'd have to ask.

'How did you get on with those three horses?'

'Sam,' I said, 'they are three of the best horses I've ever saddled.'

He laughed and slapped me on the back, then, to a chorus of approval from the crowd, he pulled the flap off a tobacco packet and playing it like a gum leaf, giving us a rollicking rendition of the old song 'Ten Thousand Miles Away'. And that, I thought as I drank my beer, would be a bloody good place for his three fat horses.

A Stitch in Time

SOME 25 MILES (40 kilometres) west of Camooweal on the stockroute stands a stone building reputed to have been a customs house prior to Federation; it is a spot that has seen its share of tragedy over the years. A particularly brutal murder is supposed to have been committed there, for which the killer was later hanged. Some years later three people, two men and a woman, died of thirst in the area. It was an oft-repeated story in the outback of people ignorant of bushcraft trying to walk to water.

None of the place's gloomy history bothered the drovers, who often camped there with empty plants on the way to pick up mobs from further out in the Territory. There was a wire yard used for station branding close by the old stone building. One year I camped there and decided to break in a clumper mare that had adopted my horse plant. No one seemed to know who owned her, so I decided I might as well get some work out of her before her owner turned up. As soon as I caught her, I realised she had a vicious streak in her a mile wide. It was also evident that someone had tried to break her in before and had given it up as a bad job.

She was an ideal type for a packhorse, so after lunging the mare and teaching her to lead, I hobbled and sidelined the uncooperative clumper and strapped a packsaddle on her back. I had a halter on her with a short halter shank, but to remove the sideline I lugged her and prevented her from seeing what was going on. I then got Ronnie Condon to undo gently the hobble strap that fastened the sideline chain to her near hind leg. After a few dry runs, during which the mare never moved, he undid the buckle and started to straighten up and move away. He never made it. The mare lashed out, kicking him full on the forehead.

The clumper mare then turned on an exhibition of bucking, with the sideline chain still swinging from her front leg. Concerned she would trample the unconscious man, I let go of the halter shank and kicked dust at her to get her out of the way, and then dragged Condon out under the bottom wire of the yard.

He looked in a bad way, so I called for help, and we carried him into the stone hut, where we surveyed the damage. Condon was still out cold, and the wound on his forehead looked as if it had been caused by a blow from an axe. Grabbing a double handful of flour, I poured it on the wound to staunch the bleeding, then placed a towel round his head. It was obvious to me that the situation was beyond the limited scope of my first aid kit, which was geared more to the treatment of horses than it was to the alleviation of human suffering. Leaving the unconscious man in the care of the cook, I caught and saddled a chestnut gelding that at one time had raced in Mt Isa and started the ride to Camooweal.

The most comfortable and natural gait for a horse is the trot. A good trotter will cover a long distance without knocking up, and do the trip in smart time. I reached Camooweal in just under two and a half hours. At the hospital I found the sister who ran the place (a doctor from the Isa visited once a week) and told her the story. She rang the auxiliary ambulance bearer, who picked me up at the Ringer's Roost after I let the chestnut go there, and we drove out to the scene of the accident.

Condon had regained consciousness, but was still a bit dazed. However, he insisted on sitting up in the ambulance and walked unaided into the hospital when we arrived there. After giving the patient a tetanus shot, the sister cleaned the wound up, then suggested that Condon be taken to Mt Isa to have the gash stitched up. When I queried the need for this, she admitted she had never stitched up a wound.

I looked at her in amazement, then said, 'Look Sister, I can't think of a better opportunity to learn. I've stitched up a few horses and I'll give you a hand if you need it.'

After some hesitation, she agreed and the job was completed to everyone's satisfaction, but she insisted on keeping Ron in hospital overnight for observation. Before leaving, I saw Ron tucked up in bed, and congratulated him on being responsible for furthering the cause of medical treatment in the drovers' town. I checked on my horse, making sure he had feed and water, then went to the pub for a rum and a meal.

Next morning, after organising a ride out for Ron, I rode back to the camp. A week later I removed the stitches from the wound with the aid of a castrating knife and a pair of stake pliers. In the meantime the clumper mare had settled down to pack work and was earning her keep in the plant. Later that year I lent her to a drover who was short of packhorses. I never saw her again.

Shoeing on the Road

THE SHOEING OF plant horses was an absolute necessity when droving, as during a season, plant horses often travelled more than 2000 miles (3200 kilometres) over all types of terrain. The way we shod was called cold shoeing and was quite different from the work done by blacksmiths, who made the shoes with the aid of a forge and anvil, then fitted the shoes hot.

Drovers bought the shoes already made up in sets of four, comprising two

Shoeing on the road using a collar rope.

front and two hind shoes. Although they came in a range of sizes, from size two (for a pony) upwards, they still had to be cut and shaped before they could be used. To cut the ends off the factory-made shoes, most drovers favoured an old axe head and a short-handled one pound hammer. Unlike stockcamps, drovers could not afford to carry an anvil, due to its weight. However, a short length of rail track made a satisfactory substitute on which to shape the cold metal.

The balance of the shoeing kit comprised a light shoeing hammer with a small head, a hoof rasp, a pair of heavy pincers and a steel pritchel to enlarge the nail holes in the horseshoes. Some drovers also included a pair of hoof cutters in the kit. Horses' hooves keep growing after being shod, and by the time the shoes had to be replaced, there was a growth of hoof or toe to be cut away before the new shoes were fitted. Hoof cutters made this task faster and easier.

Drovers and ringers on stations always liked to shoe horses 'up on their toes', as this made the mounts more agile and less likely to fall. To achieve this desired result, the horse's heels were only lightly rasped down to level them, while the toe or underside of the front of the hoof was cut back as far as possible. A good shoer always shod a horse with the hoof in the air, never on the ground.

Experienced road horses seldom gave trouble when shoeing was in progress; however, fresh horses in the plant were often a problem. At times during a trip, a drover would buy horses or swap tired ones for fresh mounts that had never worn shoes. Shoeing them in front never posed many difficulties, but they tended to play up — and sometimes kicked like blazes — when hind shoes were being fitted. The standard procedure, then, was to use a kicking strap on the horse.

The kicking strap was simply a wide strap that was placed around the horse's neck, and to this was fastened a long strap that was passed around the horse's hind leg below the fetlock, then back to a patent buckle at the shoulder. When the strap was pulled, the hoof was drawn forward and up, preventing the horse from kicking. The same result could be achieved with a collar rope made by fitting a neck loop in a greenhide rope with a bowline knot.

Occasionally we owned horses that could only be shod on the ground. The easiest way to throw them was to make a double collar rope by tying a loop in the middle of a greenhide rope with a bowline on the bite. The ends of the rope were then passed around both hind legs and back to the neck loop. As the ropes were pulled the horse sat down on its rump, and was eased over on its side by a man holding the head.

The shoeing, or rather cueing, of road bullocks was at one time a common practice. Fat cattle, because of their weight, were particularly susceptible to lameness on rough routes. Cueing enabled the drover to deliver these valuable beasts in good condition. As cattle have cloven hooves with a very thin shell, cueing was quite different from shoeing horses. The shoes used were worn-out horseshoes called slippers. These were cut in half before being shaped to fit the animal's hooves, then tacked on with the light nails used with racing plates. If no suitable yard or cueing pen was available, the beast had to be thrown before the job could be done.

Shoeing was at best an onerous and back-breaking task, by no means a favourite occupation with ringers. Nevertheless, they took pride in their work those days, and shoeing was no exception. I once worked on a station with a head stockman who had a rather warped sense of humour. We had just finished a three months' muster without a day off and at the fire that night he looked us over, then said, 'Well, lads, you've done a good job. We'll have a holiday tomorrow and reshoe the horses.'

Horse Stealing

THE WELFARE OF a drover's horses was vital to his successful operation; a man who neglected his horses never lasted long as a contract drover. After a long trip, it was essential that the horses were given a spell on good feed to ensure they would be fat and fresh at the start of the next droving season. When droving from the West, it was not unusual for plant horses to travel over 2000 miles (3200 kilometres) during a trip, and the drover's job was not finished until he had turned his horses out in a secure, well grassed and watered paddock or town common.

Security was a consideration, although genuine horse stealing was rare and, unlike poddy-dodging, was usually condemned. The reason for this was simple —

most horse owners were drovers or battlers, not wealthy station owners. A less serious and sometimes practised offence was horse 'sweating', drovers would 'borrow' horses for a trip, then return them to where the owner would find them.

The Camooweal common was without a doubt the pick of all the spelling areas; the horse feed was Mitchell and Flinders grass and the common ranger kept an eye on all that went on there. Some years I delivered bullocks well down inside Queensland and rather than walk the horses all the way back to Camooweal, I left them at places like Fort William, just above Boulia, or on the Kynuna common. The security was not the best at these places, but the only time my plant horses attracted the attention of a true horse thief was when I had taken the plant back to Camooweal.

After trucking Ord River bullocks at Dajarra, late in 1956, I walked the plant back to Camooweal in easy stages, to find the common in very poor condition. After pulling the packs off on the bank of the Georgina, I rode into town to see Jack Dally, the common ranger. Jack was an old-time bushman, who, in his heyday, had been a mate of Galloping Jones, a legendary figure in the Queensland Gulf. I liked Jack and respected his opinion. He told me that the common had been flogged with cattle, and that there was little likelihood of rain before the following February. Although the common would hold my horses, he said, they wouldn't get fat. As long as I kept an eye on them, my horses would be better off at Split Rock, where there was good feed, and agistment available.

With that said, Jack pushed his hat back and added, 'Come in and have a drink of tea, anyway.'

I followed him inside and said hello to Mrs Dally. Jack had married Count Biondi's eldest daughter and despite having a large family, they always extended true bush hospitality to visitors. I found Johnny Ormond seated at the kitchen table with a cup of tea in front of him. He looked up as I entered.

'Lock up your daughters — there's a drover in town.'

Johnny was a mate of mine, and a member of that band of unsung heroes, the bush mechanics. Before going out to the Ord, I had bought an ex-army jeep of World War II vintage and Johnny had patiently given me a crash course into the mysteries of the internal combustion engine. I had two reasons for buying the jeep: firstly, it gave me a handy run about during the slack months, and secondly, I had reluctantly come to the conclusion that courting women from the back of a horse was rapidly becoming passe. Packs were still out on their own on the road, but a packhorse at a picnic was regarded as something of an anachronism.

After yarning for a while, I rode back to the camp, and next morning, jumped in the jeep and drove out to Split Rock. The block was roughly halfway between Camooweal and Yelvertoft Station, on the road and stockroute to Mt Isa. I found the feed to be excellent and the water supply adequate. I returned to Camooweal and lost no time in organising agistment for my horses. After pulling the hobbles and neck straps off them, the next day I took them out to Split Rock, getting Johnny to pick me up in the jeep. I knew I was taking a risk leaving them there, but it would have to do until the Camooweal common improved. In the meantime I decided to check the plant regularly with the jeep. Horses that have been together on the road will continue running with their mates, making it very easy to see if horses are missing. It was a pleasant half hour run out to Split Rock and I never lacked company when checking the horses. I was delighted with their progress — that is, until the horse thief struck.

I heard that a chap I knew reasonably well was bringing a plant of horses out from Mt Isa. He had an interest in a block up in the rough country to the north. Normally he would have come through Camooweal, so when he took a short cut past the town, the alarm bells sounded. Early next morning, I threw some gear in the jeep and got Johnny to run me out to Split Rock. When we arrived at the water, I asked Johnny to wait and, grabbing a bridle, I walked out and caught a horse, jumping on him bareback. I quickly saw there were six of my best horses missing. I put the remaining 38 together on the water and, letting the horse I had been riding go, I caught Harlequin and led him over to the jeep as Johnny jumped out.

'Anything wrong?'

'Yes, the bastard has taken six good horses.'

'What are you going to do?'

'I'm going after them,' I said as I saddled the brown horse.

'Do you want me to go to the police?'

'No, I'll handle it. You could let Jack Dally know the score.'

I slipped into the saddle, told Johnny I'd see him when I returned and set out after the horse thief. The tracks of his plant were easy enough to follow, and as I knew the route he would have to take, I could lap along and take short cuts. I made good time, but despite my advantage, it was almost sundown when I rode up to the culprit's camp. There was no sign of the man himself, however his ringer was hobbling the horse plant 100 yards or so away from the packs. My six horses were standing already hobbled on one side of the mob. The man looked up as I reined in.

'Take the hobbles off those six horses.'

He shook his head. 'No, they belong to boss.'

I tapped the revolver I had stuck in my belt. 'They belong to me. Take the hobbles off now.'

He hesitated a minute, then walked slowly over and did what I had asked. He straightened up and glared at me. 'The boss won't like it.'

'He can tell me that himself. Where is he?'

'I dunno,' he said sulkily, and went back to hobbling the rest of the plant. I pushed my horses to the Camooweal side of the camp and let Harlequin go. I caught and saddled Flight, then led her back to the camp and helped myself to a drink of tea. The ringer finished hobbling up and sat on his swag in silence.

Just on dark, the man I was after rode into the camp. He stopped short when he saw me and stammered a query. 'Are those horses yours?'

'You know bloody well they are mine. A man has to sink pretty low to lift a drover's plant horses.'

'I'm sorry.'

'You're only sorry because I caught up with you. If I hadn't, you'd be thinking what a bloody smart man you were.'

'You won't go to the police, will you?'

'No, I won't, but if you ever touch a horse of mine again, you thieving bastard, I'll have your guts for garters.'

I mounted Flight and headed off with my horses, leaving him standing by the fire. I arrived back in Camooweal at ten o'clock the next morning and put the horses in the yard at the Ringer's Roost. I had changed twice on the way back and none of them looked any the worse for the experience. As soon as it rained, though, I lost no time in bringing the plant horses back to the Camooweal common.

Cattle Husbandry on the Road

THE DROVING OF store cattle from the West entailed far more than merely driving a mob from point A to point B. A boss drover charged with fulfiling the conditions of a droving contract had, in my day, a formidable task ahead of him. To be successful, a drover not only had to know the route — he had to be skilled enough to get the best out of the cattle he was responsible for. A drover who was a good cattleman could read the mood of the cattle and react quickly and correctly to the mob's response to the many and varied situations encountered on the trip. These skills were not learnt overnight; they were gained by years of experience and observation.

Despite their unpredictable behaviour at times, the basic needs of road cattle were simple: feed, water and rest. The last named was as important as the others; road cattle needed rest because, like all ruminants, they masticated their food more than once. It was essential that they were given ample time to rest, so they could regurgitate and chew their cuds.

A drover who was a good cattleman harnessed the natural urges and habits of the cattle to achieve his own ends. The benefits of doing this were threefold. Firstly, the day's stage was covered with the minimum effort — very important if the drover happened to be short-handed. Secondly, the bullocks were kept happy and contented, and contented bullocks lose less weight and give less trouble. Thirdly, it was easier on the horses, and the condition of the horses could be crucial on a long trip. Good drovers ensured that the pace of travel and the distance covered was governed by the weaker beasts on the tail of the mob.

The drover's day started early; the boss drover, who did the last watch, would call the cook and horsetailer well before five o'clock. Ringers on the road were given about half an hour to roll their swags, have a wash, have breakfast, cut their lunches, saddle their horses and take over from the boss.

If the camp was in open country, the mob was moved off camp at first light; but in rough or timbered areas, the bullocks were held back until broad daylight. After being held on camp all night, the cattle were naturally hungry, and were ready to feed as soon as they were on their feet. Good drovers were always prepared to accommodate the needs of their cattle and fed the mob along slowly in the direction the drover wanted to go. At the same time, the bullocks were allowed to spread out, so that the weaker beasts on the tail had the same opportunity as the leaders to obtain unspoilt grass.

Drovers were aware that on the station runs, the bullocks had been conditioned to walking to water from their feeding grounds, and simply waited for nature to take its course. After a couple of hours grazing, the mob showed signs of wanting to drink by walking over grass rather than eating. The mob was then eased together and turned on to the stockroute pads. There, without any urging from the drovers, the bullocks would step out, their instinct telling them there was water ahead.

Most drovers liked to be at the water by ten-thirty, even earlier after a dry day, to allow the bullocks to camp during the heat of noon, and to give them plenty of time to process the grass eaten earlier. Dinner camp also gave the drovers a chance to relax.

If the watering facility was adequate and the cattle not too thirsty, most drovers preferred to let the mob string in to drink at their own pace. If, however, the bullocks had not had water the previous day, or if the drover had doubts about the quantity of water available, the bullocks would be cut into small mobs. These small mobs or 'cuts' were watered individually to make sure that the weaker cattle were not disadvantaged in the struggle to get a drink.

As soon as the mob had drunk its fill, it was put on dinner camp and the drovers boiled their quarts. Each day the man whose turn it was did the dinner watch. Despite it being daytime, bullocks could be lost off dinner camp, particularly on a dry day when bullocks could walk off camp looking for water. When the chap on dinner watch had taken up his duties, the rest of the team could relax over a leisurely meal, then have a rest or take the opportunity to have a shave and a clean-up.

The mob was seldom taken off the water before half past two. The exact hour depended on the heat of the day and the distance to the night camp, which had been selected earlier by the cook and horsetailer on instructions from the boss drover. Before the mob was moved, it was put back on the water to top up with a second drink. As the bullocks were accustomed to walking out from water to the station feeding grounds, the drover would put the mob on the pads and walk the cattle to within feeding distance of the camp. After turning the mob onto the feed, it would be allowed to graze slowly along and would be fed up to the camp and pushed together at dusk. Once the bullocks were on camp, the boss drover or the cook would do the dogwatch, allowing the rest of the men to let their horses go and have a meal.

The routine on a dry day differed only slightly. The periods of grazing could be reduced, as dry cattle feed less than well-watered ones, and the dinner camp was, of course, a dry one. The drovers would fill their quarts from the water bags carried around their horses' necks. On an extended dry stage, great care had to be taken when using water for washing and cooking. I have seen thirsty bullocks ringing madly around a camp when a careless cook knocked over a water canteen, the smell of the wet earth being enough to drive the mob almost crazy.

When cattle lie down, they do so with their bodies upright and with their feet tucked under and to one side. When well fed and watered road bullocks lay down on a night camp, air was expelled from their lungs with a quite audible whoosh. It was a sound that drovers enjoyed hearing, for it signalled full and contented cattle.

When bullocks moved off a night camp, they left behind clear evidence of the drover's husbandry. Weeks later a good cattleman could ride past the camp and tell at a glance how the mob had been faring. Small, dark dung that was almost nodular in composition indicated the mob had been having a hard time, while large, light-coloured, flattened pats clearly showed all was well.

Back in the days when cattle were walked to their destination, instead of being trucked as they are today, there were three types of mobs on the stockroutes; fats, breeders and stores. Drovers often specialised in one class of cattle droving and were described in conversation as being of that ilk.

The droving of fat cattle from the fattening depots in the Channel Country to the railheads provided work for a large number of drovers. The trips were short — weeks rather than months — and the mobs were restricted to about 700 head. The big, placid fats seldom gave trouble and after a few nights, most fat cattle drovers gave watching away, merely camping behind the mob. All in all, the job of droving fats was regarded as something of a sinecure, although it was essential to nurse the mob along and deliver the cattle in prime condition.

The droving of breeders, or cows and calves, was, in my opinion, sheer drudgery. Circumstances forced me once to take on a mixed mob that included cows in calf, and it was a mistake I vowed never to repeat. The long-suffering characters who followed this type of droving usually had a conveyance called a calf cart in which they put the newly born calves for transportation to the next camp. No self-respecting cow and calf drover would be without his calf cart, for without one, the calves would have to be knocked on the head and the mothers thrown and hobbled each night until they forgot about the unhappy event. Cow and calf droving was not for me, but I suppose someone had to do it.

Store cattle drovers were a breed apart. Many of them were larger than life characters who had a lot in common with the wild restless cattle they brought down the unfenced stockroutes. Despite their often reckless behaviour, those of them who were successful were all top cattlemen. If they regarded themselves as an elite group — if they dismissed other forms of droving with cynical amusement — it is perhaps understandable.

Stockroute Characters

NORTH-WEST QUEENSLAND and the Territory were at one time full of hard cases — men who drifted to the outback, there to find scope for their unique individuality and general acceptance of their most outrageous behaviour. Among them were the adventurers, the drifters, the ne'er-do-wells, and those reckless characters who left wherever they came from in haste and for a very good reason. There was an unwritten law in the Territory — you never asked a man about his past. If he talked about it, well and good — otherwise his anonymity was respected. Many an outback character took his past to the grave with him.

In the outback the use of nicknames was common. These were, as a rule, descriptive, colourful, and not without humour. Here are a few examples: One Potato Tom, Wirrawarra Mick, Jerida, The Dancing Duck, The Gilgai Crab, The Blue Bull, Beef Eye, The Territory Tick, Up and Down the River Jack, Cornbeef Jack, Shortstop Turner, The Pregnant Goat, Twenty-One, The Pic, Robbo the Lair, Robbo the Horsetailer, Looking Glass Joe, and Knock 'em Down Tommy.

Droving, because of its mobility, attracted many of these characters. They were colourful, larger than life figures who thrived in an environment where the social graces and conventions meant nothing, but where guts and self-reliance were essential for survival.

Vale Rusty Reagan

Old Rusty Reagan's cashed his chips
No more he'll go on droving trips,
And no more grog will pass the lips
    Of drunken Rusty Reagan.
He died of drink, or so they say,
Or pure neglect, but anyway
The sands of time have slipped away
    For luckless Rusty Reagan.

Although he camped upon the flat,
The bar was his true habitat,
And home was underneath the hat
    Of drifter Rusty Reagan.
There's none to say from whence he came,
Not sure, in fact, if that's his name,
To Rusty, though, it's all the same,
    Dead finish Rusty Reagan.

No relatives with reddened eyes
Will weep at Rusty's sad demise,
No lowered flag at half-mast flies
    To honour Rusty Reagan.
We'll miss perhaps his ugly dial,
His raucous voice and toothy smile,
We'll miss him for a little while,
    Then forget Rusty Reagan.

Perhaps somewhere someone will wait,
A mother, sister, brother, mate,
Who'll wonder as they vainly wait
    For absent Rusty Reagan.
I'd like to think some tears might fall
For Rusty's ilk, no-hopers all,
Who answer that last trumpet call
    Unmourned like Rusty Reagan.

The now abandoned police station at Anthony Lagoon. IAN TINNEY.

The Stockroute Dips

OVER THE YEARS Australia has had many problems with introduced pests: rabbits, prickly pear and cane toads, to name just a few. One of the major threats to the cattle industry in this country had its beginning in 1880 when cattle ticks were brought in on Asian cattle imported to Glencoe on the Adelaide River. From there the ticks spread like wildfire.

The ravages of this blood-sucking parasite have been dealt with in detail elsewhere. It is sufficient to say here that they cause serious debility in stock, and are carriers of red water fever, a bovine disease that virtually wiped out some stations in the early days of Top End development. Tick infestation led to serious restriction of stock movement and the introduction of tick lines, as well as tick-free areas.

The main method used to stem the spread of ticks was to put travelling stock through plunge dips containing an arsenic solution. In an attempt to keep the cattle tick out of Queensland, a plunge dip was constructed at Lake Nash, on the Northern Territory–Queensland border, in 1907. The walls and floors of this dip were built of puddled clay and are a monument to the enterprise of outback Australians.

It soon became apparent that cattle had to be dipped more than once before they could be guaranteed to be free of ticks. To avoid holding cattle at Lake Nash, dips were put in at Austral Downs on the Georgina and at the Rankine in 1918. From then on, cattle going down the Georgina to Queensland were dipped three times, with at least one week between dipping. Later still, dips were built at Wendy Bore on Anthony's Lagoon and by the Queensland authorities at Camooweal. Dipping at Austral was later abandoned.

In response to the huge movement of stock walking to Queensland after World War II, a number of actions were initiated. The Territory was under martial law during the conflict and in 1945 the army ordered that all drovers' horses travelling to Queensland were to be sprayed for cattle ticks. In 1949 an additional dip was constructed at No. 7 bore near Elliott, and by the 1953 droving season, another dip at Connell's Lagoon, between Brunette and Alexandria, was ready for use. This latest addition to tick control prompted an old-timer to growl: 'The bastards will have us swimming the bloody bullocks to Queensland soon.'

The early 1950s saw a large increase in the number of Northern Territory stock inspectors and this took some of the load off the shoulders of the Territory police, who had previously done a great deal of the work relating to travelling stock. In the early 1960s the old dip at Wendy Bore on Anthony's was relocated to No. 1 bore on the stockroute between Anthony's Lagoon and Eva Downs.

The introduction of compulsory spraying for drovers' horses caused immediate protest and ongoing bitterness that was not helped by the actions of the character in charge of the dip on Anthony's Lagoon, who plunge-dipped some horses. Drovers had good reason for concern: after spraying, horses cut up badly in the cold south-easterly winds that swept across the tableland.

Many of the road mobs were difficult to yard for dipping and drovers who put the horse plant up front to lead the bullocks in found the horses becoming as yard shy as the cattle. Dips were never popular with drovers, who, while accepting them as a necessary evil, cursed them whole heartedly for what they did to the cattle. At best, dipping knocked the road bullocks about and stirred them up, causing bad nights and rushes well into the trip; at worst, if the arsenic solution was too strong, cattle could be driven half mad.

One of the worst nights I ever experienced on the road was after dipping at the No. 7 bore near Elliott. When the lead split off and got away, it was close to daylight and our nighthorses were exhausted from a night of hard riding. My brother Jeff, who stuck with the leading mob, did not get back to camp with them until eleven o'clock in the morning.

The day I dipped Willeroo bullocks at Anthony's Lagoon, the late 'Wogga' D'Arcy put his mob of Mallapunyahs through behind me. Wogga was quite a character; the eldest son of George D'Arcy, he was reared with the rest of the family on Mallapunyah Springs, the family property. He was a big man, big enough, some said, to hold a bull out to piss, and he had huge feet. So large were his feet in fact, that he never managed to get boots that would fit him — so Wopgga went through life quite happily without them. A good all-round man, he never let the lack of boots inhibit his riding ability; he hung his spurs on his bare heels and put only his big toe in the stirrup irons.

That night, after dipping, Wogga camped about a mile behind me, with the turpentine scrub at his back. Near midnight the Willeroos splashed, and soon after, the Mallapunyahs rushed and hit the scrub. I heard Wogga bellowing at them as he crashed through the turpentine on a nighthorse. It must have been hell on his feet, but next day when I met him he seemed none the worse for the experience.

The Eva Downs bullocks were usually good on the road, but they could turn it on if things went wrong. One mob I took got a bad fright after dipping at Connell's Lagoon and for the next few weeks they kept us on our toes, as the rather laconic entries in my 1958 diary show.

16TH JUNE. Camped out from Plain Bore. Mob rushed at daylight.

17TH JUNE. (No entry)

18TH JUNE. (No entry)

19TH JUNE. Dipped 1395 bullocks Rankine.

20TH JUNE. Camped back from Coolibah Bore. Mob rushed. Two crippled bullocks shot.

21ST JUNE. Watered. Went out from bore. Bad rush. Two bullocks shot.

22ND JUNE. Went back. Watered at bore. Camped at point of timber. Rush. One beast shot.

23RD JUNE. Watered. Camped at the same camp to settle the mob.

24TH JUNE. Watered and went out. Left crippled bullock.

25TH JUNE. Watered at Bell Hole. Bad night. Little feed. Raining.

26TH JUNE. Horse plant cleared out during night. Took mob on with nighthorses. Camped on ridge back from Five Mile. Horses caught up late. Raining.

27TH JUNE. Weather clearing. Watered at gilgias. Same camp. Bad night.

The mob finally settled down, although it was a rough trip, as the feed down the Georgina was little more than goose picking. Five months to the day after taking delivery, I trucked the mob away at Longreach.

The Woodstock Hills

THE CATTLE PADS of the Boulia–Winton stockroute wound their tortuous way through the hills of Woodstock Station; dry, rugged, scrub-covered hills that seemed to us road-weary drovers to be unending. I eased myself in the saddle as I watched the leaders of the store mob pick their way gingerly through the spinifex and stones. They had travelled over 800 miles (1300 kilometres) since leaving Eva Downs in the Northern Territory, and it was obvious that the rough going was not to their liking. All the fire that had characterised their behaviour in the first weeks of the trip was gone, and all that remained was the disciplined resignation of bullocks that had marched 9 miles (14 kilometres) a day for too long.

I rode back along the straggling lines of cattle stretched almost half a mile (800 metres) from lead to tail, and as I rode, I cooeed through the lifting dust to keep them moving. I was short-handed. Two men had pulled out in Boulia, leaving only myself and two Aboriginal stockmen, Splinter and Isaac, with the cattle. With my brother Jeff doing both the cooking and horsetailing, that made four men in all to handle 1350 bullocks and 46 horses. Droving is a hard game at best, but being short-handed meant each man had to work so much longer and harder than normal.

As I rode around the point of a hill, Splinter rode towards me. One of the old school of Aboriginal stockmen, Splinter had proved his worth many times.

'How is the tail travelling?' I asked as he reined in beside me.

'Orright, maluka. Them sore-footed fellers are a bit slow. Mebe a little bit spell help 'im.'

Splinter would never be more direct than that, but I knew him well enough to accept the implied advice.

'Right oh,' I agreed. 'There's a flat just ahead of the lead. I'll block them up there and you can give them a spell while I trot ahead and see where the camp is.'

About 2 miles (3 kilometres) on, I saw where the plant horses had turned off the stockroute. I found the camp over a low ridge, with a fair expanse of open ground to camp the mob on. The eight packs were lined up, with the fire between them and the cattle camp, and behind the packs a sapling had been selected for the nighthorse tree.

Jeff was busy working around the fire as I rode up. I swung down from my horse and tied it to the sapling. Strolling over to the fire, I greeted him with: 'How is it going?'

'How the hell do you think it's going? I've got to take the horses on six miles to water yet, and make a damper before I go.'

I took stock of the situation, agreed it was a dog's life, and got my quart pot from my saddle.

'How about a drink of tea?'

'Look in the billy.'

I sat on my heels and sipped the tea.

'What's the horse feed like?'

The acting cook did not answer at once. He was slamming flour into a mixing dish with careless abandon. Finally, he looked up.

'There's enough for them tonight, about half a mile down the flat. Nothing much for the bullocks, though, apart from spinifex tassels.'

'Well, that will have to do them.'

I put down the quart pot and rolled a smoke. Jeff quickly added rising and salt to the flour, poured water into the mixture, then began to work the dough as though he was intent on belting the bottom out of the dish.

'Take it easy,' I said. 'You've a couple of hours of daylight yet.'

He looked at me. 'I've got plenty of time to do what I have to do, but I don't have time to sit round the fire smoking and drinking tea.'

I said nothing. I knew he was dog tired, for the long hours were taking their toll on all of us. Tossing out the tea dregs, I walked over to my horse and rode over to inspect the cattle camp. In area it was not a lot bigger than a normal size house block, but it would do. Road bullocks can be eased into a surprisingly small camp once they are broken in.

On the way back to the mob I rode past the fire, where my young brother was shovelling coals onto the camp oven that held the newly made damper.

'One thing,' I said. 'If you ever leave the bush, you could get a job cooking at Lennon's Hotel.'

His initial reply was unprintable, but then he laughed. 'Get back to your bullocks, you slave driving bastard.'

I saluted him and rode back to where I had left the mob.

We put the bullocks on camp just on dusk, riding around them and pushing them together until they were in a roughly circular configuration about 5 yards in front of the fire.

Jeff, in his capacity as horsetailer, then had to take the horses we had ridden that day on to the water 6 miles (10 kilometres) ahead. I changed to a nighthorse and watched the mob until he had returned and hobbled the day horses out with the rest of the plant.

He nodded to me as he rode out to take over. I tied up the nighthorse and got stuck into a frugal meal of corned beef and damper. I had done half of my brother's watch while he was tending to the horses and I was still sitting by the fire, albeit half asleep, when he was relieved by Splinter.

He came over to the fire for coffee and saw me.

'Why the hell aren't you in your swag?' He shook his head. 'You've got to be on watch at three.'

'It's all right,' I assured him. 'I've been dozing here.'

I lay on one elbow and listened to the corroboree that Splinter was singing drift across the sleeping mob. It had been a hard day, but at that moment I was at peace with the world.

My brother broke the spell. 'I've had droving,' he stated. 'Never again will I work on the road with Territory bullocks.'

'At least you'll be able to tell your grandkids about the time you did two men's work on the road with Territory bullocks.'

'I'll also be able to tell them I did it for one man's wages. Anyway, after the pizzling I've had this trip, I doubt if I'll be able to sire anything.'

I laughed. 'Don't worry, you'll get a fat bonus when we deliver this mob.'

'When we deliver,' he snorted. 'This mob had been for sale ever since we left Eva. I don't think they'll ever sell them and you'll probably end up in Victoria.'

'Oh well, I wouldn't mind. Look, we'll be out of these blasted hills in a few days. When we get to Winton we should be able to pick up an extra man or two.'

'Fair enough.'

He pulled out his tobacco tin, opened it, then put it down in disgust. I was about to throw him mine when he got up and walked to the dry ration pack for a fresh tin.

'I'll tell you one thing,' he said, rummaging about in the packbag, 'you'll never get me back in this part of the world. It must be the last place God made. I doubt if it would carry two goannas to the square mile.'

I looked over at the rugged ridge tops outlined against the starlit sky. 'It's pretty rough all right,' I agreed. 'I might give this route a miss myself in future.'

Fate, however, can play some funny tricks. These same Woodstock hills were to play an important part in both our lives at a later date. Deep under their rough surface were sandstone levels that contained a sparkling treasure: that most beautiful of all nature's gems — opal. In time we would both fall under its spell.

Trials and Tribulations

HAVING FINALLY LEFT the rugged woodstock hills behind us on what would be an epic journey from Eva Downs Station, the soft going was more to the liking of the bullocks. Feed was still scarce, though, and we were entering an area of closer settlement, and would soon be in the heart of the sheep country. The day before we reached Winton, I camped a few miles out and watered at a bore west of the town.

Being short-handed, all of us were feeling the pinch. After the bullocks had a drink at the bore, I let them lie down around the trough on dinner camp. Splinter and the other ringer lost no time in catching up on some sleep while I did dinner watch. I was sitting on my horse, one leg cocked over the pommel of the saddle, when I saw a car approaching at speed. The vehicle swung around the mob and braked to a stop in from of me. A smartly dressed chap of about 30 stepped out and walked over. I picked him to be a stock and station agent, and soon discovered I was right; I also found him to be a smart alec.

He greeted me with: 'Where's the boss?'

'I'm the boss.'

'How long has your name been Chambers?'

I was in no mood for repartee. 'Look, mate, my name is Simpson, I'm in charge of this mob. If you want the bloody owner, bloody well ask for him, otherwise piss off and don't bother me.'

He ignored my outburst.

'Do you know where Alf Chambers is?'

'No, I don't.'

I uncocked my leg and rode off around the mob.

Later that afternoon Alf put in an appearance. I asked him about my visitor, and he laughed.

'He's a bit of a hard case, but he's no fool. I think he will sell the mob.'

The cattle had been for sale for a long time and had been in the hands of a number of agents. Alf was right about my visitor at the bore. Within a week he would have the mob sold.

Alf and I yarned over a cup of tea for a while, then he suggested we both take a run along the stockroute towards Longreach. The feed got worse rather than better, but in the fenced off-rifle range just past Winton the Mitchell grass was 2 feet (60 centimetres) high.

The rifle range was seldom used, but nonetheless it was illegal to put stock inside the fence. On the way back through Winton, I called on the common ranger. I gave notice I would be crossing the common and handed him two large pieces of corned beef. I had ideas about the rifle range and I wanted to keep the common ranger on side. The following day I took a calculated risk and told my brother Jeff, who was doing two jobs, those of cook and horsetailer, to camp in the rifle range. I thought I would be able to get rid of the common ranger before we got to the camp, but in that, I was wrong.

The common ranger was an old drover, and a friendly bloke. The gift of the meat may have been a mistake, for he took a shine to me and stayed with the mob all day. As we neared the rifle range, my mind was working furiously.

Suddenly the common ranger reined in his horse. 'The camp's in the rifle range.'

'What the hell does he think he's doing? He must have misunderstood me. Mind you, he's just about dead on his feet — he's been doing two jobs for nearly a month.'

'Well, you can't stay there.'

The common ranger had a job to do, and that job was to move the camp. The only chance I had was to take the initiative away from him.

'Of course not. He'll just have to pack up and shift the camp.'

We rode into the camp, with me winking furiously at my brother.

'What are you doing here? We can't camp here — this is the rifle range.'

Jeff ignored my winks. 'You bloody well told me to camp here.'

'Well, I'm afraid you'll have to shift the camp.'

'But I've just cooked a bloody feed, and it's nearly sundown.'

'Sorry mate, but the common ranger says we have to move, so move it is.'

My brother let go a string of oaths, put the boot into a billy of tea and, still cursing, turned towards the packs.

'Hang on, hang on,' said the common ranger. 'Look, leave the camp here, but I didn't give you permission — and I didn't see you here.'

I nodded my thanks to the common ranger, who wheeled his horse and left the scene of the crime at a hard gallop. Grinning, I turned to my brother, to find him looking daggers at me.

'You're a nice type of bastard. You know bloody well that you told me to camp here.'

'Of course, but I tipped you the wink. The only chance we had of staying here was to make him feel sorry for you.'

'I don't need any bastard to feel sorry for me. I reckon you'd sell your soul to the devil to get feed for those f...ing bullocks.'

I laughed. 'I did that a long time ago.'

I left Jeff refilling the tea billy and rode back to the mob feeling rather pleased with myself. The common ranger had disappeared, but he was no fool — he would have known that I had put one over him, and he would have known why, for he was an old drover himself.

Late the next afternoon Alf Chambers ran out to the camp with a cook. He was busy around the fire as I put the mob on camp and the aroma of a stew wafted across the bullocks. When I finished the dog watch, he had done the washing up and was sitting on his rolled-up swag. I nodded to him and helped myself to a plateful from the camp oven and grabbed a drink of tea. When I had finished, I rolled a smoke and looked at the cook. 'That was a damned good feed.'

'Make the most of it — I won't be cooking another; I'm finished.'

'Finished! You've just bloody well started.'

'Well, I'm pulling out. I won't work with packs.'

'I suppose you expect to get paid?'

'No, I've had a feed. We'll call it square.'

Without another word he stood up, shouldered his swag and was gone. I've had some short-term employees, but that cook still holds the belt.

The grass improved quite a bit in the next few days, and when the agent brought two potential buyers out, the mob was on dinner camp looking full and contented. My friend the agent bustled over to me.

'Can you lend these chaps horses to look through the mob?'

'Yes, they can take those,' I said, indicating the horses Splinter and his mate were riding.

'What about yours?'

I was riding a smart chestnut mare. She was one of four I had bought back in Boulia. She was still fresh and was a bit lively to mount.

'She's a bit hard to get on. They would be better to use the others.'

'Oh, if you can ride her, this chap will handle her,' he said, nodding towards one of the buyers.

I dismounted and handed the reins to his client, who looked far from confident. The moment he reined up the mare, I knew he was in trouble. As he swung for the saddle, the mare ducked away, leaving him sprawling on the ground. I caught the chestnut mare and rode around to the back of the mob, leaving them to sort things out for themselves.

Despite the bad start to the inspection, the partners bought the mob and advised me that they would be trucking the bullocks from Longreach. Alf Chambers was of course delighted, the agent had has commission, and the buyers, who came from Jericho, seemed pleased with the deal; it was, in fact, happiness all round. The only cloud on the horizon was the trucking date. The first available one was three weeks away. At the normal rate of travel, it would only take me eight or nine days to reach the trucking yards at Cramsey. There was little feed for the mob there, so I decided I would have to waste time on the route.

Store bullocks are supposed to travel 9 miles (14 kilometres) per day, and the stockroute ranger is employed to see this is done. Stations along the route also send men, usually jackaroos, to see you don't leave the stockroute. Despite the attentions of these characters, it is still possible to take things easy: a day's spell here and there because of lame bullocks, a few days held up because of lost cattle while a man rides back along the route on a wild goose chase — and then there is the organised rush.

It is very easy to step a horse over a sheep fence; horsetailers do it all the time to get feed for the horses. A sheep fence is not very high. If you take your belt off and tie the wires together, a horse can step over the fence very easily. When organising a rush, a drover uses this method to take a horse into a well-grassed paddock after dark. Most drovers have a horse that will pull with their tail; with a horse like this, it is an easy matter to hook a rope on to a post and pull 20 or 30 yards of fence out into the paddock. The bullocks are then driven through the gap and scattered far and wide. The drovers then return to camp for a good night's sleep.

When, the next morning, a jackaroo would bum-trot up to see the mob along the route, I always would make a point of galloping about in the pretext of mustering the bullocks. The 'roo usually took one look and galloped back to the station, giving me additional time to scatter the mob. By the time the furious sheep cocky had arrived and I had explained about the rush, the bullocks were as full as ticks and starting to camp. I explained then that it would be easier to muster them onto the water, and all hands started on the job. By the time the mob was pushed back through the gap, it was usually late afternoon and the bullocks had paunches on them like poisoned pups. The moment they saw the camp, they went over and lay down. I always gave the cocky a hand to put the fence back up and invited him to camp with us if he was worried about a reoccurence. It was an offer that was never accepted.

I had no compunction about doing this, for as far as I was concerned, drovers who pinched grass were only getting a bit of their own back. Many graziers regarded the adjacent stockroute as part of their property and used it as an extra paddock early in the season. By the time the first mobs moved down the route there was little grass left.

By devious means such as this, I arrived at Cramsey with the mob the day before I was due to truck the bullocks. Over the next two days I sent them east by stock train to their new home.

Further In

On the road with Eva cattle we've at times had quite a battle,
But we've struck good grass at last past Winton town;
All the squatters look us over: 'Just another drunken drover',
As we're heading down through Queensland further down.
It has been a sad old story since we left the Territory,
Old man drought has had the country by the tail,
But the grass is growing sweeter, and the jillaroos we meet are
Getting fairer as we travel on for sale.

We have seen the stubble blacker than our native trade tobacco,
And the drought, some say, is worse than 'fifty-two;
What with trials and tribulations and the squatters' altercations,
'Twas the OP rum alone that pulled us through.
Now the bullocks look in wonder at the sound of muffled thunder,
As the boundary rider passes in his jeep;
For the gates are coming quicker and the 'pills' are getting thicker,
And it's plain enough the country carries sheep.

Oh! the gates are crazy tangles, swung a dozen different angles,
And the source of many blasphemous tirades,
For a bloodhound soon would find us by the hide we've left behind us,
On those blasted, buckled, twisted barricades;
Some are mantraps made of wire that a trapper well might hire,
Should he wish to catch the bear that hibernates,
They're of wood and steel and cable and we shut them when we're able,
Oh! they keep us pretty busy with their gates.

It seems these blanky squatters look on droving men as rotters,
As one fellow said who found us on his run;
Oh! his manner grew quite shirty and the words he used were dirty,
But we told him that we took it all in fun.
Oh! their boundary riders haunt us, but they very seldom daunt us,
And the stars alone look down and see us pass,
With a fortnight still to squander, we must let the bullocks wander,
And it keeps us pretty busy pinching grass.

We've a camp of native ringers and they really are humdingers,
At wolfing red-hot rib-bones off the coals,
Now our killers are all eaten, but a drover's never beaten,
For a drover is a man of many roles.
They of course prefer goanna in their ancient tribal manner,
But a stock of them is rather hard to keep,
Tho' at first they wouldn't try it, now they're on a mutton diet,
And they keep us pretty busy pinching sheep.

Oh! this droving game is chancy, there's no cop in being Clancy
If you're not awake and haven't any clues;
For your friends are few, if any, and the pitfalls they are many,
Though old Eva Downs of course pays all the blues.
Up to date we've dodged the rangers, but we're wary still of strangers;
Being caught, we're told, is far the greatest sin.
But the grass is growing sweeter, and the jillaroos we meet are
Getting fairer as we travel further in.

Yes, the worst of it is over and we'll really be in clover,
When we truck the mob away at Longreach town;
Then like modern guided missiles we'll head straight to wet our whistles,
And we'll toast the little steers bon voyage down.

Cattle Duffing

CATTLE DUFFING HAS always been prevalent in Australia. When one considers the number of poachers and sheep stealers transported to this country, it is not surprising. Add to that the influx of people with an inherited antipathy toward the landed gentry, together with the opportunity created by the bush, and the result was inevitable.

It is a fact of life that Australian bushmen have always regarded cattle duffing with a sneaking respect. Take the case of Harry Redford, the greatest cattle duffer of them all: the evidence was overwhelming, the judge's summing up damning, yet the jury, without hesitation, found him not guilty. In reading the report of the case, one almost gets the impression that the members of the jury stood and applauded Redford as he left the court.

The attitude of bushmen to cattle stealing probably rose from two facts: firstly, the theft, as a rule, was from big stations; secondly, those stations were usually owned by southern or overseas interests.

The stealing of stock falls roughly into three categories: killing other people's beasts for beef; stealing unbranded stock, called poddy-dodging; and the stealing of branded stock, or cattle duffing.

The first type of offence has always been widespread. There's an old story that the only time a station owner knows what his own beef tastes like is when he visits a neighbour. The second of the above was, in the past, common practice, and many a respected cattle baron got his start by poddy-dodging. The third, and most serious, offence is cattle duffing. It is a risky business, to say the least, but at times it still goes on.

I was involved for a short time in a poddy-dodging block with Looking Glass Joe Dowling, who was one of the smartest men with wild cattle I ever met. Looking Glass Joe got his nickname because he was a bit of a dandy; shaving daily was something of a ritual with him and he spent a great deal of time admiring himself in the mirror-like inner surface of his tobacco tin lid — rolling a smoke was usually a leisurely exercise for Looking Glass Joe. Recognised as a top cattleman, he was also a notorious poddy-dodger. Mind you, he had never been convicted of the offence, and he remained in the eyes of the law a cleanskin, like the cattle he lifted.

I did not take our venture into the cattle business too seriously, and perhaps that was just as well, for it had many of the elements of a second-rate theatrical farce. The owner of the property was in gaol in Alice Springs, but he had agreed to sell the place to Looking Glass Joe, and also agreed to let us have possession of the run while the sale was being finalised. Joe, who believed in the old adage 'The early bird catches the worm', moved in, and we began mustering at once. Looking Glass Joe was totally uneducated, but he was no fool.

The block had some unusual land formations on it as well as quite good grazing country. Out on the edge of the desert there was a rather strange spring that ebbed and flowed with the phases of the moon like a tide; when the moon was full, the spring ran out for at least a mile, then gradually dried back as the moon waned. When the new moon put in an appearance, the process was reversed. The block lay south of Newcastle Waters, not far from the Powell Creek telegraph station, and west of Helen Springs. Newcastle Waters was a big station and always good for a few poddies, so Looking Glass Joe reckoned we had it made.

He did, however, have one problem; neither of us had a Territory cattle brand. I had a Queensland brand — no use at all for our present circumstances — and Joe had never held a brand, as all his past efforts in poddy-dodging had been for other people. He had made application to have the property brand and earmark transferred to him after the sale went through, but with his reputation, that was no certainty. Looking Glass Joe, however, did not seem to be worried, so we mustered merrily on.

Stations had a long-standing agreement that whenever country near a boundary was to be mustered, both stockcamps would be involved. Looking Glass Joe sent word to Newcastle Waters that we would be mustering around Powell Creek on a certain day, then made sure we were there two days before the given date. The evening before the Newcastle camp was due to arrive we had a small mob of cattle in hand in which was a fat barren Newcastle Waters cow that Joe decided would make good eating. He had just ridden to the camp for the rifle when out of the timber jogged the Newcastle horse plant.

In charge of the horses was a jackaroo who told Joe that the head stockman, who was coming along behind with the rest of the ringers, had decided to get to Powell Creek before us. Quite undaunted, Looking Glass Joe handed him the rifle, pointed out the cow and got him to shoot it. By the time the Newcastle Waters camp arrived the beast was butchered and we were wolfing into rib-bones freshly cooked on the coals.

The property had a rough but fairly comfortable homestead on it, so Looking

Glass Joe arranged for his wife to join us. She had been a nursing sister at the Quilpie hospital before she met Joe on his last trip into the Channel Country.

By this time we had close to 300 head of cleanskin cattle mustered, but still no brand, and no news of the sale being finalised. Looking Glass Joe and his wife decided to go into Renner Springs to pick up the mail and to try to find out what was going on, while I rode the horse paddock fence where we were holding the cattle.

They returned late that afternoon looking as miserable as bandicoots. Looking Glass Joe handed me a letter advising him that the deal was off. Whether the owner received any help in changing his mind was debatable, but in any case, we were up the proverbial creek without a paddle. Next morning we opened the horse paddock gate and bushed the cattle that were to have been the nucleus of our herd. Looking Glass Joe and I rode off the place with nothing — at least, I got nothing. A few days later Looking Glass Joe received a broken jaw from the head stockman from Newcastle Waters, who apparently took umbrage at our activities, regarding them as a personal insult.

That was the closest I ever came to becoming a cattle king. However, Looking Glass Joe eventually obtained a run in the Top End. Sadly, his wife was killed off a horse soon after.

Galloping Jones

Where the Gulf rivers run, in the days that are past
The runs that bred cattle were fenceless and vast,
The stockriders mustered while e'er there was light,
But the duffers of cattle rode only at night.
They were reckless and daring, a larrikin band,
They took what they wanted and rode where they plann'd.
The troopers who chased them, though chafed to the bones,
Were sure the ringleader was Galloping Jones.

Many sovereigns have sat on a great many thrones,
And the King of the duffers was Galloping Jones.
His throne was his saddle, his realm it was vast,
The horses he rode were sure-footed and fast.
He travelled by starlight, unchallenged and free
To colour the pages of Gulf history.

He would go to a ball and he'd dance half the night,
Then be forty miles distant before it was light,
With a nice mob of poddies he quickly would sell
To a battler, then back to Kajabbi Hotel.
The tired troopers knew by the smile on his face
He had done them again, for they hadn't a case.
He took what he wanted and rode where he pleased,
The troopers who cashed him were taunted and teased.

Now the cattlemen argued the troopers are fools
We have got to do something to alter the rules.
They employed a sharpshooter on cattleman's pay
To hunt the wild duffers and keep them at bay.
But the message he got from the duffers was clear,
They stalked him at midnight, and shot off an ear.
He resigned very promptly and said, 'I'll refrain
From combat in future', then caught a fast train.

Quite a legendary figure was Galloping Jones,
Though the cattlemen viewed him with curses and groans.
He was straight in his dealings, a good mate in strife,
A friend of the battlers the whole of his life.
Though the police had been told: 'Bring the Galloper in',
He greeted them all with a wave and a grin.
He could ride, he could fight, and he galloped at will,
Now in legend and story he's galloping still.

Many sovereigns have sat on a great many thrones,
And the King of the duffers was Galloping Jones.
His throne was his saddle, his realm it was vast,
The horses he rode were sure-footed and fast.
He travelled by starlight unchallenged and free
To colour the pages of Gulf history.

Now the duffers have gone from the Gulf and the West,
And old Galloping Jones has been called to his rest.
But up in the Gulf, when the mist's on the ground —
When the night wind is stirring the treetops around —
It is then you may see them as wraith-like they go
With cleanskins in front, with the troopers in tow.
The stars pale and shiver, the dark forest moans
As fast flies the spirit of Galloping Jones.

A Letter 'Inside'

No doubt, perforce, you've settled down to prison's grim routine,
But I suspect you often think of how things might have been.
For one so used to distant hills it must be very hard
To find horizons shortened to a crowded prison yard,
But you have seen hard times before — have struck a snag or two
And though the going may be rough, you'll doubtless see it through.
I meant to write you long ere this, but you know how things are,
With us who live the same old life by bit and stirrup bar.

Although of late you've found that fate can play a fickle game,
Back here beyond the Queensland fence things still are much the same.
The Wet has come and gone once more and in the drovers' town
The same old crowd have had their fun and drunk their quota down.
Out bush it's like a garden now, the weather's fine and fair,
The scent of turpentine in bloom drifts on the freshened air,
The waterholes have overflowed, and on the blacksoil plain
The Mitchell grass and Flinders grass are tall and sweet again.

The travelling stock are rolling down the old Georgina route,
And I am on the road again with stores from further out;
As to the shaded dinner camps the bullocks slowly string
I wonder what you'd give just now to ride upon the wing —
To watch the mob these autumn nights on timbered camps starlit,
And feel a good and willing horse again upon the bit —
To yarn around the fire again as stockmen always do,
While close beside the feeding bells there mourns the lone curlew.

A mystic spell the outback weaves beneath the Milky Way
That ever holds a horseman's heart though half a world away.
And when the slate is clean at last, as it must surely be,
You'll find the old life waiting here, the same old company,
And on the day you meet old mates upon the blacksoil plain
You'll know the firm and friendly grip of bridle hands again.
Though men must bear misfortunes cross, and bow to unkind fate,
Unchanging, loyal to her own, the bush will always wait.

Maloney's Luck

Once a battler named Maloney owned a run so rough and stony
That the only way to prosper was by quietly pinching calves.
Now this very crafty codger was an expert poddy-dodger,
One who never cruelled his chances or did anything by halves.
With a conscience never troubled and a herd that quickly doubled,
It appeared our friend Maloney was enjoying fortune's smiles.
For the seasons made to order and the cleanskins on his border
And the attitude of bankers seemed reward for all his wiles.

Then alas the good years finished and his fortune soon diminished;
To prevent the wolf from calling, he was almost out of clues.
For his herd was gaunt and bony on his run so rough and stony
And it seemed at last the devil was desirous of his dues.
Now the drought gave him no quarter, he was almost out of water,
Just one soak, a creaking windmill and a tank of many years;
Though the banks had cancelled lending and discouraged wanton spending,
His appeal to them for money would have moved Shylock to tears.

But Maloney's star was waning, as were chances of it raining,
And Maloney's credit rating now was rather on the nose.
They appeared to think it funny that he'd write to them for money,
So they answered and advised him that they shortly would foreclose.
Well Maloney felt quite bitter, but he'd never been a quitter,
So he reckoned he would front them, he would meet them face to face.
He fuelled up the old Land Rover and he cranked the motor over
And he set off through the dust clouds at a very lively pace.

Now the road to town was shorter by his one remaining water;
There the sight that met Maloney wasn't one to create mirth,
For the tank so badly rusted had thrown in the towel and busted
And had spilled ten thousand gallons on the dry and dusty earth.
All the cattle he had cherished, those of them that hadn't perished,
Were now bogged down most completely in sad and sorry state.
Well Maloney cursed creation and he cursed his stony station
And he wished on money lenders a most agonising fate.

Then he drove his old jalopy through the quagmire wet and sloppy
And he dragged each beast to freedom with a trusty greenhide rope.
Through the bog on foot he struggled, then with clutch and gears he juggled,
For to save his last few cattle was Maloney's only hope.
When the job at last was over, mud had caked the old Land Rover
And Maloney too was filthy from his hard, back-breaking toil,
For his shirt was mud bespatted and his hair was badly matted
And his boots and duds were plastered with a yard of sticky soil.

'Ah, to hell with boots and trousers and to hell with lending houses,
And to hell with bloody cattle,' wild Maloney loudly swore.
'They can take me as they find me, for the devil's close behind me,'
Then he drove to town and pulled up by the bank's rapacious door.
In the bank he grabbed a teller: 'Is the big boss here, young feller?'
And the manager thought quickly: it's far better I am out,
But Maloney wasn't dozing — as the boss's door was closing,
He just put his shoulder to it, striking hard the banker's snout.

Quickly choking back a groan, he cried: 'Come in, my dear Maloney.
That mud's a welcome sight, sir; no there's no need to explain.
I will make no protestations, my sincere congratulations,
It is evident to me, sir, that you've had drought-breaking rain.
Well, that loan will be no trouble, we in fact can give you double;
The interest rate will suit you and the terms will quite astound.
Here, Maloney, have a whisky, some investments can be risky,
But I've always told head office you are one man who is sound.'

Well Maloney never faltered, from that day his fortunes altered;
Soon with assets and investments he was up there with the best,
And today his boundaries wander out across the wide blue yonder,
He's respected, well regarded, through the North and through the West.
But there's always speculation in this region of the nation
On just how Maloney started, on just how he got his wealth,

Jimmy Charles, left, *and the author*
with Sam Fuller's plant in 1951.

And his bankers all acknowledge though he never went to college
He has got a head for business, then they drink Maloney's health.

Now Maloney doesn't prattle of the start he got in cattle
Or the lucky reprieve given by a ruptured iron tank;
But the servants who attend him note that mud does not offend him,
For Maloney still remembers it was mud that beat the bank.

Buckjump Shows

THE BUCKJUMP SHOW in Australia was the first step in the evolution of rodeo as
we know it today, and has always been popular in the outback. Most of the early
buckjump show arenas were merely a roped ring with an outer wall of hessian.
Spectators stood in the space between. Despite their humble beginning, the
Australian buckjump shows have had a long and colourful history, many of them
surviving long after the introduction of organised rodeos. Over the years some
illustrious names have been associated with buckjump shows: Martini, the
Skuthorpes, Thorp McConville, the Gills and the Tulipans. The cry of 'Roll up, bowl

*Frank Douglas, a top horseman
in the bush, winning the buckjump event
at Normanton in 1959.*

up, tumble up, bring your sheila up to the buckjump show' once was an oft heard invitation throughout the land.

Many of the buckjump shows added to their attraction by having whip cracking, sharp shooting and rope tricks in the program. Some even had a pug on hand who was prepared to take on all comers. Probably the last of the buckjump showmen is Larry Dalhunty, a colourful character from North Queensland, who ran a traditional-type show until recently.

Sam Fuller, a legendary figure in his own lifetime, ran his buckjump shop as late as the 1950s. Sam made Longreach his base, and at that time he also had a plant doing contract mustering and short droving trips. As he used some of the plant horses in the buckjump show, the plant was called to town whenever a show was planned. I put in a season with Sam, and to me, the difference between the plant and the buckjump show was fairly academic.

Sam always had good buckjumpers and the first I remember was Send 'em. When I was with him, his top horses were Depot Glen and Wait and See. He also had two creamy mares, Wattle Bough and Icecream. As the hour to start the show approached, Sam would stand outside and bellow: 'Prizes for riders and busters for windbags, just a few canvas chairs left.' There were as many chairs in the show, however, as there were feathers on a horse.

Sam Fuller was a born showman and a good horseman. Among his stunts were playing a mouth organ as a horse bucked, and riding a buckjumper he knew whilst blindfolded. Most of the showmen used a long flank rope, which they held as a horse bucked. Sam's own men were given the nod to jump off before a horse was bucked out, but if a rider from the crowd backed himself to ride a horse for money, Sam had no scruples about helping to unseat the rider with the aid of the long flank rope.

The buckjump shows remained traditionally Australian to the last and did not succumb to American influences as rodeos did.

Tall Stories in Verse

THE TALL STORY is an important part of our outback folklore. I doubt if there is a single facet of bush life that has escaped the outrageous attention of the spinners of tall yarns. Such stories are another example of how isolated people created their own entertainment. Whether it was around a gidgee fire, on a stockroute, or in the bar of a bush pub, the teller of tall yarns never lacked an audience.

Duckabrook Dan's Ride

In legend and story we constantly read
(Until we're emotionally spent)
Of tales like the man and his suffering steed
Who galloped from Aix to Ghent.
For love and for honour men galloped pell-mell,
They galloped for better or worse,
The Light Brigade charged to the entrance of hell,
As Tennyson told us in verse.

The man from the Snowy, a tedious lout,
Is very well known to us all.
With galloping yarns there is never a doubt
Most epics we clearly recall.
We all know of Phar Lap and old Peter Pan,
They raced with and humbled the best,
But who's heard the story of Duckabrook Dan
Who once raced a storm in the West?

It was out at the ten mile the contest began,
It was run at a furious pace,
A wild western storm and old Duckabrook Dan,
One gut-busting hell of a race.
Dan was riding that evening his favourite steed,
An ancient and flea-bitten grey,
Dan swore that the horse had a fair turn of speed
Though he'd once known the shafts of a dray.

Old Dan was enjoying an afternoon nap,
Unconscious of peril or rain,
When the wild tempest struck with a great thunder-clap
And the noise of a runaway train.
Dan leapt to the saddle and gathered his wits,
He whistled his dog to his side,
As the mill on the dam bowed down to the blitz
Dan started his marathon ride.

Ahead and beside them the lightning would strike,
Behind was a curtain of rain,
Dan wished for a moment he'd ridden his bike,
Then spurred over Bandicoot plain.
The grey galloped on with his blaspheming load,
The lightning had made him near blind,
But he kicked up the dust on the deep-rutted roar,
With the dog only metres behind.

To get to the station Dan knew was a must,
The old grey was still going strong,
The storm wind blew harder, a cyclonic gust,
A tail wind that helped them along.
The thunder boomed out through the scrubland beside,
The wind shrieked a fiendish refrain,
Behind came the rain like a billowing tide
And never a foot could they gain.

At the four mile the old horse was covered with foam,
He was spavined and short of a feed,
Dan crouched on his back like an oversized gnome
And prayed that they stayed in the lead.
At the two mile the grey seemed to break in his stride,
He had thrown off one of his shoes;
Dan swore to the saints if he finished the ride
He'd give up bad women and booze.

Dan wished he'd been born with the wings of a dove
As down went the grey on his knees,
The wild wind that roared through the timber above
Blew the fauna right out of the trees.
To be killed in a storm is a terrible fate,
It preyed on old Duckabrook's mind,
But they finally lurched through the horse paddock gate
With the dog only metres behind.

Old Dan asked the grey for an effort supreme,
The station was looming ahead,
The grey crossed the yard as he ran out of steam
To stop in the stable near dead.
But old Dan was the winner, he never got wet —
Was not even damp from the spray,
He had beaten the tempest by three lengths and yet —
The dog had to swim all the way.

Murranji Mick

Now old Murranji Mick was a tiger to talk,
A rough Territory stockman as wild as a hawk,
He would booze and he'd bellow and blaspheme and fight
And talk a blue streak without pausing all night.
He was rugged and rough and addicted to drink,
And could wreck a bush bar-room before you could wink.
He was ugly and sinful and fond of a brawl,
With a temper as short as his stories were tall.

He proclaimed he was born in the midst of the Wet
On a dark Monday morning he'd never forget,
The North-West monsoon had made things rather damp,
And at midday the flood rose and covered the camp.
When his crib sank beneath him, the outlook was grim,
He had one chance, he reckoned, and that was to swim.
So he floated and swam till he reached higher ground,
And was nearly a month old before he was found.

But he got by all right, eating crocodile eggs
And the Burdekin ducks that he caught by the legs.
Mick was good in the bush, he would calmly relate
How he ran mustering camps long before he was eight.
But he shot through soon after to go to the war,
And exceedingly strange were the sights that he saw.
But he won fame and honour and seven VCs,
And he soon had the enemy down on his knees.

When the fighting was over, Mick headed back quick,
Swimming most of the way just to get into nick;
His renown as a fighter was well known of course,
He'd a punch in each hand like the kick of a horse.
He was tougher than greenhide — as quick as a cat,
And he'd once flogged a bunyip to death with his hat.
He had challenged Jack Johnson, and Johnson turned white
And pleaded with Mick that he'd no wish to fight.

But his hardest fought battle, he said to us, was
When he went fifteen rounds with the Wizard of Oz;
They fought and they struggled and tore up the ground,
And Mick took an eight count in the very first round.
When the Wizard was cornered, he'd just disappear,
Then hit Mick from behind on the butt of the ear.
In the end Mick had wheeled him, but only because
He had pointed the bone at the Wizard of Oz.

'Twas an art he'd been taught by the Bullwaddi blacks,
But the thing he excelled in was following tracks,
He could track a black ant down a bitumen street

And then tell you what grass seeds it took home to eat.
On a horse that could buck Mick would stick like a flea,
When he rode Curio he'd been pretty to see;
He got on her blindfolded with saddle reversed,
But he'd thrown that away when the surcingle burst.

There are some who claim Mick is a terrible liar —
And some say that the devil himself was his sire,
But to question the truth of his tales is unwise,
As the sceptics have learned to their painful surprise.
Now if Mick ever dies, and of that there's some doubt,
I wonder sometimes just how things will turn out;
Where he'd finally end up isn't hard to foretell,
But they'll hear throughout heaven the uproar in hell.

The Territory Rouseabout

Now Brumby George was broke and sick and looking for a job —
A week before he'd snatched his time and left a travelling mob;
He'd had his spree, and sober now his troubles had begun,
Far from home and stranded in this town of Hughenden.

For Brumby George was born and bred where scrubs are deep and dense,
In God's own land where pikers roam across the border fence.
He'd cut his teeth on bronco ropes, at breaking colts he'd played,
His greenhide whip and Wave Hill spurs were hallmarks of his trade.

And many a ride he'd had at night, when troopers were abed,
Thru distant runs on business that is better left unsaid.
But Brumby George grew tired of life where poddy-dodgers ride,
So with a droving plant he went to 'look about' inside.

And as he tramped those dusty streets from whence all joy had fled,
A shearing team prepared to leave to start at 'Blowfly' shed.
The agent glowered in his door, his thoughts a bitter cup,
In vain he'd tried all over town to find a picker-up.

Just then o'er Brumby's doleful face his searching optics ran,
And as he called the bushman in, he knew he had his man.
The cunning agent rubbed his hands and spoke of added pay,
'Out there,' he said, 'they eat the best and work an eight hour day.'

Now Brumby listened, to his woe, to what the agent said,
Next morning saw him signed and set to start at Blowfly shed.
'Your duties are,' the classer said, 'as shown by the award,
You bring the fleeces here to me and sweep the shearing board.'

Just then the board-boss rang a bell and with a hungry shout,
Five shearers sprang into the pens, each dragged a wether out.
No doubt to Brumby's startled eyes it was a crazy sight,
And then the fleeces light and loose were off to left and right.

Like falling snow the stubborn wool slipped thru his horny hands,
And soon a foot in depth it lay in drifts about the stands.
The classer cursed and screamed for wool to fill the empty bins,
Until devoutly Brumby wished that he'd been born twins.

In high-heeled boots and beaver moles he sprinted down the board,
While 'wool away' and 'tar boy, tar' the grinning shearers roared.
With growing wrath yet icy calm, he let them have their fun,
Until alas, the last straw came, when halfway thru the run.

It may have been a trick of fate, or yet a studied plan,
No one ever found out where the root of it began.
Perhaps the shearers weren't to blame (though shearers mostly are),
Five fleeces all came off at once, and each man yelled for tar.

Then something snapped in Brumby's head, for Brumby went berserk,
He tore a top rail off a pen and with that went to work.
They say that shearers like a stoush where freely flows the gore,
They never had a bolter's chance when Brumby went to war.

He stacked the shearers in a heap, put jackaroos to flight,
The classer, struck behind the ear, was outed like a light.
The 'bogis' freed from nerveless hands went clattering o'er the board,
And like a Scot at Bannockburn, old Brumby smote and roared.

Fresh-shorn sheep went flying by like signals of distress,
In mortal fear the presser-bloke sprang headlong in the press.
Quite calm, the expert grabbed a wrench, he looked a worthy foe,
As Brumby charged with levelled lance, as knights did long ago.

His aim was good, without a doubt the blow was neatly dealt,
The expert with a gentle sigh collapsed across the belt.
The air was thick with oaths and screams and fleeces torn to bits,
When Brumby deftly felled the boss, and cried: 'We'll call it quits.

'I'm going back to Camooweal, and then to further out,
No more I'll tramp your crimson board as ruddy rouseabout.'
And there today old Brumby toils where scrubs are deep and dense,
In God's own land where pikers roam, across the border fence.

Although he's no philosopher, his views have stood the test,
He sticks to beer and bullocks, and to blazes with the rest.
And in his whole vocabulary, without the slightest doubt,
The most soul-searching epithet is 'ruddy rouseabout'.

Top: *'Old drovers never die, they just keep meeting at reunions.'*
Author Bruce Simpson and Les Teece. NORTH QUEENSLAND REGISTER.

The Transports Take Over

MARION DOWNS IN the Channel Country introduced road transport for cattle as early as the late 1940s. However, other stations were slow to follow, and droving continued to boom during the 1950s.

Drought and higher cattle prices finally saw the introduction of road trains throughout the cattle industry, and in the early 1960s the long trips from the East Kimberleys to the western half of the Northern Territory stopped forever. Droving did continue, on a drastically reduced scale, on other routes, and today a few mobs still walk into Queensland from the Barkly Tableland.

Disease control has cleaned up herds on the outback runs, and today the demand is for younger beef. As a result, cattle moved now are little more than weaners — a far cry from the big wild store bullocks that once came down the Murranji and other routes in their thousands.

Above: *The mechanised replacement for drovers:*
a road train at the Victoria River. IAN TINNEY

And Yet Sometimes . . .

Now the droving is done and no more from the scrub
Come the drovers to camp by the Newcastle pub.
They are gone from the routes with their horses and packs
And the tall grasses blow o'er their deep trodden tracks.
Now there's never a campfire the stockroute along,
For the transports have silenced the night-watcher's song.
And yet sometimes on nights filled with thunder and rain,
In my dreams I am back on the stockroutes again
With a wild restless mob ever ready to rush,
On a camp mid the ant beds and dry underbrush.

'Twas a grim hundred miles down the Murranji track
Where the night camps were bad and the scrublands were black,
A vast wasteland unwanted that seemed without end
From the scrub-covered jump-up to Bucket Creek bend.
Then we prayed for fine weather — a clear autumn sky
When we entered the scrubs of the grim Murranji.
And we doubled the watches and cursed long and plain
When the Murranji met us with thunder and rain,
For when big mobs rushed there, there was little recourse,
Save to trust to your luck and to trust to your horse,
And there many a drover when things went amiss
In the Murranji scrublands faced grim Nemesis.

And the big bullocks knew, for they gave us no rest
As they grudgingly walked from their runs in the West,
For they sulked and they pined for their far distant hills
And they scorned the long troughs at the Murranji mills.
They would moan soft and low for their pandanus springs
And they watched us like hawks from the lead and the wings.
But they'd ring in rebellion and baulk in dismay
When the Mitchell grass plains stretched ahead and away.
Now there's never a campfire the stockroutes along,
For the transports have silenced the night-watcher's song.

There is bitumen now where the big diesels roll
And the dead men grow lonely by Murranji hole.
Now the shy curlews wail and their sad chorus swells
As though missing the music of Condamine bells,
For the droving is done and the drovers no more
String their mobs to the lake by the Newcastle store.
They have hung up their whips and like me settled down
In a job that's secure mid the comforts of town,
And yet sometimes on nights filled with thunder and rain
In my dreams I am back on the stockroutes again,
With a good horse beneath — with the timber a-crack
'Round a mob of wild stores on the Murranji track.

Travelling Stock — 1969

Southward the road trains thunder,
    On through the hours of light,
Never a halt this morning,
    Never a rest tonight.
Hollow, and gaunt and hopeless,
    Dusty, and dim of eye,
By night and day on their weary way,
    The travelling stock go by.

On through the noon day silence,
    On through the dust dry air,
Away with the drought time harvest,
    The loadings of dumb despair.
Weary, and weak and wasted,
    Famished, and sinking fast,
Two tiers high 'neath a brassy sky,
The travelling stock go past.

Pet Food

I was passing by in the blazing heat,
Past the transport parked in the empty street,
When I saw the grey in the pet food crate
With a brumby mob that would share his fate.
He appeared to be of the game old breed
With an honest eye and a turn of speed;
We had known the type, we had known their worth
In the cattle country that gave him birth,
But they'd sold the grey, and without regrets
Had consigned his flesh to the city's pets.
Then the truck moved off with its sorry load
And was lost to sight on the Longreach road . . .

That was long ago, but I can't forget,
For the old grey stockhorse haunts me yet,
Standing there betrayed in the heat and flies
With a look of trust in his weary eyes,
With his dumb brute's mind that could never know
Of the lengths to which human greed will go.

*Don Dawson, a horse tailer
for Jimmy Charles.* LANCEWOOD.

Glossary

Babbler   short for babbling brook — cook

Bang-tail, to   to cut the tassel off the end of a beast's tail as an indication that the beast has been counted

Bang-tail knife   knife used for the above

Bang-tail muster   muster cattle for the above

Beaver moles   a type of moleskin trousers

Belar   a type of tree

Board-boss   supervisor of the shearing shed

Bogan fleas   small, low-growing burrs

Bogis   shearer's handpieces (pronounced 'bog eyes')

Blow-out   a spree

Blue   a fight or argument; also a summons

Bolter's chance   no chance at all

Bronco rope   a greenhide rope used to catch unbranded calves

Brownie   bush cake

Bull's head   brand of Victoria River Downs; road mobs from VRD were known as 'Bull's head bullocks'

Bullocks   fully grown male cattle that have been castrated as calves

Bum trot   sit on a trotting horse without rising in the saddle

Bush a horse   turn the horse out for a spell, or for good

Choked down   fall into a drunken sleep

Clatter   a rattling sound

Cleanskin   unbranded cattle

Clumper   a heavy type of stockhorse

Curio   a famous buckjumper

Dawn patrol   a gathering of drinkers served at the back door before the pub opens

Dinner camp   a break during the heat of the day

Dogwatch   a short watch before the regular watches start and after they finish

Drafting   cutting selected beasts out of a mob

Dough roaster   a camp cook

Duffer   someone who steals branded cattle

Flinders grass   a very nutritious native grass

'The Fort'   Fort William, just north of Boulia

Founder   to break down

Front leg, to   to throw a beast by the front leg

Gibber   a stone

Gidgee   a species of Acacia

Gilgai   shallow depression holding water after rain

Goas   Aboriginal tribe in the Winton areas

Gooly   a stone

Goosenecks   spurs

Goose picking   short, scattered grass shoots after rain

Greenhide   untanned hide

Guyver   style
Hand (as in horse height)   4 inches (10 centimetres)
Hip shot   standing with the weight off one hind leg
Hobble or **hopple**   a chain with two short straps to tie a horse's front legs together; the horse can walk, but it can't stray far
Hobble up   the act of putting hobbles on a horse
Holt   corruption of the word hold
Horsetailer   a ringer or stockman whose job it is to look after the horse plant
Jackaroo   a company man sent to the station for experience
Jibs   refuses to move
Jillaroo   female version of a jackaroo
Jump-up   a steep incline leading to a tableland
Killers   beasts killed for beef
Knackered   exhausted
Knock up   become exhausted
Lug or **to lug**   to get a firm grip of a horse's ear to mount
Maluka   Aboriginal term of respect for a boss or old man (pronounced mul-a-ka)
Mick, micky   a young wild bull
Min min light   an unexplained phenomenon of the outback
Mitchell grass   a nutritious native grass
Monkey strap   a short strap on the off (right) side of the saddle sometimes used in mounting a horse
Munjon   myall native
Murranji   the stockroute between Newcastle Waters and Top Springs (pronounced Murran-jai, to rhyme with 'eye')
Near leg   front of hind leg on the left side
Nick, get into   get fit
Nighthorse   a special horse for nightwork with cattle
North-West   usually refers to North-West Queensland and part of the Northern Territory
On the road   droving
Packs   pack saddles used to transport equipment on packhorses
Peter Pan   a winner of the Melbourne Cup back in the 1930s
Pills   sheep dung
Pikers   big wild scrub cattle
Plant   a drover's horses and equipment
Poddy   an unbranded calf
Poddy dodgers   someone who steals unbranded calves
Pound   a small yard
Pug   a boxer
Quart   quart pot, a small flat-sided billy carried on the saddle
Reef (at the bit)   pull hard on the reins
Reined up   pulled on the reins to pull a horse up
Rooter   a pig jumper, a horse that does not buck badly
Rouseabout   semi-skilled worker in shearing shed
Rush   a maddened gallop of cattle, usually at night
Salvos   the Salvation Army

Scrubbers   wild scrub cattle
Shank   a short rope tied to a halter
Sideline   a chain fastened to both the front and hind leg of a horse
Silver-leaf box   a type of timber
Spayed cows   de-sexed female cattle
Store-conditioned   not fat
Stores   store-conditioned beasts; not fat
Stoush   a brawl
Stunner   a good sort; an attractive girl
Surcingle   a strap that goes over the saddle to secure it
Swinger   top notch
Tailing cattle   to shepherd or keep under control
Tucker   food
Turpentine   low scrubby native bush
Turkey nest   an earth tank for water storage
Two-pot screamer   a cheap drunk
Utility or **ute**   a light commercial vehicle
VRD   Victoria River Downs
Waler   a famous type of Australian cavalry horse exported in large numbers
Watching cattle   riding round road cattle at night
Wave Hill route   the route west of the Murranji was often called the
Wave Hill route
West   that part of the Northern Territory that was west of the Murranji, including
the East Kimberleys
Windy (of something)   afraid

NOTE ON CURRENCY

The following is an approximation of the decimal equivalent of currency mentioned in the text; the actual value of the original currency at the time in question would be considerably higher than that of its decimal equivalent today:

sixpence (or zac)	5 cents
a shilling (or bob)	10 cents
a quid (or pound)	2 dollars

BIBLIOGRAPHY

The Pastoral Review, May 1905

The Pastoral Review, August 1929

The Pastoral Review, September 1929

Gordon Buchanan, *Packhorse and Waterhole,* Angus & Robertson, Sydney, 1933

Hudson Fysh, *Taming the North,* Angus & Robertson, Sydney, 1933

Catherine Drummond Cotton, *Ludwig Leichhardt,* Angus & Robertson, Sydney, 1938

Ion L. Idriess, *The Cattle King,* Angus & Robertson, Sydney, 1947

Ernestine Hill, *The Territory,* Angus & Robertson, Sydney, 1951

Margaret and Colin Kerr, *The Overlanders,* Rigby, Adelaide and Brisbane, 1975

*Cattle horses and men
all share the same water at an earth tank
on Glenormiston.* IAN TINNEY.